# RESEARCH *and* RECONCILIATION

# RESEARCH *and* RECONCILIATION

## Unsettling Ways of Knowing through Indigenous Relationships

*Edited by Shawn Wilson, Andrea V. Breen, and Lindsay DuPré*

Toronto | Vancouver

**Research and Reconciliation: Unsettling Ways of Knowing through Indigenous Relationships**
Edited by Shawn Wilson, Andrea V. Breen, and Lindsay DuPré

First published in 2019 by
**Canadian Scholars, an imprint of CSP Books Inc.**
425 Adelaide Street West, Suite 200
Toronto, Ontario
M5V 3C1

**www.canadianscholars.ca**

**Library and Archives Canada Cataloguing in Publication**

Title: Research and reconciliation : unsettling ways of knowing through indigenous
    relationships / edited by Shawn Wilson, Andrea V. Breen, and Lindsay DuPré.
Names: Wilson, Shawn, 1966- editor. | Breen, Andrea V., 1975- editor. | DuPré, Lindsay,
    1990- editor.
Description: Includes bibliographical references.
Identifiers: Canadiana (print) 20190131470 | Canadiana (ebook) 20190131519 | ISBN
    9781773381152 (softcover) | ISBN 9781773381169 (PDF) | ISBN 9781773381176 (EPUB)
Subjects: LCSH: Indigenous peoples—Research. | LCSH: Reconciliation. | CSH: Native
    peoples—Research—Canada.
Classification: LCC GN380 .R47 2019 | DDC 305.80072—dc23

Page layout by S4Carlisle Publishing Services
Cover art created by Jeremy McLellan with images by Tasha Fiddler, Falco Wassenas, and
Francesca Breen Kurtz
Cover design by Dean Pickup


19  20  21  22  23        5  4  3  2  1

Canada

# ABOUT THE COVER

The drawings used in the cover design were contributed by three important young people in our lives: Tasha Fiddler, Falco Wassenas, and Francesca Breen Kurtz. Thank you for reminding us of the essential perspectives that children and youth bring to these conversations. Also, a big thank you to Jeremy McLellan for your graphic design work, which beautifully ties together this artwork and the stories of this book.

# CONTENTS

# INTRODUCTION

*by Andrea V. Breen, Shawn Wilson, and Lindsay DuPré*

The conversations that led us to put this book together began early in 2016, just a few months after Canada's Truth and Reconciliation Commission released its Final Report and Calls to Action. Canada was abuzz with talk of reconciliation and improving relationships between Indigenous and non-Indigenous peoples. Schools, businesses, and governments were eagerly striking committees on Indigenization and incorporating Land Acknowledgements into meetings and conferences. Settlers were learning, many for the first time, about the history of the Indian residential school system, and there seemed to be a surge of researchers newly interested in doing research with (or on) Indigenous people. The three of us co-editors—Shawn, Andrea, and Lindsay—shared a vision for what we wanted this book to be. We wanted to profile stories, art, and conversations by researchers about their experiences engaging in research that was aligned with Indigenous worldviews and striving to advance processes of reconciliation. We also wanted to challenge Eurocentric conceptions of what research is, who it is for, and who gets to do it.

Over the months and years that have passed since then, we have engaged in many conversations about research and our changing understandings of reconciliation, including its possibilities, limitations, and contradictions. We have understood this word to mean many different things to people—reconciliation as attempts to improve social relations between Indigenous and non-Indigenous peoples; reconciliation as specific calls to action and processes outlined by national governments; reconciliation as healing within our families and communities; reconciliation within ourselves. We have also understood this word to be associated with exploitation and ongoing colonialism. Basically, #itscomplicated.

Our circle of conversation has expanded from the three of us to include the incredible authors and artists who have contributed their research stories to this volume. As editors, we have tried to preserve each contributor's unique ways of seeing and speaking about the world and we are grateful to the wonderful team at Canadian Scholars for supporting this vision through the publication process. Readers might notice that there are some discrepancies between chapters in spelling, grammar, and some of the terms used. This is intentional—we wanted to ensure that each author's story is told in a way that is true to them and so we made space for some inconsistencies rather than enforcing uniformity across chapters. Readers will also notice that many of the chapters incorporate words in Indigenous languages. While it is common practice in publishing to italicize words in non-English languages, in this case, italicizing feels to us like a kind of othering. We have elected to have Indigenous words stand tall in regular font beside their English counterparts.

As Shawn highlighted in his book *Research Is Ceremony*, Indigenist research is all about relationships: with ourselves, one another, the land, spirit, and with ideas. Our relationship with ideas is like every other relationship—it is alive and it changes over time. The way we see it, research and reconciliation are both ultimately about processes of growing, learning, and changing. We learn most when we are open to new ways of seeing, and there is nothing quite like a good story or conversation to get us to see things in a new way.

**Shawn:** What is the collective noun for a group of editors? A pack? A flock? A gaggle?

**Lindsay:** A gaggle—I like it.

**Shawn:** Alright then, let's go with gaggle. As the gaggle of editors of this book, what is the story that we want to tell?

**Lindsay:** For me, when I talk about what we're doing with this book I've been using the term *navigation* a lot. I think all of the stories that we're sharing are about navigation in one way or another. Contributors are coming from all different entry points or intersections of research and reconciliation, and their stories are uncovering a wide range of tensions and possibilities.

**Andrea:** I like that a lot because readers will also be coming from different entry points and navigating in different ways through the stories.

**Shawn:** A lot of people will be coming at the book thinking, "What does reconciliation mean to me? What is the theory behind it and what are some examples of people putting it into action?" I don't think any of these chapters specifically address the theory behind reconciliation.

**Lindsay:** You're right, they don't.

**Shawn:** We probably would have booted out a theory chapter in our abstract vetting process because it sounds too academic-ish. All of the chapters demonstrate reconciliation in practice, but no one has really unpacked it theoretically.

**Lindsay:** Yeah, I think we should keep the book as accessible as possible. Conversations about research, and about reconciliation actually, can be really inaccessible for a lot of people—usually the people who are affected the most. I want us to hold space for diverse and even conflicting perspectives that can help show just how complicated this work is and how relevant it is to all of us.

**Shawn:** Okay, I guess I could write more about this theoretical stuff myself, as it does tie in with the work that I'm now doing. A lot of people look at theory as being disconnected or purely abstract, so I can try to write something that brings in theory through story.

**Andrea:** One word that isn't explicit in the way we have organized the book and chapter headings is *healing*. It's really present in a lot of the chapters: it's there in the ones about identity and about institutions healing and moving forward.

**Lindsay:** I agree, healing is an important piece to this. It seems like there are two opposite things happening in reconciliation right now. The healing and moving forward, and the violence and moving back—and they're happening at the same time. The concerning part is when the moving back is being confused with moving forward and ongoing colonial violence is being masked as reconciliation.

**Andrea:** When you talk about the violence of reconciliation, Lindsay, I think of how I'm sometimes seeing people using the word *reconciliation* without thinking deeply about what they're doing, without reflecting. I've been asking Indigenous and non-Indigenous people who are actively involved in reconciliation work, "What does reconciliation mean to you?" The answers vary. In the Canadian context, some say reconciliation is about following specific recommendations of Canada's Truth and Reconciliation Commission, while for others it's about giving back land or creating entirely new institutions and practices together, and some people's answers are still along the lines of "saving Indigenous people." The saviour narrative is still really present for a lot of settlers, including those who are doing work relating to an idea about reconciliation. Obviously, this isn't what it means to the authors here and there's increasing awareness that there are those problematic narratives. But people are engaging in reconciliation in a range of ways and some of these ways are not so different from past versions of colonialism. The word *reconciliation* is being used as a shield, like a protective armour of good intentions, when the work that is being done isn't always different from other ugly things that came before.

**Shawn:** The contributors in this book are trying to move things forward, but with the recognition that other forces are at play that are moving things back. We have to recognize our part in this as editors—we were careful not to include chapters that looked like they were ticking the box of reconciliation in a bullshit way.

**Lindsay:** Definitely. We hold power in this process by choosing which stories we are connecting readers to. Some of the chapters talk about reconciliation fairly explicitly and others don't use the word at all. From what I've been seeing, the most meaningful work that's being done to improve relationships between Indigenous and non-Indigenous people in Canada doesn't actually touch the word *reconciliation*, or at least doesn't centre it. It can really get in the way.

**Andrea:** We also hold power in being able to highlight certain ideas. We really do this with the introductions to each of the three sections of the book. Each of us wrote one of the section intros, but the writing is based on conversations among us. We talk about ideas that we think are especially important right now in relation to reconciliation. It's stuff that we've talked about together over months and months of working together on this project. And we ask a lot of questions, questions we've asked ourselves, too. We want people to make their own connections with the ideas in this book and to really think of what reconciliation means for them and their communities at this time. We don't define reconciliation for people, instead we show a range of meanings and approaches that people are taking in different contexts and we invite people to think and feel for themselves.

**Lindsay:** And hopefully it will make some people uncomfortable. Like Shawn said, there are a lot of box-tickers engaging in bullshit ways. There are also a lot of spaces where people are appropriating concepts like Indigenization and reconciliation for their own purposes and I'm tired of it. I want those people to read this and to be a little bit uncomfortable—actually, a lot uncomfortable. I want them to have more questions than answers in relation to reconciliation and to become more critical of their role within these relations and their responsibilities to the territories they are on.

**Andrea:** Speaking of readers becoming uncomfortable, I think it's important that people know that this isn't a how-to guide. There is no "follow these four steps to do Indigenous research" here. Some people might not be comfortable with the approach that we've taken, but we've done it with a lot of intention. Indigenist approaches to research are as much about who we are as they are about what we do. We don't learn lessons about who we are and how we should be with one another through how-to guides. We learn these lessons through stories and experiences.

**Shawn:** And that's why it's so important that the book isn't written in conventional academic style. We were able to pull out a lot more of people's knowledge by inviting them to get creative and asking them not to just write about storytelling, but to write through stories—there's a difference.

**Lindsay:** I think that was one of the most rewarding parts of this project for me.

**Shawn:** Seeing how people responded to our invitation?

**Lindsay:** Yeah, it was hard for some people and freeing for others. You can really see that across the chapters. There's some disjointedness in the writing, but I really like it that way—I'm glad that we didn't try to influence their voices too much. It says something about how important it is to respect where people are at in their journeys and to maintain openness in how we try to understand one another.

**Shawn:** And also about learning through humour. It's fun how we tease each other, and I think it is a kind of stress release for us, or maybe protection from some of the serious bullshit and pain that we've had to deal with. I like that we were able

INTRODUCTION    xv

to incorporate some *Walking Eagle News* pieces into the book for this reason. People from outside of Canada might not get some of the context, but hopefully the intent of writer Tim Fontaine's humour comes through regardless.

**Andrea:** That reminds me, Shawn—recently we were speaking with one of the authors who talked about your book *Research Is Ceremony* as being a form of intellectual protection. For him, it created a space to do a different kind of work. I think there are a few different purposes at work here. There are the people who we want to make uncomfortable and that's really important. And the flip side, I think, is something like protection, creating safer spaces for people to do different kinds of intellectual work.

**Shawn:** The protection is important and so is the discomfort. An Elder I was talking with the other day referred to my family as "intellectual terrorists." We don't blow people up, but hopefully we can blow their minds. Sometimes we need a provocateur to give us impetus to move outside of our safe spaces.

**Lindsay:** And, in order to do this, having humility and patience is important. Pushing each other to learn in new ways, but trusting that knowledge will come to us as we need it and when we are ready for it. I see that with this book. Someone may pick it up and at first connect with one chapter's stories, then they might come back to it another time and find what they need in a different piece. They also might not find what they need in here at all, but hopefully that will motivate them to seek out knowledge somewhere else.

**Shawn:** I agree.

**Andrea:** I keep thinking that what we're asking of the reader is similar to what you encouraged in your book, Shawn, *Research Is Ceremony.* We're inviting people to enter into a relationship with ideas. To be open and challenged, to pay attention to the discomfort zones and not just close the book on them. We want people to enter into the parts of the book that are difficult and to have openness.

**Shawn:** That idea of inviting people along is important. Maybe that's how we are practising reconciliation in what we're doing—saying, look, here is this broad range of ideas. They don't all say the same thing, they aren't all pointing in the exact same direction. But that's what reconciliation is about: accepting that people can be going in different directions and doing their own thing and providing some freedom for them to do that. Well, not just providing freedom but giving some serious thought to why they're doing that.

**Lindsay:** Like holding space for each other's realities and the stages we are at in our learning and unlearning.

**Shawn:** It's also kind of like allyship. It's recognizing that we've got our struggle in this way, but just because our struggle is this way doesn't mean that others' struggle is the same as ours. Being a good ally is not saying that their struggle is exactly the same as ours or that they're going to find the exact same solution as us. So, like you said, being a good ally is finding that space.

**Lindsay:** Exactly.

**Shawn:** One of our students just handed in his thesis and he's such a good writer. His thesis is on rainforest restoration because this whole area where I am living now used to be rainforest and he's been working with people who are actively trying to replant rainforests. One of the chapters that he wrote is called "How I Weed and Write." One of the people in the project said that she doesn't actually regenerate the rainforest, all she does is pick out invasive weeds and then the rainforest regenerates itself. It's that whole idea that you don't have to actively go and promote reconciliation or healing for someone else. All you have to do is pick out the weeds. All you have to do is remove barriers and provide the space and people will do it for themselves, or the rainforest will do it itself.

**Andrea:** I really like that as a metaphor for allyship.

**Shawn:** That's what I thought, it was really good. It's a metaphor for writing, too. Using writing to edit ideas.

**Andrea:** I think it can also be about weeding out ways of doing things. The act of noticing, paying attention, and making space for something different.

**Lindsay:** And sometimes it's just about getting out of the way.

**Shawn:** Yes, and using your leverage as people who know how the Western system works to clear space for others to do what they want to do for themselves. When we use our own power to create and protect space for others it also helps them to find their own place: who they are and the tools that they have to bring to this reconciliation process.

**Lindsay:** The change that is needed isn't going to happen all at once, but we can use these tools and the opportunities we have now to start getting some things done.

## REFERENCES

Truth and Reconciliation Commission of Canada. (2015). *Honouring the truth, reconciling for the future: Summary of the final report of the Truth and Reconciliation Commission of Canada*. Retrieved from http://publications.gc.ca/collections/collection_2015/trc/IR4-7-2015-eng.pdf

Wilson, S. (2008). *Research is ceremony: Indigenous research methods*. Halifax: Fernwood.

# SECTION I

# BEING, LONGING, AND BELONGING

*by Lindsay DuPré*

Unsettling truths of settler colonialism involves messy processes that uncover not only new information, but also new questioning and understanding of who we are in the world. We are challenged to reflect on our collective histories and to reconsider the ways in which we are in relation to one another. This navigation of relationality requires us to simultaneously hold space for the past, present, and future so that despite our different locations—both geographic and social—we can realign ourselves in more just ways. Research offers possibilities to understand our ontological gaps, but can also create more confusion.

As I've been working with Shawn and Andrea on this book, the theme of belonging has emerged from our conversations with each other and the contributing authors. In some of the chapters, the idea of belonging is raised in regard to how people are using research as a tool for reconciling their individual identities and healing journeys. In others, authors discuss more systemic explorations of belonging, looking at how reconciliation is—or isn't—being taken up within institutions through the presence of Indigenous knowledge. While some authors have chosen to focus on one more than the other, their stories indicate how closely tangled our longing to belong and individual identities are within larger systems of power. There is reciprocity within this entanglement, where Indigenous knowledge and research paradigms can help us find belonging as individuals, and our work as individuals can also influence how Indigenous knowledge and methodologies find new—or old—ways to belong.

## WHAT DO OUR IDENTITIES HAVE TO DO WITH RECONCILIATION?

The short answer is: everything. Who we are and our experiences in the world are shaped by the history of the land that we are on. In Canada and other places mentioned throughout this book, this includes a history of violent colonization. Settlers have tried to control Indigenous lands through dehumanizing policies that have attempted to disconnect us from our identities and land-based knowledge systems. Some families have been able to hold on to their cultures and languages, while others have had their ties to community more gravely severed and they will never return home. For those of us who fall somewhere in between, reclaiming our stories and cultural knowledge presents pathways to belonging.

But it is critical that Indigenous–non-Indigenous relations not be oversimplified. Reconciliation needs intersectional analysis and theories of change that reflect the diverse identities and realities of people living on these lands. Part of this requires understanding that colonization is a global project that has displaced, and continues to displace, people from all over the world. Forced migration due to war, slavery, human trafficking, and climate change have also contributed to this movement and will continue to influence why and how people are moving on (and leaving) Indigenous lands. At the same time, however, love can also be found in this movement. Families and communities continue to grow with connections to different places, peoples, and cultures. These identities beautifully complicate reconciliation and speak to why our belonging cannot be defined through an identity check box.

The complexity of reconciliation and belonging also includes other dimensions of identity, including gender, sexuality, class, and ability. The chapters in this section touch on a range of these dimensions and speak to how they influence our experiences in the world and, consequently, how we approach our research. While reading them we encourage you to reflect on your own identity, and to think about the following: What is your relationship to settler colonialism and heteropatriarchy? In what spaces do you feel a sense of belonging? How does your longing to belong inform your work? What is the relationship between power, privilege, and belonging?

## WHAT DOES IT MEAN FOR INDIGENOUS KNOWLEDGE SYSTEMS TO BELONG TODAY?

Government and institutional interest in reconciliation is rapidly changing. We need to seize opportunities to confront the dominance of colonial institutions while we have them, and to find new ways for Indigenous knowledge to breathe life into how we understand, live, and work together. True belonging, however, does not rest in inclusion to these spaces. Increasing the number of Indigenous people, courses, and content in academia opens some possibilities, but it does not necessarily translate into a meaningful, or sustainable, presence of Indigenous knowledge. Similarly, research ethics boards can improve guidelines for working with Indigenous communities and recognize Indigenous research methodologies, but this does not mean that researchers are doing work that actually advances justice for Indigenous peoples or our ways of knowing.

Determining how Indigenous knowledge can belong within colonial systems is also difficult because we are still in a time of healing and resurgence. Indigenous people are at different places in our connection to Indigenous knowledge and, depending on where we are from, we may carry different protocols for how this knowledge should be accessed and cared for. Because of this, we might not agree on what these inclusion processes should look like and this is further complicated when we are working on territories that are not our own. If institutions rush to increase Indigenous presence through tokenism and oversimplified, pan-Indigenous understandings of Indigeneity then the result will continue to be more colonial paternalism. This work is political and requires firm grounding in place, with significant investments of time and resources.

Rather than seeking belonging solely through inclusion, there is also important work to do outside of these institutions. Relationships with Indigenous knowledge are being strengthened through the revitalization of Indigenous languages, ceremonies, governance, food systems, art, and other cultural practices. Without people dedicating their lives to this work, we would have little connection to the ways of knowing that (some) colonial institutions are trying to include. These people are also researchers and knowledge mobilizers, and so appropriate resources must go into their work in order to rebuild our own institutions. This also includes investments in the protection of water and land rematriation as essential steps in decolonization.

Indigenous knowledge systems have lived through these lands since time immemorial and will continue to be here long after the current buzz and definitions of reconciliation die out. Whether or not institutions make space for this knowledge does not change this, but it can present possibilities for advancing justice and belonging for Indigenous peoples while we are operating within these systems. As you read through these chapters, think about what it means for knowledge to belong while considering the following: Where does your knowledge come from? What are the risks and possibilities of colonial institutions integrating Indigenous ways of knowing? How can Indigenous knowledge be protected and revived outside of these institutions?

## CHAPTER 1

# Why Research Is Reconciliation

*by Shawn Wilson and Margaret Hughes*

––––––––––

Tansi, I'm Shawn Wilson. I'm Opaskwayak Cree, from northern Manitoba in Canada, but I currently live on Bundjalung territory along the east coast of Australia. I generally introduce myself as a dad, community psychologist, great-great-grandfather and grandson, a teacher, and an Indigenist researcher.

I'm Margaret Hughes. I'm White Settler American from Fort Worth, Texas. I also currently live in Bundjalung Country. I'm a mum, a community worker, a queer woman, a practising Buddhist, and an Indigenist researcher in training.

––––––––––

**Shawn:** When Andrea and I first started talking about this book, it was exciting. (Lindsay joined us a bit later.) It seemed like a natural next step from some of the other research work I've been doing, and a carry on from the book *Research Is Ceremony: Indigenous Research Methods.*

For me, reconciliation is all about action. Indigenous reality is relational: we are our relations with family, ancestors, environment, ideas—with everything. When we realize that reality is relational, we also become accountable to all our relations. It requires us to use our power as researchers in line with our values. I choose to act upon the foundational Cree values of Caring, Sharing, Compassion, and Truth. To care is not enough, to be compassionate is not enough, to know the truth is not enough. We must use this awareness to guide our actions— as researchers and as human beings.

**Margaret:** That's really compelling to me—that we are accountable as researchers and as human beings, and that it's active. My work has been around racial disparity in the criminal justice system, both in America, where I'm from, and here in Australia. In Chicago, I was working with communities to develop or revive alternatives to the dominant system. Now my research is about how the broader Australian community can respectfully learn from Aboriginal systems for maintaining balance. So, to me, the context of reconciliation is colonization, but the activity—the actual change work—is personal and relational. My experience of community work in Chicago, especially circle work, is that you have to be in there as a person. You can't be outside of it. I feel like I learned how to be a person from sitting in circle. I think it's the same with research. If it's going to affect change, it has to be personal. I have to be putting myself in there.

That being said, I've been reluctant to join this conversation, partly because I feel very new to Indigenist research, and also because as a White person, I'm still learning to listen. But I recognize that it doesn't make sense to write about relationality and the importance of being in the research, and then pretend that I'm not here!

**Shawn:** Yeah, we can't just think or write about relationality and accountability, we have to demonstrate it, too. And an important part of that relational accountability might be building relationship with whoever is reading this chapter—that could be people just starting to learn about reconciliation and research, or people who've been working on that process for decades. I've written before about how research is a ceremony for engaging with ideas and actively shaping reality, a reality that is relational. As we become truly accountable researchers, we become agents of reconciliation. We become the peacekeepers with/in relations, responsible for the restoration of harmony in all our relations.

**Margaret:** At first that feels like a big claim, but when I think about the activity of research, if it isn't about respectful engagement and restoration of relationships, it doesn't make any sense to me. On the one hand, if the research process itself isn't aligned with my values and the values of the people I'm doing research with, or doesn't reflect a long-term commitment to respectful relationships and accountability, well beyond a discrete project, then I don't think meaningful change is going to come out of it either. On the other hand, if there is respect, accountability, and open-hearted communication happening in the research relationship, that's powerful in and of itself.

**Shawn:** We have to recognize that as researchers we have power. We have to use our power and knowledge responsibly. We have to act. That might be acting to resolve differences or acting to ensure accuracy or acting by refusing to follow the status quo. It requires us to use our power as researchers to change ourselves as individuals, but also all of humankind. These are big claims, and we have some equally big aims for this book. But we also have to remember that we don't have to achieve all of these goals right this minute. We're working on a thousand-year plan. So this chapter will start things off by building some of the theoretical background and justification for why and how we've developed the book the way we have, and we'll see where we can take you (yes, *you*) from there.

## INDIGENIST RESEARCH

First off, let's talk about what we mean by *Indigenist*, so we're all speaking the same language. We're using *Indigenist* to describe a philosophical approach to research that centres Indigenous ontology, epistemology, and axiology (Wilson, 2008), or Ways of Knowing, Ways of Being, and Ways of Doing (K. Martin & Mirraboopa, 2003). Indigenist research is about who we are, how we know and engage with Knowledge, what we do as researchers, and the ways we enact relational accountability (all of which we'll talk more about in this chapter). So, we're using *Indigenist* to label a philosophy that includes a relational and emergent understanding of reality and Knowledge, and requires a particular way of behaving in the world.

Within the broader context of Indigenist philosophy and theory, researchers develop and utilize methodologies grounded in local and specific tribal epistemologies; for example, Indigenous scholars have articulated Nêhiýaw epistemology (Kovach, 2010), Quandamooka ontology (K. Martin & Mirraboopa, 2003; K. L. Martin, 2008), and Varvateten/Tolai research design (Lubett, 2018). The term *Indigenist* is therefore not meant to be prescriptive or exclusive, but rather to point to common elements of research approaches born out of Indigenous philosophies and conducted by and with Indigenous communities.

It follows that just because a researcher is Indigenous, doesn't mean their methodology is Indigenist; Indigenous researchers pursue research using all sorts of philosophical and methodological approaches. And, by extension, non-Indigenous researchers can also undertake Indigenist research, provided they are working from a relational understanding of reality, engaging respectfully with Indigenous Knowledge and Indigenous Peoples, and learning how to behave themselves properly.

## Relational Ontology

Indigenist ontology and epistemology—what is, and how we know what is—are based on an understanding that reality is relationships. We are our relationships: to self, family, Nations (other peoples), our environment, ideas, ancestors, the cosmos, everything that IS (Wilson, 2008). We are not all separate entities that are interacting within relationships—we are the relationships.

Put another way, our relationships make us who we are and locate us within a whole system. For example, in Cree there is no word for "grandmother"; someone is either "my grandmother" or "your grandmother." You can't be a grandmother without being attached to a grandchild.

Similarly, we don't exist outside of our relationships to Place, which are continuous with our relationships to people. Kombumerri Elder and scholar Auntie Mary Graham (with Morgan Brigg and Polly Walker) writes,

> Connection with Place, whether direct or mediated through Place's role as a template for social relatedness, provides Aboriginal people with a type of unconditional ontological security. A basic precept of Aboriginal worldview is that "you are not alone in the world." Place serves as a sentient companion, a calibrating device that informs Aboriginal people of "where" and "who" they are at any time. (Graham, Brigg, & Walker, 2014, p. 81)

Reality as relationships includes our relations to ancestors, family, and Place, as well as ideas and cultural understandings that make us who we are. In the context of research, a relational understanding of reality requires that we acknowledge where and how we are connected and co-emergent with the ideas and questions we research. So, we must attend to how we fit into the web of relationships that make up our research context—the People and Land and Stories with whom we co-participate in the research ceremony (Kovach, 2010).

**Margaret:** For me, a key aspect of doing respectful work in this space is position-ing myself as a researcher. Part of preparing for the research ceremony (Wilson, 2008) is doing personal work to strengthen my existing relationships: with my-self; with my family and ancestors and lineage—the people who make me who I am; with the places I am from; with the ideas I have been engaged with for a long time, which continue into this work; and with my heartful intentions in pursu-ing the project.

**Shawn:** That's certainly what I've been taught by various Elders. Our relational ontol-ogy means things from everyday life aren't separate from ceremony, including any research ceremonies that we perform. So, living a lifestyle that is congruent with what you are trying to achieve through your research is crucial, as is incor-porating what you learn from your research back into your lifestyle afterward. The knowledge that you gain, from research or any other way, is also relational, so you will only understand it fully if it is incorporated into all the other relations—that's how knowledge becomes wisdom.

## Indigenous Knowledge Is Relational

Indigenous epistemology, or Ways of Knowing, is also relational and emergent. Indigenous Knowledge is alive, it has agency, it moves (Adams, Wilson, Heavy Head, & Gordon, 2015; Graham, 2017; Sheehan, 2011). Therefore, Knowledge can't be "discovered" or "owned" but instead it reveals itself, is experienced, is shared (Adams et al., 2015). As researchers, we aren't separate from the pro-cess, but rather participate in relationship with what we are learning. As Dawn Adams, a Choctaw scholar explains,

> In a relational system, participation—being in relationship to the thing you are learning about and to the knowledge itself—is essential to the learning process. I mean, if knowledge is generated through relationship, you literally cannot learn if you take an objective "apart" stance outside the thing you're trying to understand. Which does take us back to relationality as a core process. (Adams et al., 2015, p. 24)

Knowledge participates in this relationship. The alive and agentive quality of Knowledge is evident in the central place of Stories within Indigenist epistemol-ogy (which is also why this is a book of Stories!). Dawn Adams again:

> We see Story as conveying meaning to people in its own way—Knowledge having and expressing agency—so we do not overtly state the Story's meaning.

The meaning is left ambiguous because we cannot, ourselves, say what it's go-ing to be to any particular person. The meaning arises within the relationship between the Story and any specific listener. (Adams et al., 2015, p. 19)

Stories are a way that Knowledge communicates and participates in relation-ships, which can occur whether Stories are shared orally, visually, through dance, song, poetry, or sometimes, through writing them down in English. Indigenist Knowledge is not made up of discrete or arbitrary relationships, but rather rep-resents a system of relationships that encompasses worldviews and cultures that arise from their Place.

**Margaret:** For me, to approach research in a way that respects the emergent and agentive quality of Indigenous Knowledge involves an orientation that Nia Emmanouil describes as "ontological openness" (2017): a willingness and com-mitment to open to ways of knowing and sources of knowledge that may be new and unfamiliar (to me); and to persist through uncomfortable experiences of not-knowing and having my existing ontology challenged. Developing new relationships (with research participants; with Place; with new ideas and Knowl-edges) requires a level of vulnerability on my part as a researcher, as well as a willingness to learn and grow and change, and take cues from the broader environment.

**Shawn:** You've touched on another important point, in that there are whole systems of knowledge, or systems of relationships working through all of this. So those relationships aren't just individual or interpersonal, they are with *everything*. They include environmental and spiritual relationships that we hold with the Land, as well as relationships with ideas themselves. These relationships make up our cultures, our worldviews, our languages and histories, and our place in the cos-mos. Our systems of knowledge inspire us to be open to learning from all of these relationships.

**Margaret:** There is also a moral component to ontological openness, in the context of decolonizing research practices. My intention in my own research is to privi-lege the ontological perspectives of research participants and ensure that their perspectives come through in my analysis and final presentation of the research. This moral component is reflected in a commitment to relational accountability, which we need to talk about more.

To engage with Indigenist epistemology in research is to engage respectfully with these systems of Knowledge and understand our place in the relationships.

We will talk more about respect a bit later, but part of this engagement is the quality of our listening, or how we attend to the way Knowledge is moving in our research context. This is the process of knowing, rather than the content (Adams et al., 2015). As the Bawaka research collective explains,

> These messages are part of the way we communicate with Country.[1] And they are part of the way Country communicates with us. To hear those messages, we need to attend with great care to the world. When the wärrkarr[2] is in flower, we know it is time to hunt stingray. You know the sweat you felt when you sat drinking tea on the sand earlier this evening? That sweat tells you that the fruits are ripening. We know that when it is hot there will be good fruits to eat. The thirst we feel in our bodies is linked with the trees that give the fruit. We know and the tree knows. We feel these messages in our body, and our body sends messages to the fruits and the animals. In our heart and our soul we feel the season unfolding. The fruits will be ready when we go out on Country, when we need them. These messages are part of our very being. To hear these messages, you have to be aware of the connections and relationships which bring everything into being. You have to be attentive and open. You need to be alert to the world in all its complexity. (2015, p. 275)

The research collective describes this as a methodology of attending, which has to do with caring, bringing one's whole being to the process of engaging and communicating with the human and more-than-human entities that make us who we are. This way of knowing includes honouring the "messages in our body" and the feelings in our "heart and soul." Whereas Western academic knowledge systems privilege cognitive knowing to the exclusion of other ways of knowing, Indigenist epistemology includes cognitive knowing as well as experiential understanding; sensory, emotional, and spiritual knowing; intuition; dreams; and cultural knowing (Adams et al., 2015; Meyer, 2001). Again, these ways of knowing emerge in the context of our relatedness.

**Margaret:** To me, part of being an Indigenist researcher is bringing my whole self to the project. I am still finding the words to describe what this means for me, but it includes seeing the research process as more than an intellectual exercise involving my mental faculties. My desire to work in an Indigenous Knowledge context has to do in part with a deep respect and resonance with a more holistic approach to being a human being; an acknowledgement that we are not brains on sticks, and the way we "come to know" involves our whole selves. Being a researcher in that sense has to do with being willing to engage my intuition and my spiritual commitments in the research process. I believe finding a holistic approach is important to the integrity of the research and the extent to which I am able to respectfully engage with Indigenous forms of inquiry.

**Shawn:** Yes, that's why I have come to understand that research is a ceremony. It is a ceremony that knowingly builds relationship with Knowledge, so that we allow that knowledge to move through us. What we hope to get out of the research ceremony is the miracle of enlightenment—to inform us and help us to better understand the cosmos around us. We can use that enlightened understanding to better fulfill our role and responsibilities in all of those relationships.

This book explicitly privileges Indigenous Ways of Knowing through telling research stories and including visual and poetic presentations of Knowledge as well as soundscapes and the written word. We have organized the book this way both because it is an appropriate and respectful way of communicating, and because Indigenous Knowledge and Indigenous Ways of Knowing have been deliberately excluded, marginalized, and denigrated through the ongoing process of colonization. In the spirit of moving toward balance, it is necessary to reclaim a privileged space for these Stories and appreciate the sensitive political context within which this communication takes place.

## RELATIONAL ACCOUNTABILITY

### Indigenist Methodology and Axiology

It follows from understanding reality and Knowledge as relational, that our process of undertaking research should be accountable to those relationships. The methodology by which we gain new Knowledge is a process of strengthening or building our relationships—with community, with Place, with new ideas or insights. The moral component, the axiology of Indigenist research, is that everything about the research process must align with our values and communicate respect and accountability to all our relations. For example, the Bawaka research collective's methodology of attending is underpinned by a relational ethics of care (2015). In an Indigenist research paradigm, both methodology and axiology are about relational accountability.

Relational accountability is significant because of the context of ongoing colonization in and through research (Smith, 2013), and because relational ontology and epistemology dictate that we can't actually learn anything without relating properly, which means being accountable. The Bawaka research collective describes how relational ontology and epistemology lead to accountability:

> A methodology of attending requires more than listening closely, being radically open to feelings and messages, it also requires relating to the world in a different way, understanding ourselves in a different way. And once you do that, you have to act in a different way, with a different kind of ethics. You see, for Yolŋu, humans are not inherently separate from non-humans, from Country, or from the world in which we live. We are part of it and are bound in relations of responsibility, care and reciprocity. We relate to animals, plants, weather, geology, songs, dances as kin. They make us who we are, just as we make them who they are. (2015, p. 275)

Relational accountability points to the experience that when we recognize reality as relationships, we have to act differently. We become bound by our relations of responsibility, care, and reciprocity. We have to act in accordance with our values—well beyond the limited framework of academic ethics requirements (K. L. Martin, 2008)—and fulfill our responsibility to care. Relational accountability therefore comes into every aspect of the research process, from formulating research questions, to developing appropriate methodology and methods, to analysis, and, finally, to how research is presented and to whom (Wilson, 2008). At every stage, we have to ask ourselves, am I fulfilling my responsibilities to my relationships? Is this of benefit to the community? Am I being true to my values? Am I being true to the values and wishes of the communities with whom I'm working? Is this research approach enacting an ethics of care?

Cora Weber-Pillwax, a Métis scholar, explains the way responsibility to community provides a primary reference point for ethical research:

> When we actually deconstruct systems, what does that mean in real language, day-to-day, sitting around the table? Rather than university students sitting around talking about it, that's one thing. That's useless to me. I cannot waste my time doing that unless I know this discussion is going to lead to some change out there in that community. That's critical to me. That's the most important aspect of research and I don't waste my time on anything that doesn't go there for me. That is my axiology. (as quoted in Wilson, 2008, p. 110)

Indigenist research must ask questions that are relevant to participating communities and must engage with Knowledge in ways that reflect a shared understanding of what is important. In a recent seminar on the research agenda for Aboriginal Affairs in New South Wales, a presenter commented, "What we don't know about Aboriginal health disadvantage could be written on a post-age stamp. We don't need more research about health disadvantage, we need to know what is working to improve Aboriginal health" (Sarra, 2018). Research questions matter, and part of relational accountability is ensuring that research questions are genuinely aligned with community priorities and, as Cora states, are going to "lead to some change out there in that community."

Noonuccal scholar Karen Martin talks about the importance of relational accountability in the context of analysis and research presentation. She describes a process of harmonization whereby research stories are interpreted and conveyed to reframe and restore Aboriginal Stories in a contemporary context. Martin presents her research findings through oral, written, and visual stories to ensure that the process is culturally meaningful both to herself as a Noonuccal Quan-damooka researcher and to the Burungu, Kuku-Yalanji research participants. The potential of such a research approach is powerful: Martin describes the Indigenist research paradigm as a "means to restore our Stories towards reclaim-ing our sovereignty" (2008, p. 35). When we are accountable in our research relationships, the research process moves toward relatedness and contributes to restoration.

**Shawn:** I choose to act by the Cree values of Caring, Compassion, Truth, and Sharing. Caring is a state of mind that is aware within relationships. It is the opposite of apathy and extends on an emotional, physical, mental, and spiritual level. If I care about you, I care what you think, but I also assume some sort of responsibility for the way we are in relationship; what happens to you will affect me as well. You have to be aware of the relationship, that it's a two-way thing. Caring and com-passion are really closely related—you have to be compassionate, otherwise you wouldn't care. So, I care about someone, but it's not in a selfish way. Truth has to do with not deluding self or others. And sharing is the process of acting on the first three. Because you are compassionate and caring, it forces you to act on that, so I'm going to share. It's through enacting sharing that truth can come about. To do all of these things is to be a loving person; then you are practising Sakihewaywin—love in action. Truth is about not allowing self-delusion, and also knowing true history. So, our actions are based upon truth and congruent with values. And the purpose of those actions is to resolve differences, to restore har-mony in relationships.

Martin, K. L. (2008). *Please knock before you enter: Aboriginal regulation of outsiders and the implications for researchers.* Teneriffe, Australia: Post Pressed.

Meyer, M. (2001). Acultural assumptions of empiricism: A Native Hawaiian critique. *Canadian Journal of Native Education, 25*(2), 188–198.

Reconciliation. (2018). *OxfordDictionaries.com.* Retrieved from https://en.oxforddictionaries .com/definition/reconciliation

Sarra, C. (2018). Keynote presentation at A Research Agenda for Our Time, Lismore, Australia.

Sheehan, N. W. (2011). Indigenous Knowledge and respectful design: An evidence-based approach. *Design Issues, 27*(4), 68–80. doi:10.1162/DESI_a_00106

Smith, L. T. (2013). *Decolonizing methodologies: Research and Indigenous Peoples* (2nd ed.). London, UK: Zed Books.

Wilson, S. (2008). *Research is ceremony: Indigenous research methods.* Halifax: Fernwood.

## CHAPTER 2

# Breath as Research:
# Finding Cracks in the Wall

*by gzhibaeassigae jen meunier*

———

gzhibaeassigae n'dishnikaaz. baskatong minwaa kichesipirini n'doonjibaa. migizi n'dodem, niizh manidoweg n'dow. my colonial name is jen meunier. i'm a queer non-status algonquin half-breed without the words to thank those who call me auntie, niece, brother, sister, partner.

———

I wish we could sit together for this story. You could come to my house and we'd sit at the table we made out of an old skid, I'd make you a good strong coffee, and we'd talk as the light moved across the room. That's a good way to hear a story. But instead you're reading these words on a page.

Who knows where you might be. You might even be in jail. Or worse, in school. If you are, imagine taking pages out of this book and sliding them in between the cracks that inevitably appear in old colonial buildings that are made to hold people in or out. Imagine those pages can be blown full of breath—not just the breath that read these words out loud in my kitchen, but all of your ancestors who speak to you, and my ancestors who speak to me. Imagine the force of all of our lungs together, filling the interstellar and interstitial spaces in between the atoms of that page til the breath becomes a roar and the crack splits open. Can you pull it apart with your fingers yet? Can you stick your head out and look around? Now can you pull your body through (watch yer balls!) until you're standing there on the outside?

You might blink and miss a story. You might drive past a corner every day and miss the greatest story that no one but someone sitting there will ever hear. You just might want to be careful and listen. For a long time. You might want to.

This is a story about a queer half-breed who slid their fingers along the wall and found a crack. That wall was York University and it was 2005. You know that town you grew up in that never felt like home? Remember the day you left. That's how it felt. I left home looking for home and landed in Mi'kmaw scholar and professor Bonita Lawrence's classroom in a course called Aboriginal Peoples and Colonization: Identity, Recovery, and Sovereignty. Her strong, sure arms reminded me of an old picture of my aunt Cecile, who never married and lived on the laker boats that traversed the Great Lakes. On the first day of class, Professor Lawrence told us we'd be smudging and that the fire alarms might go off but hopefully not, and she rolled her eyes at the racism of administrative policies. We had this huge book of readings. That was the first time I'd heard of Maria Campbell, Ward Churchill, Linda Tuhiwai Smith. My fingers slid over the surface, looking for a handhold, landmarks, something. All those closed White faces and well-adjusted clothing left no roughness to distinguish souls or geography. Fingers slid. Looking for a crack.

I made my way through readings by Thomas King about a million porcupines crying in the dark in residential schools, the sarcastic and brilliant disproving of the Bering Strait theory by Vine Deloria Jr. The loneliness and existential fear began to make sense and take shape, but so did the feeling that I belonged somewhere. I scanned the faces of people on the long bus rides to and from the university until it became an unconscious radar, looking for other Indians. On one bus ride, I heard someone shouting in this desperate voice that every hydro post was a tree crying out for the woods. We got off the bus together and played the jukebox in a basement bar, then we just walked around for hours in the cold Toronto night. She was Cree. She had cancer. She called me her daughter and smoothed down my hair. I never saw her again. How does anyone survive this city?

I dreamed of bodies and bodies and bodies. I began to look at the other people in the class and wondered if the White students were lying in their beds at night and thinking about genocide. As time went on, that seemed to be part of the widening gap between colonizer and the colonized. There were about three or four of us in the class who were Indigenous and from what I remember, mostly we listened. Mostly. One of the first things Professor Lawrence stood up and said was that she wasn't going to expect us to answer for our Nations or communities or our own experience. So, we had the choice to speak or to listen. I listened a lot. For a long time. It was hard to speak when it felt like my heart kept tearing open. There was this homesickness that came on so hard that it stopped up my throat and weighted every move and there was no relieving it by going back to that small town. It was a supernatural homesickness. I don't tell too many people that but I knew what it was. Fingers sliding with no traction on the slick streets.

After class one day, Bonita said she had something to talk to me about. She was doing this project and it was about non-status Algonquins. "I'm a non-status Algonquin," I said. "I know," she said, "that's why I asked you." There was another student who was also Algonquin and she'd asked him, too. I had no idea what a research assistant was and had never held any job that paid above minimum wage. She explained that she was going to give me a tape recorder and some cassette tapes, just a few to start off with. I had to play the tape a little ways, then transcribe exactly what was said. They were interviews with Algonquin people: community leaders and ordinary people who'd been around for a long time, Elders, family members, organizers. They told family stories in hushed tones. Some of them told stories for the first time in a long time. They talked about the history of our people. Not the kind of history you read in textbooks, but the kind of knowledge that gets remembered and told in families who hold on for hundreds of years. Some of the Elders told stories of windigo. Some of the knowledge concerned the government and their twisted ways of stealing the land and getting us to fight each other so we wouldn't think about fighting them. Stories about stories.

I have this thing with books. When I was a kid, I thought they could take you away. Not in the metaphorical sense but for real, like, out of this world and into another reality. Especially old books, the kind that smell good. I cried so hard the day I realized that the magic wasn't going to happen. Until the day it did, through those voices. There was this rush of breath and it was like being able to see a thread that has always been there but you couldn't see it til it was struck and thrummed back down through time and stirred something deep that you could feel with fingers and heart, that could be filled with breath. My fingers found a crack in the wall and I hung on.

I sat alone through the cold winter in a small apartment in Toronto that I shared with two White women. Sometimes I just sat there and listened to those tapes and cried. It was the first time in my life that I didn't feel alone. I never knew another Native kid growing up or another family like mine. Now I knew. But what came with that knowledge was homesickness, and listening to those stories didn't make it go away. It got stronger. It got worse. I had the TV tuned to APTN constantly. I went a little crazy and fell in love with Rebecca Veevee and the way she laughed with her mouth open as her knife thwacked through a goose neck. I stole a Kashtin CD from the library. I went to the Native Centre on Spadina when they had Thursday night socials, but everybody had their own friends already and I felt too gay and too weird to fit in. At the end of the day, though, the tapes waited for me. I started writing back to them and talking back to them. In a way, it was a little like getting letters from people all of a sudden but still being locked up in solitary confinement. You go a little more crazy but you get a little less lonely. Hanging on, I was starting to crack a little, too.

I think it was Bonita who told me about this Elders conference that was going to be at Trent University that February. Everybody was really excited because William Commanda was going to be there and he was the carrier and keeper of wampum and would be bringing them with him to this conference. I went to see him. I remember he was very old and we were all very quiet.

It felt like those wampum were the real books and they could take us not into another world, but the real world, the spirit world, of this world. It felt like we were real and the buildings around us were not.

That was the last day of the conference and I didn't want to stick around after that. I had brought the tapes, of course, and one of them was from this Elder who lived in a community not too far from Peterborough. "I'll just drive up there," I thought. "I'll just drive up there and maybe I'll see him and maybe we'll talk but probably not. But I'll drive up there." It was seven hours. By the time I got up there it was pitch black and near midnight and I drove down the roads slowly, and then suddenly, the signs were in Anishinaabemowin. I learned the word for "road" that way: mikan. I followed the road down and drove around the lake and of course everybody was asleep. I just drove and drove, listening to the Elder on the tape and following my headlights with his voice surrounding me.

Then all of a sudden, I didn't feel it anymore. The homesickness. It was just … gone. I turned off the ignition, got out, and stood shivering in the cold night air on the side of the road with no lights from the car and no lights from the city. The stars were very clear and bright and it was very quiet. The pain and weight had left. There was just breath and air, floating out into the darkness around me. I hadn't been homesick for people. I'd been homesick for the land.

I got back in the car and drove back to the city. No happy ending. The decade following that was all about coming home and I couldn't tell you the moment when the homesickness went away for good because there was no single moment. Maybe it happened when I moved back to Algonquin territory and lived there for a while. Maybe it was because of the people who call me sister and auntie and friend and partner. That crack widened as we shared breath, around kitchen tables, on long car rides, late at night holding an occupation in land defence, sometimes in the backseat of a car outside a reclamation, in sweat lodges and in ceremony. I felt the breath and strength of writers who, incredibly, can transmit words and experience spirit-to-spirit through the transmission of a page. Those walls are not so strong that they can hold up under our breath. There always were too many of us for them. There always will be. Think of it. Even when we die, we stick around. There will never be enough settlers to overwhelm all our spirits for the thousands of years our bodies have been buried and lived and made love all over the land that loves us. The crack is widening. It widens in spite of, not because of, the racist and colonial institutions whose gates we often found ourselves dancing around and in and out of.

"My auntie used to be like you," that good woman sister-friend said. "Going around here and there living in her car, looking for a home. She found it," she said. "You will too."

Maybe it was because I finally took a trip up north and talked with my Uncle Clem. He told me where we were from was called Baskatong, but it wasn't like we could just go there because in 1929, the government flooded it. There was this priest who was in charge of digging up the graves of those who were buried at the mission before the land was flooded. They reburied our dead in Grand-Remous, a very small town in rural Quebec. There's a sign there at the reburial site. I went and looked for it but couldn't find it and the White folks there didn't know what

I was talking about. Our home was flooded to make way for the construction of the Mercier Dam. I did find the dam. Hard to miss.

I asked my uncle why he thought his mother didn't speak to him in the language. We were walking through the Walmart parking lot in Timmins going to visit his buddies at the McDonald's. He looked thoughtful for a moment and then he said, "I think, maybe she was ashamed." Then he told me a story about outsmarting the Ministry of Natural Resource guys.

That project that Bonita Lawrence started became a book. It's called *Fractured Homeland: Federal Recognition and Algonquin Identity in Ontario* (2012). I had mailed Uncle Clem a copy of the book shortly after it was published. He came down from Timmins for the funeral when my mother's oldest brother, Bob, passed away suddenly, and he brought it with him. He came up to me and my mom excitedly, waving the book in one hand. "It's all here!" he said. "Everything I told you, it's all in here! I got so excited when I got to the end of it, that I just had to go back and read it all over again!" That was the last time we got to talk to each other. He left this world not too long after that. But not before he got to read the same stories that held me together in those early years of finding home.

We find these cracks in the walls of the institutions, we dance around their edges and widen the crack through our breath and we hang on to each other and pull each other through. In the interstitial and interstellar spaces between our words and in the silence of a dark night sky and alone in some apartment. We breathe life into each other and thrum the threads between us, the voices crackle to life and underwater, the graves might be gone but the land is still there. The land is still here.

We could make these stories about redemption or salvation or reconciliation, we could put a spin on them that blurs them just enough so they resemble something the colonizer will find useful to his own machines. Is there a word in your language for reconciliation? What, exactly, are we reconciling ourselves to?

Widen the crack. And when you stick your head out, look around. When you find yourself breaking through the wall, look back at me and tell me what you see. Tell me everything. I want to know it all. Tell me about the cracks so I can find my own. All our breath together can split them open. Put your body through the wall. Watch yourself dancing in the mirror to see how your ancestors moved.

Maybe those cops and those politicians and those smooth-talking negotiators you dance around will not see your dancing for what it is and you might dance right on past them through those cracks in the wall and they'll forever be scratching their heads wondering how it was you escaped.

Maybe you will transcribe that breath onto paper. Maybe you will whisper stories in the dark. Maybe you will call that "research" and someone will read the book before they die or maybe they will hold it close to their chest and find their way home.

But be careful. And listen. You might drive past a corner every day and miss the greatest story that no one but someone sitting there will ever hear. You just might want to be careful and listen. For a long time. You might want to.

## ACKNOWLEDGEMENTS

Chi miigwetch to my auntie Marilyn Maracle, Jaret Maracle, who first heard it, Dr. Bonita Lawrence, Dr. Minqi Li, Vinh, Ratanak Ly, and Kwaku Agyeman, without whom none of this would have come together the way it did.

## REFERENCE

Lawrence, B. (2012). *Fractured homeland: Federal recognition and Algonquin identity in Ontario.* Vancouver: University of British Columbia Press.

## CHAPTER 3

# Proclaiming Our Indigenous-Black Roots at a Time of Truth and Reconciliation

*by Ciann L. Wilson and Ann Marie Beals*

————

My name is Ciann Wilson and I am of Afro-, Indo-, and Euro-Caribbean descent. I am an assistant professor at Wilfrid Laurier University. My body of work aims to utilize research as an avenue for sharing the stories and realities of Indigenous, African diasporic, and racialized peoples, and improving the health and well-being of these communities.

My name is Ann Marie and I am an Indigenous-Black L'nu from Nova Scotia, Canada. I am Indigenous to both Turtle Island and the continent of Africa: I am First Nation Mi'kmaq and from a tribe somewhere that has existed on the west coast of the motherland for millennia. I am now entering my second year of the community psychology PhD program, under the wonderful and critical tutelage of my mentor, Dr. Wilson, at Wilfrid Laurier University in Ontario, Canada.

————

## OPENING

We are Ciann and Ann Marie and in the pages to follow we share with you our journeys of how we come to this deeply personal, historic, and tension-filled space of working with Indigenous-Black communities, that is, communities of mixed Indigenous (i.e., First Nations, Inuit, and Métis) and African diasporic (i.e., African, Caribbean, and Black) ancestry. Indigenous-Black communities have been recognized in the United States for hundreds of years (Smith, 1994), but do not hold the same recognition in Canada, despite an over 400-year presence (Mills-Proctor, 2010). Our collective goal in our work together has been to centralize the voices, perspectives, and stories of Indigenous-Black people in the Canadian nation-state, and so, in many ways, this is a story of an often erased community on Turtle Island. Too deeply melanated to fit the White man's conception of the "imaginary Indian," in the words of our friend Keisha Roberts, but not quite "Black enough" either (Proclaiming Our Roots, 2017). A space between seems to be the uncomfortable place many Indigenous-Black people are left to occupy. Through our work, and the stories that have been shared with us, we hope to facilitate the carving out of a space just for Indigenous-Black communities in the midst of this national dialogue about truth and reconciliation, and an international dialogue at a time when the United Nations has declared 2015 to 2024 the International Decade for People of African Descent (United Nations, 2015).

I am Ann Marie, and I am going to share with you *how I walk in this world…*

As a many-spirited mixed-blood Indigenous-Black person on a land that was created with the beautiful universal interconnectedness of all things, but is now reborn in violence, I long to understand where I fit, where I belong, as I experience mental, physical, emotional, and spiritual disconnect in a White, dominating colonial settler-state. I feel like I have never fit, never belonged. I believe this is the result of the nebulous but nefarious and far-reaching colonial patriarchal forces that have shaped the lives of those who have come before me and will affect the lives of my children.

We can only trace back my heredity on my father's side to the War of 1812; however, it is assumed that we originally hail from one of the many regions of West Africa. We will never really know for sure. During that war, my father's ancestors escaped plantation slavery in Virginia to fight for the British, with payment for their sacrifices promised as freedom, land, and the rations required to start a new life in Nova Scotia; hence, I am African Nova Scotian. However,

British/European racist attitudes of superiority over and subjugation of those they deemed inferior did not change simply because my ancestors walked and sailed an arbitrary border; anti-Black racism was alive and well in 19th-century British North America, as it is today in colonial Canada.

This account has been told many times, but I share it again, briefly, as it is part of my story. From 1813 to 1815, my ancestors settled in North Preston, Nova Scotia, still considered to be the largest historical Black community in Canada, on land that was not suitable for even subsistence farming. It is possible that prior to eventually receiving land, they were held in prisoner-of-war camps on Melville Island in Halifax Harbour, or imprisoned in poor houses in Halifax, where many died of smallpox. Policies were enacted by the British government to not spend undue amounts of money providing rations for the new residents, which meant no rations for anyone who did not have a permanent residence (consider that most refugees did not receive land immediately, and many had to petition for years to receive a plot of land that was too small to farm). George Ramsey Dalhousie, the British lieutenant-governor in 1816, wanted to send my newly

Communities such as North Preston were situated close to Mi'kmaq communities.

*Source:* Photo taken by the Proclaiming Our Roots Team.

freed ancestors back to their "masters" in the United States. "Slaves by habit & education, no longer working under the dread of the lash, their idea of freedom is Idleness and they are altogether incapable of Industry" (personal communication of Dalhousie, as cited in Winks, 1997, p. 122), bemoans Dalhousie as he sets to cease all rations promised to the refugees, while providing transportation back to slavery. Such policies and edicts set the tone for relations between African Nova Scotians and the White colonial settler-state.

Racism was ever-present in the lives of my ancestors, with no political power, lack of adequate schooling, and poverty shaping their lives. Self- and imposed segregation became a way of protecting each other from the outside, from anti-Black racism, as much as possible; however, they still needed to work and farm to survive, which meant interacting with White settlers who were resistant and bigoted in their response to the new arrivals, and did not want them on "their land."

It must be acknowledged that the land on which my paternal ancestors eventually settled, though considered poor of quality, was nonetheless stolen Mi'kmaq land. The areas of North Preston, East Preston, Cherrybrook, and Lake Loon were adjacent to Mi'kmaq communities, as is the unceded land that Dalhousie University, George Ramsey's namesake, now occupies.

As my paternal ancestors were struggling to survive, First Nation Mi'kmaq were fighting for their lives in a genocide enacted by Lieutenant-Governor Cornwallis, recorded in colonial revisionist annals as the "founder" of Halifax, who issued the order now known as the "Scalping Proclamation." In this decree of 1749, his government paid a bounty to anyone who killed a Mi'kmaq child or adult (including pregnant women, the infirm, the unborn, the Elders), receiving 10 guineas (imperialist stolen gold from the Guinea region of West Africa) per scalp (Paul, 2006, p. 116–118), in an attempt to rid himself of the "Indian Problem" ("Edward Cornwallis," 2008; Paul, 2006). Though the Mi'kmaq as a Nation survived, by the 1800s, they were "reduced to beggars in their own homeland and were, for all intents and purposes, without viable means of support. At the dawn of the nineteenth century, the Mi'kmaq of Nova Scotia were moving slowly but surely to the brink of extinction" (Paul, n.d., p. 1). Colonial state violence on Mi'kmaq territory has been maintained since the arrival of the White man, as it was perpetuated on African Nova Scotians exchanging death for freedom and the Mi'kmaq in a fight for their existence.

In my adult life, I learned that my maternal grandfather was Mi'kmaq; however, I know nothing about him, except that he was downtrodden. My mother spent the majority of her childhood and youth, 16 years, at the Black residential school known as the Nova Scotia Home for Colored Children (the Home). She did not know her father and her mother sent her to the orphanage at the age of five. Her mother, my grandmother, is believed to be African Nova Scotian and White, but I do not know for sure, and I may never know—this is my colonial legacy. That would make sense, though, as the Home, which opened in 1921 (Luck, 2018), was built because White orphanages would not accept Indigenous or Black children, or children of colour, as segregation was alive and well as an arm of colonial racism. (The last segregated school in Canada closed in 1983, in Nova Scotia [Historica Canada, n.d.]). Currently, there is a provincial inquiry and a class action lawsuit pending for many residents (and their families) of the Home who were subjected to physical, emotional, psychological, and sexual abuse during their time in placement (Nova Scotia Home, n.d.). To participate in this lawsuit, one needed to verify the abuse to secure an award; however, because of the mental toll of reliving the inflicted trauma, some eligible former residents chose not to participate in the lawsuit. They could not relive the experiences that, to this day, have affected their physical, mental, and spiritual health so profoundly, and likely for the rest of their lives. These experiences are not altogether dissimilar from Indigenous Peoples who are participating in the Truth and Reconciliation process, who deserve to not be reified or objectified as they lay bare their trauma in this vulnerable process (Manuelito, 2015; Truth and Reconciliation Commission, 2015).

The Black residential school: The former Nova Scotia Home for Colored Children.[1]

*Source:* Photo taken by the Proclaiming Our Roots Team.

I cannot help but notice the parallels between the Indian residential schools (which my grandfather may have attended in Shubenacadie, Nova Scotia) and the Home for Colored Children. Both were endemic with abuse; in the residential schools, abuse was perpetuated by staff of various church denominations, with the unmitigated blessings of the colonial state. In the Home, abuse was maintained by undertrained or untrained staff who were paid less than staff at White orphanages (which is not an excuse for the behaviour, but merely an example of racism and segregation supported by the province of Nova Scotia). And now, the trauma that Indigenous and Black children suffered at both institutions passes on to the next generation, who pass it on to the next generation, and so on, until there is recognition of the trauma that allows for healing; then the cycle can be broken.

As an Indigenous-Black L'nu who walks in both worlds, I am keenly aware of how imperialist colonial violence has affected both sides of my family. The intergenerational effects of such violence reverberate from the time of the snatching of my ancestors from the west coast of Africa, and the crushing of the Mi'kmaq spirit and near annihilation of an entire Indigenous Nation, to me and my children. The Nova Scotia where my mother and father grew up in the 1940s and 1950s, as children and young adults, was rife with segregation, abuse, and overt and systemic anti-Black racism and Indigenous oppression, and they found themselves living just to survive, as their forefathers and foremothers had in 1749 and 1812.

Note: While I acknowledge my Indigenous heritage, as I have not grown up in Mi'kmaq culture and community with relations to the land and cosmos, I do not claim to be an Indigenous researcher. I have been socialized as a Black woman and am perceived as a Black woman by White society. As such, I grew up in impoverished circumstances as a result of structural violence. This violence set my path in not being able to attain the power, resources, health care, and education that others were born into, or have access to the same chances of success as those of the White dominant society. Now, I look to level the playing field for those who are oppressed and treated in unequal and uncaring fashion in colonial Canada. I am unapologetic in that my social location defines the work I wish to pursue, that is, the raising up of Indigenous-Black folk on Turtle Island.

My name is Ciann, and *I'll tell you about my journey...*

As I have written elsewhere (Wilson & Flicker, 2018), my story begins in the Caribbean on the island of Jamaica, which is the Hispanic form of the Indigenous Taino name for the island, meaning "the land of wood and water"

(Hall, 1990). Jamaica, like most Caribbean islands, is a site of the massacre of Indigenous people, with the importation of African enslaved labour and, in more recent history, South Asian and Asian indentured workers for the creation of a plantocracy within the empire-building project of British North American Empire. Jamaica, being part of the Americas, is an island nation-state still dealing with the implications of centuries of colonial violence. "The Caribbean Islands were the petri dish–sized test-sites for the atrocities colonists rolled-out on the mainland (i.e., Canada and the United States)," my friend LLana James frequently reminds me. You cannot get to North America without passage through the Caribbean and so there are important parallels and connections between the histories and contemporary realities of the Caribbean and North America. Thus, it is important to me that we collectively acknowledge that Turtle Island spans from present-day Canada to Mexico and the Caribbean.

It is within this context that I was born within a multiracial family of African, South Asian (Indian), and European ancestry in the Jamaican parish of Westmoreland. My mother, a South Asian beauty, is third-generation Indo-Jamaican. She hails from a Hindi-speaking, historically affluent family that migrated to the Caribbean not as indentured workers, but imperial subjects afforded passage by the Crown to the then famed and widely talked about "West Indies" in the "New World." The Caribbean was historically referred to as the West Indies, forever memorializing the tale that European colonists—being banned from easterly travel by the Muslim world—voyaged west and thought they had found India and the Orient (the site of the historic spice route) when they first sighted the Americas. As such, they referred to the Caribbean as the West Indies, and subsequently practiced transplanting crops from Asia and South Asia in their re-creation of the fabled Orient.

The transplantation of crops and people to the Caribbean is a practice that marks much of the history of the region. My father is the descendant of African slaves and European colonists. African enslaved people literally fuelled the ships of colonists in their journeys to the Americas, and so even in the history of the middle passage through the Atlantic and into the Caribbean, we see deep connections between the Indigenous Peoples of the African continent and of Turtle Island. That being said, the influence of Indigenous cultures and people in Jamaica and other parts of the Caribbean is often erased or relegated to romanticized symbols such as the Jamaican coat of arms, which consists of an image of an Indigenous-Arawak man and woman on either side of the national crest. The Jamaican creole language, colloquially referred to as patois, incorporates Indigenous words that go unacknowledged. Indigenous presence on the island is often relegated to being "part of the barely knowable or usable past" (Hall, 1990, p. 235; Newton, 2013). Very little of Jamaican folklore or popular culture acknowledges or alludes to Indigenous past and present. As a result, individuals who acknowledge their Indigenous identity within the Caribbean are often questioned about the integrity of their claims. There is much silence about Indigenous heritage in our families, as it is my generation that is finally in a place to ask the difficult questions of our Elders, who tell us of our familial origins through stories.

Displacement from land is a recurring theme that surfaces in my narrative quilt, as African diasporic peoples seem to be signifiers of migration—"modern nomads of the New World," to quote Stuart Hall (1990, p. 234), mandated to perpetually roam this earth, with no claims to—and perhaps no need to lay claim to—the land. Due to neo-colonialism in the form of globalized capitalism, Jamaica remains economically dependent on international trade and externally controlled capital. The country never really experienced the promise of independence from British rule. Structural adjustment programs and international loans became attractive sources of capital intended to boost the economy of the former colony. These efforts were further undermined by the international community, namely Canada, the United States, and the United Kingdom's extraction of the educated class of Jamaicans from the island for labour as domestic caregivers, teachers, health professionals, etc. within the empire. After centuries of enslavement and a plantocracy built from the blood and bones of Indigenous and African diasporic peoples, the Jamaica my ancestors imagined would never materialize. How could it? The nation simply exists in a state of enslavement by another name. This perpetual state of impoverishment is what motivated my parents to migrate with my siblings and me to Toronto, Canada.

Upon migrating to Canada, I was largely ignorant of Indigenous realities and, given the intentional gaps and deficiencies within Jamaica's and Canada's colonial education systems, which erase Indigenous history, I did not come across information about Indigenous Peoples until grade 10. It wasn't until my graduate studies that I was confronted with the personal and political implications of residential schools, assimilation policies, displacement from land, and reservations for Indigenous Peoples across the Canadian nation-state. During my graduate studies, I worked with both Indigenous and Black communities and gained a proximate look at our similarities and differences, as well as the implications of colonialism for our respective communities. It was this early work, and the paucity of Canadian research in the area, that inspired me to work with people of both Indigenous and Black ancestry to artistically create and write their stories into being within national conversations about Indigenous identity and truth and reconciliation. This was the catalyst for the initial conceptualization of the Proclaiming Our Roots project.

## THE STORY OF THE PROCLAIMING OUR ROOTS PROJECT

The Proclaiming Our Roots (POR) project became a reality as a result of a culmination of many thoughts I (Ciann) shared and conversations I had with my friend and soul sister, Denise Baldwin, who is of Black and Anishinaabe Kwe ancestry. Ideas started to percolate around the time I was completing my doctoral work in 2015, which focused on the connections between Indigenous youth leaders and Black youth leaders in the HIV movement. Unsurprisingly, as is the trend with most chronic diseases such as HIV, Indigenous and Black communities are disproportionately affected. My doctoral work at the time was really aimed at exploring the ways our young people could work across community differences in sharing resources for our overall well-being. Denise, seeing the value of the cross-community connections I was trying to make, quickly got to talking about her experiences as an Indigenous-Black woman and the lack of acknowledgement and resources for Indigenous-Black people in Canada. We discussed the more prolific Indigenous-Black groups in the United States, some of which had become so politicized over the years that they demanded and received international recognition. These conversations sparked the initial inspiration for the POR project, which is led by community leaders, scholars, and activists of Indigenous, African diasporic, and Indigenous-Black ancestry in Ontario and Nova Scotia.

The POR project has three main objectives: (1) to gain an understanding of the nuanced and unique intersectional forms of (personal, institutional, and structural) violence and erasure Indigenous-Black people face, and how this relates to service access; (2) to situate their lived experiences in current discussions about truth and reconciliation and imagine new models for support; and (3) to create a written, visual, and narrative archive of the histories, geographies, and realities of people of both African diasporic and Indigenous ancestry in Canada.

Through the POR project, we intend to historicize the existence of mixed-blood Indigenous-Black people in the Canadian mosaic and explore how Indigenous-Black people survive in the context of colonial structures such as capitalism, racism, intersectional oppression, structural inequities, lack of territory, and social, cultural, and geographic displacement. The project aims to bring understanding to how these intersecting forms of violence impact the mental health, well-being, and service access of Indigenous-Black communities. Moreover, it interrogates what the Truth and Reconciliation process has meant and what is now required for Indigenous-Black people to move forward with inclusion in the process. Toward this end, we combined traditional qualitative methods such as interviewing with arts-based methods such as digital storytelling, which afforded community members the opportunity to layer their images, sound, music, and text in the creation of personal videos about their lived experiences, realities, and histories. Community mapping, in which community members were able to pinpoint their family histories and geographies on a digital map, was another arts-based method we employed, allowing community members the chance to disrupt the White settler hegemonic narrative.

We are currently in the knowledge sharing phase of the POR project. We are adding the wonderful stories and knowledges to the project website (www.proclaimingourroots.com) and launching our community-dialogue sessions in the Toronto, Ontario, and Halifax/Dartmouth, Nova Scotia, communities in which the project originally took place. The intent is for the website to become a repository for the community maps and digital stories of Indigenous-Black people across Canada. We will also continue to populate the website with articles, community reports, project-related events, and other associated resources and content produced by project team members and community members. We hope this digital repository will serve as historical documentation of Indigenous-Black people and will provide generations still with us, and the generations to come, a platform for understanding the historical and cultural contexts of living as an Indigenous-Black person in this society.

## CLAIMING SPACE: THE ART OF STORYTELLING

An integral intention of the POR project is the empowerment, self-determination, and political sovereignty of Indigenous-Black communities. Through this work, we hope to empower Indigenous-Black people by centring their voices, histories, and realities through the grassroots production of alternative ways of sharing knowledge (namely, digital stories and community maps) that challenge Euro-Western ideas of what constitutes knowledge and history. By invoking their historical and contemporary realities, Indigenous-Black people are able to triumph over colonial structures and revive Indigenous ontologies and epistemologies through the art of storytelling (Sium & Ritskes, 2013), and reframing, restorying, and reshaping their colonial histories (Corntassel, 2009) from the African continent to Turtle Island.

The art of storytelling is an act of liberation, testimony, reclaiming, and truth-telling that is integral to the sustaining of the knowledges and the recognition of Indigenous-Black presence on Turtle Island (Sium & Ritskes, 2013). Through the act of sharing their stories for others to witness, but more importantly for themselves, Indigenous-Black people are joining other colonized communities around the world that have documented their livelihoods, presence, and resilience as they struggle for justice (Dupagne, 2010). As such, media produced by and for Indigenous-Black people disrupt the colonial revisionist narratives that have usurped these communities' rightful place on this land. Through this process, community members told their stories in ways in which they had complete control over the symbols, representations, and texts used, effectively reversing the colonial gaze. Consequently, they created a liberating process.

One of the most transformative outcomes of this work is witnessing the upliftment of Indigenous-Black people who are naming and claiming their identities and space within their communities. They had felt silenced and shamed from doing so before, but are now empowered with the self-determination to move their agenda forward in that they will not be chained to oppressive and divisive policies, laws, and social mindsets, not only in their communities but also throughout Turtle Island. Community members in the project and Indigenous-Black people who've come out to the community events have remarked how they had never before had the opportunity to share space with so many other Indigenous-Black people. "We have been waiting for you and this project for a very long time," commented an Elder attending the first Toronto community dialogue session in July 2018. As such, we view this process as reconciliatory for those sharing their truths and reclaiming space, as Indigenous-Black people resist the colonial glare of the settler nation-state, which has denied their existence.

## WHAT DOES TRUTH AND RECONCILIATION MEAN FOR INDIGENOUS-BLACK FOLKS?

We fight for our identity and right to be, as we collectively memorialize the stories and knowledges that have maintained our ancestors through the infernos of colonization and slavery. Our voices will ring loud and clear, and we will not be silenced into submission. We are here to stay, and we will know who we are. Our ancestors were strong, we are strong, and we are empowered!

—Ann Marie

In our examination of what truth and reconciliation might look like for Indigenous-Black communities, we must consider the traumatic and oppressive intergenerational implications of colonial ideologies around "blood quantum," and colourism, which are often used to categorize Indigenous-Black folks based on how they phenotypically present—which often means being categorized as Black under the colonial "one-drop" rule. Explicitly defined as "not Native enough," and conversely "not Black enough" or able to fully partake in African diasporic communities and cultures, Indigenous-Black people may experience a fracturing of their identities and a feeling of a tug-of-war over their identification with one part of their heritage versus another. It is difficult when an individual is not able to explore both parts of their identity or feels shame in attending to only one part of their identity, due to the society-wide negation of their more complete self. As a result, for mixed-blood Indigenous-Black people, identity formation can be a complicated and challenging process experienced throughout the life course, as identity is not static or homogeneous. Indigenous-Black communities are also dually affected by the manifestations of colonially entrenched trauma that impacts both Indigenous and Black communities (Lawrence, 2004).

With opportunities such as the POR project to tell their stories, give testimony, and witness the testaments of others, Indigenous-Black people are engaging in a decolonizing process of self-determination and liberation. They are also learning more about who they are and where they come from, and claiming space in an act of declaring where they would like to be. This is a form of truth-telling, which is imperative for any form of reconciliation to take place. Given the erasure of Indigenous-Black people, the lack of national recognition of these communities, and their negation from engagement in the Truth and Reconciliation process, these kinds of spaces and opportunities are imperative for Indigenous-Black communities to write themselves into these national discourses.

There are a number of truths that Indigenous and Black communities must contend with internally, outside of and in addition to the demands for truth and reconciliation placed on the nation-state; these include the following:

1. There is rampant anti-Black racism prevalent in many Indigenous communities, which is often used by some Indigenous people to distinguish themselves from African diasporic peoples and deem themselves superior in the Euro-Western racial hierarchy (Klopotek, 2011). Reductionist dichotomies between "full-blood and mixed-blood Natives" and ideologies that "blood equals culture" are often used to diminish the degrees of real "Nativeness" ascribed to Indigenous-Black people

(Pack, 2012). The thought here is that the mixing of blood is associated with cultural loss, and the only way to ensure the continuation of Indigenous cultures is to keep the blood lines pure. This "blood hegemony" has become internalized by Indigenous communities and expressed through lateral violence as, according to this line of argument, only full-bloods can be the arbiters of Native culture (Pack, 2012, p. 179). This has real implications for Indigenous-Black people, who are often considered not "Native enough." It affects their ability to access membership to and participate in their communities, and to benefit from Indigenous services (both on- and off-reserve) (Amadahy & Lawrence, 2009, p. 114), as many participants expressed throughout the POR project.

> For mixed Black and Indigenous people, I think we are always questioned about our identity, not like Indigenous and Europeans, they are always accepted into the community without being questioned. The space is already opened but for a Black *and* an Indigenous person, the first thing they see is Black and then Indigenous or they don't even see Indigenous, so you are constantly being questioned about your identity to the point you don't want to be part of the community, because you feel like you are in a museum because people are constantly questioning you. (POR interview)

2.  African diasporic communities across Turtle Island, from the Caribbean region to the mainland, must contend with their tendency toward perpetuating colonial narratives about the "disappeared Native" and their replacement by the African slave, who magically becomes Native by proxy (Newton, 2013). The death of the Native is imperative for the legitimization and belongingness of African peoples and cultures on the Caribbean islands (Newton, 2013), much like Indigenous erasure is integral to the legitimization of the Canadian nation-state. While we acknowledge that African diasporic peoples are, for all intents and purposes, displaced Indigenous Peoples in the context of Turtle Island, to participate in conversations about Native extinctionism is to ascribe to White supremacist, colonialist logic.

3.  Further, such colonial narratives were often written in tandem with proclamations of creolization and creole nationalisms that—much like multiculturalism in colonial Canada—have been understood to usher the Americas into modernity as epicentres of exhaustive diversity and

hybridity, which has simultaneously signified the erasure of Indigenous Peoples (Hall, 1990; Newton, 2013). In this, multiculturalism and creolization are not critically regarded as the by-products of colonial violence that they are (Wilson & James, 2018). A more recent manifestation of this is the declaration by some Indigenous-Black people in Canada of an "Afro-Métis" identity, described as "the genetic and cultural mixing between Canadian Blacks (particularly from Nova Scotia) and Indigenous Peoples that has occurred frequently, beginning over two hundred years ago" (White, n.d., p. 1). This racially and culturally specific definition of mixed blood perpetuates the manifestation of colonial violence in settler Canada. This context matters, as we witness recent attempts to introduce the context-specific term *Afro-Métis* into the national discourse without a critical interrogation of what it means to take-up the term *Métis* as a signifier for creolization and being mixed race.[2] The underlying assumptions here are that Indigeneity is a race, which reputable scholars have refuted (Amadahy & Lawrence, 2009; Razack, 1994), and that Métis identity—whether that be a mix of Indigenous and European ancestry or Indigenous and Black ancestry—is anything but the result of the need for survival in the face of colonial violence. In this critique, there lie many questions about racial formations, identity, and Indigenous nationhood.

## CONCLUSION

In closing, with the cultural uniqueness of dual Indigenous-Black identity and the similar but distinct colonial histories of Indigenous and African diasporic peoples, the theme of identity is ever-present in our work. Our exploration of Indigenous-Black identity is of particular importance in the context of colonial Canada, given the nation-state's problematic erasure of Indigenous-Black communities while simultaneously recognizing and ascribing nationhood to mixed Indigenous and White communities (Lawrence, 2004; Wilson & James, 2018). Such inherent ascriptions to Whiteness and blatant anti-Black erasure affect Indigenous-Black people in myriad ways, including how they think about themselves; the legitimacy of their claims to Indigeneity on Turtle Island; their mental, emotional, and spiritual health; and the ways in which their historic and current realities impact their overall well-being (Beals & Wilson, 2019). In an effort to problematize this erasure and spark national conversation, we continue our engagement around these issues through our collective work on the Proclaiming Our Roots project.

**Ann Marie:** I am honoured to be able to contribute to the raising up of Indigenous-Black people—my people—through the POR project. We are rewriting the stories as we reveal our resilience and share pride in who we are. The work of the POR project offers Indigenous-Black community members an opportunity to share their stories, come to an understanding that we are not alone, and work toward building a critical consciousness amongst Indigenous-Black people on Turtle Island. We feel a sense of pride in that we have survived, and we honour our ancestors for their strength and guidance. This is necessary and transformative work. *I am grateful.*

**Ciann:** I am honoured to bear witness to Indigenous-Black communities that are artistically expressing and writing their histories and stories into being. It has been an honour to steward and share these stories and to witness the transformative impact of this process for Indigenous-Black people who are directing the next phases of the POR project, how their stories are shared, and what is done with the project outputs. I am humbled to be a part of this history-making project, meant precisely for a time such as this.

## NOTES

1. The building is now undergoing a major retrofit to become an incubator for local businesses. Former residents of the Home feel that this renovation will wipe away the history of the abuse that took place there. Some community members want the building to stand as is, so that the harmful history of the Home is not forgotten.

2. Notably, in Northern Turtle Island, there is a distinct Métis Nation, who are a people within a defined history in a defined region—the Western Prairies (with some in other regions of Turtle Island)—with their own political and cultural definitions of Métis identity. People of the Métis Nation understand that their ancestors fought for the political decision (*R. v. Powley*, 2003) to identify as Métis "based on shared histories and culture" (Canadian Geographic, n.d., p. 1).

## REFERENCES

Amadahy, Z., & Lawrence, B. (2009). Indigenous Peoples and Black people in Canada: Settlers or allies? In A. Kempf (Ed.), *Breaching the colonial contract: Anti-colonialism in the US and Canada* (pp. 105–136). Dordrecht, Netherlands: Springer.

Beals, A. M., & Wilson, C. L. (2019). *Mixed-blood: Indigenous-Black identity in colonial Canada*. Manuscript submitted.

Canadian Geographic. (n.d.). Identity: Métis. In *Indigenous Peoples atlas of Canada*. Retrieved from https://indigenouspeoplesatlasofcanada.ca/article/identity/

Corntassel, J. (2009). Indigenous storytelling, truth-telling, and community approaches to reconciliation. *English Studies in Canada, 35*(1), 137–159. doi:10.1353/esc.0.0163

Dupagne, M. (2010). Story circle: Digital storytelling around the world. *Journal of Broadcasting and Electronic Media, 54*(3), 532–533. doi:10.1080/08838151.2010.498704

Edward Cornwallis. (2008). *The Canadian Encyclopedia*. Retrieved from https://www.thecanadianencyclopedia.ca/en/article/edward-cornwallis/

Hall, S. (1990). Cultural identity and diaspora. In J. Rutherford (Ed.), *Identity: Community, culture, difference* (pp. 222–237). London: Lawrence and Wishart.

Historica Canada. (n.d.). *End of segregation in Canada*. Retrieved from http://blackhistorycanada.ca/events.php?themeid=7&id=9

Klopotek, B. (2011). *Recognition odysseys: Indigeneity, race, and federal tribal recognition policy in three Louisiana Indian communities*. Durham, NC: Duke University Press.

Lawrence, B. (2004). *"Real" Indians and others: Mixed-blood urban Native peoples and Indigenous nationhood*. Vancouver: University of British Columbia Press.

Luck, S. (2018, June 26). Former Nova Scotia Home for Colored Children to be transformed. But what of its past? *CBC News*. Retrieved from http://www.cbc.ca/news/canada/nova-scotia/renovations-home-for-colored-children-business-incubator-1.4721470

Manuelito, B. (2015). *Creating space for an Indigenous approach to digital storytelling: "Living breath" of survivance within an Anishinaabe community in Northern Michigan*. Doctoral dissertation, Antioch University. Retrieved from https://aura.antioch.edu/cgi/viewcontent.cgi?article=1219&context=etds

Mills-Proctor, D. (2010). Born-again Indian: A story of self-discovery of a Red-Black woman and her people. *Kola, 22*(1), 44–137.

Newton, M. J. (2013). Returns to a Native land: Indigeneity and decolonization in the anglophone Caribbean. *Small Axe, 17*(2/41), 108–122. doi:10.1215/07990537-2323346

Nova Scotia Home for Colored Children Restorative Inquiry. (n.d.). *A different way forward*. Retrieved from https://restorativeinquiry.ca/

Pack, S. (2012). What is a real Indian? *AlterNative: An International Journal of Indigenous Peoples, 8*(2), 176–188. doi:10.1177/117718011200800206

Paul, D. (n.d.). *We were not the savages: First Nation history; Mi'Kmaq, Maliseet, etc., & European relations with them*. Retrieved from http://www.danielnpaul.com/Mi'kmaqStarvation1763-1867.html

Paul, D. (2006). *First Nations history: We were not the savages; Collision between European and Native American civilizations* (3rd ed.). Black Point, NS: Fernwood.

Proclaiming Our Roots (Producer). (2017). *Not half of anything by Wapahkesis* [Digital story]. Retrieved from https://www.proclaimingourroots.com/partners

R. v. Powley, 2 SCR 207, 2003 SCC 43 (CanLII)

Razack, S. (1994). What is to be gained by looking White people in the eye? Culture, race and gender in cases of sexual violence. *Signs: Journal of Women in Culture and Society*, *19*(4), 894–923. Retrieved from https://www.journals.uchicago.edu/doi/abs/10.1086/4 94944?journalCode=signs

Sium, A., & Ritskes, E. (2013). Speaking truth to power: Indigenous storytelling as an act of living resistance. *Decolonization: Indigeneity, Education and Society*, *2*(1), 1–10.

Smith, M. (1994). Behind the lines: The Black Mardi Gras Indians and the New Orleans second line. *Black Music Research Journal*, *14*(1), 43–73.

Truth and Reconciliation Commission of Canada. (2015). *Honouring the truth, reconciling for the future: Summary of the final report of the Truth and Reconciliation Commission of Canada*. Retrieved from http://publications.gc.ca/collections/collection_2015/trc/IR4-7-2015-eng.pdf

United Nations. (2015). International Decade for People of African Descent. Retrieved from http://www.un.org/en/events/africandescentdecade/plan-action.shtml

White, C. (n.d.). Definitions of "Métis" and "Afro-Métis." *Afro-Métis*. Retrieved from http://afrometis.ca/definitions-of-metis/

Wilson, C. L., & Flicker, S. (2018). *It's about relationships: The decolonizing potential of digital storytelling and collaborative mural making as research methods*. Manuscript submitted for publication.

Wilson, C. L., & James, L. (2018). *Imagining possible futures for Black and Indigenous relations and well-being*. Manuscript in preparation.

Winks, R. W. (1997). *The Blacks in Canada: A history* (2nd ed.). Montreal: McGill-Queen's University Press.

———

Tim Fontaine is the Founder, Editor-in-Grand-Chief, and Head Writer of Walking Eagle News, which he started as a means of setting his illustrious journalism career on fire and dancing in its ashes. Since launching in 2017, Walking Eagle News has emerged as the pre-eminent leader in the world of satirical Indigenous news and humour.

Tim Fontaine was a real journalist for almost two decades before becoming a pretend journalist and had worked for APTN National News, iChannel, CPAC, and CBC Indigenous. Since establishing Walking Eagle News, he has also hosted and produced The Laughing Drum, a satirical news and talk show on the Aboriginal Peoples Television Network.

A member of the Sagkeeng First Nation, an Anishinaabe community in Manitoba, he grew up mainly on the Hollow Water First Nation and in Winnipeg. He currently lives in Winnipeg where he single-handedly invented and refined Indigenous journalism.

———

## Canada's Spy Agencies Struggle to Balance Reconciliation with Spying on Indigenous Peoples

Canada's intelligence services say they're struggling to balance reconciliation efforts with continuing to spy on Indigenous Peoples.

Agencies like the Canadian Security Intelligence Service have been tasked by the Liberal government with implementing the Truth and Reconciliation Commission's 94 calls to action and the United Nations Declaration on the Rights of Indigenous Peoples.

However, many operatives are complaining that it's hampering their ability to spy on Indigenous communities.

"We decided we would smudge before conducting surveillance on a rally but the activists saw what we were doing and came and joined us," said one CSIS agent who asked not to be named.

"I suppose that's reconciliation right there, us coming together like that, but our cover was completely blown."

Another problem arose when the RCMP's national security wing invited renowned Indigenous academic Peyton King to deliver "Aboriginal awareness training" to operatives in that agency.

"The operatives learned about the history of Indigenous Peoples, which is great," said a senior RCMP official.

"But it worked too well because the agents eventually refused to spy on Indigenous people, saying they didn't want to contribute to ongoing settler colonialism and state violence."

While some Indigenous leaders praised the federal government's efforts to push reconciliation, others say it's too skewed.

"I mean, good for them for trying, I guess," said Chief Herman Boushey, from the Long Lake First Nation in Ontario.

"But I'd prefer if they just stopped spying on us."

A spokesperson from the federal government said the Solicitor General, which oversees intelligence, would review the reconciliation process sometime after the next election.

## CHAPTER 4

# You Do Not Belong Here: Storying Allyship in an Ugly Sweater

*by Andrea V. Breen*

———

My name is Andrea Breen. I currently live in Toronto/Tkaronto with my partner and our two children. I am a settler of Western and Eastern European heritage and I was raised in the place we call Burlington, Ontario, along the Niagara Escarpment. My work focuses on identity development, family relationships, storytelling, and resilience. I am an associate professor in Family Relations and Human Development at the University of Guelph.

———

I imagine an image of a book. It's a thick book with pages closed tight between hard, still-blank covers. I imagine people across the world, hunched over tables, intently writing words in invisible ink that will eventually darken to fill its pages. In my mind, as I write this, I feel like I am trying to nudge the book open, to find my way in. I imagine what the book would say to me if it could speak.

*You do not belong here.*

That seems right. I close my blank document, check my email, move on to other tasks. But I can't leave it alone. I wonder about my reluctance to take space in this book that I am co-editing, a book that I have been working hard to bring into the world. Over many months, Shawn Wilson, Lindsay DuPré, and I have worked together to imagine this book and it is now taking shape with the labour of collaborators whom I am so grateful to be working with, each creating and reshaping the book for themselves as they write. I speak to the contributors about their chapters in process and there is an exciting mix of creativity, searching, vulnerability, and wisdom in their stories. It is all more than I imagined a couple of years ago when I first had the idea for a book of stories about Indigenist research and strivings toward reconciliation(s). I feel honoured to be part of this work. And yet I do not feel like I belong in the book. I think about the feeling I have of not belonging over days, between writing and teaching, in committee meetings, on the Greyhound on the long commute to and from work, while I'm cooking and when I am putting my kids to bed.

I can't let it go.

I am most comfortable listening to others, learning and finding ways to support the work of Inuit, Métis, and First Nations friends and collaborators from behind the scenes. I prefer to be the one helping—chopping vegetables for the feast, following directions to help set up an art installation, writing the grant proposals and ethics applications for projects to be led by others, providing a place for students to stay and connect when they can't make it home from the south for holidays, working behind the scenes to help make the institutions that I have power in places of belonging for Indigenous colleagues, students, and their families. At this time, I feel at home in an allyship role that involves working in mostly quiet ways that can enhance other people's voices and gifts. I gravitate toward this role because it provides ways for me to contribute while I learn and ensures that I am not taking up space that would be better occupied by someone who is Indigenous.

My hope is to write a chapter with Jamie Bell and Ethan Tassiuk, my friends, collaborators, and co-dreamers of alternative possibilities. Ethan is an emerging young Inuk filmmaker. Jamie Bell is of Oji-Cree and Métis heritage and, along with Ethan, was one of the founding members of the Arviat Film Society and Arviat Television. We've spent days together in Arviat, Montreal, and Toronto talking about reconciliation, connectedness, colonialism, trauma, dreams, education, family, technology, loss, and hope. Last year we wrote a presentation together on the problems of words like *reconciliation* and *resilience*; words that try to put harms in the past and gloss over ongoing settler colonialism in education and research institutions. We wrote the paper together and had planned to travel and present together at the Pathways to Resilience Conference in South Africa, but in the end Jamie and Ethan weren't able to make the trip from Arviat to Cape Town. So, I found myself presenting at the conference for us in a role that was deeply contradictory, a White academic presenting alone without my Indigenous collaborators on the problems of settler colonial research practices.

Jamie, Ethan, and I start to work on a chapter for this book but we can't seem to get a hold on what to write. We start and stop. Jamie and I bounce ideas back and forth over email. We have daily conversations over Twitter, linking to others' ideas that we'd like to explore, ideas that strike us as perspectives and points that ring true with our own experience or challenge us in new ways. We sit in a coffee shop and talk through ideas, but we can't quite find the story we want to tell together. The timing just isn't right and these things can't be rushed. We give up for now. But it doesn't feel right. So much of what I think and feel about allyship, Whiteness, decolonization, and reconciliation comes from a couple of years' worth of our conversations.

Should I think about writing something alone?

Shawn, Lindsay, and Jamie all tell me that maybe I should write a chapter, even if that chapter focuses only on my own story. "Reconciliation is a two-way street," Jamie reminds me when I tell him that I'm not comfortable writing alone as a non-Indigenous author in a book meant to centre Indigenous voices. When he says this, I realize that there are dangers in my desire not to take space—my comfort with invisibility could look to others like apathy or laziness. Others will not know that behind the scenes I am striving hard to understand myself and my own culture, to see how the past, present, and future of my own existence relate to the ongoing settler colonial project and how it impacts others on these lands. While I need time to learn and reflect, there is also danger in not speaking up. There is a fine line between a silence that is needed to learn and a cowardly sort of shrinking that lets others do the dangerous work of putting their voices in the world and coping with the violence that all too often gets hurled back at the truth. The quietness of my work obscures my deep commitment to finding ways to contribute to ongoing efforts to challenge worn lies, disrupt power imbalances, and create narratives that offer possibilities for a finally different future. "You're an editor on this book," says Lindsay. "People are going to want to know who you are and where you stand."

But I don't quite know what to say. The story isn't coherent yet. I have fragments of experience, feeling, and insight. And I have words, individual words not yet bound together in a way that makes sense to me.

*A collection of words is not a story.*

Maybe if I write the words down, they'll get me somewhere. If I'm lucky maybe my individual words will start to take shape into something I can't see yet, something that I hope is worthwhile. I think about my academic research on storytelling and identity that has taught me that we make sense of our experiences by getting outside of them and looking in; experience becomes abstracted into story when we can see the big picture and we shape our sense of ourselves and our identities by putting the pieces together.

I start writing the words that are on my mind. Putting pen to paper to see where it leads.

*White.*

   *Settler.*

These words don't feel right as I write them. They feel tight and constricting, like an ugly, itchy sweater that is too small for me. I feel myself wanting to escape these words, to justify why they don't fit. The words feel ugly because they speak truths that are ugly. They place me in relationship to a brutal, menacing history that has consumed so much of the present and threatens our future. They place me on the wrong side.

I'm the daughter of a man whose Irish-Scottish-English family began settling near what we currently call London, Ontario, almost 200 years ago. I was raised with the privilege that Whiteness can afford. I'm also the daughter of a refugee from Eastern Europe who never met her own grandparents. I carry many gifts from my parents' families along with an inheritance of hidden, unknown traumas that have stolen the place of family stories. I never learned the language that my mother spoke with her parents. I was never able to speak to my grandfather in a shared language before he died when I was six, in a house just a few blocks away from the home I am writing in today in the city we currently call Toronto. Sometimes I've felt justified in trying to squirm out of the imaginary too-small, itchy sweater. I've thought that coming from a family with its own history of trauma, forced migration, and the absence of a homeland to return to makes me different from others whom I have been tempted to think of as somehow more complicit in the colonization of these lands. I have been squirming against the reality that being a *settler* means that I may not fully belong here, in this place that I love so deeply.

If not here, where?

Grappling with my place in relation to colonization, racism, privilege, and Whiteness is something I've been doing for a long time and, despite having very good teachers all along the way, it is taking me a long time to learn. I can trace my growing awareness along a timeline of flashpoints: Reading the Indian Act in high school. Learning about residential schools from a friend who worked as a research assistant on the Royal Commission on Aboriginal Peoples in the 1990s. Working with youth in detention, mental health, and child welfare settings and seeing for myself how the violence of colonization plays out for kids in my own time. I learned more as I spent years developing education programs for youth with histories of violence who had been pushed out of schools and I started to recognize, more slowly than I'd like to admit, that most of the kids and families I worked with were from racialized communities, and their experiences could only be fully understood by examining the roots of the displacement, surveillance, poverty, violence, shame, and forced separations that are the offshoots of colonization, hidden beneath the surface of our institutions. I started to see how much I have gained and gotten away with in my life because I am White.

Recently, I've been learning most deeply through my relationships with Jamie, Ethan, and other friends in Arviat, Nunavut, with the youth, families, program leaders, artists, and filmmakers I've been meeting in my program evaluation work with First Nations and Inuit communities, and through the nIshnabek de'bwe wIn//Telling Our Truths research project with Susan Dion, Carla Rice, Hannah Fowlie, Tanya Senk, Nicole Robinson, Krista Tucker Petrick, Vanessa Dion Fletcher, and the many urban storytellers—Indigenous and non-Indigenous—who have shared their experiences and relationships with Indigeneity and education over the last several years. My research relationships and my accountability to specific people, families, and communities provide the ethical compass from which I find direction in my work. More than this, they provide the orientation for my ongoing explorations and shifting understandings of my own identity.

I think a lot about colonial violence, how it permeates our society, and who I am in relation to this. The violence of White supremacy and racism can sometimes be sneaky and subtle, but of course it isn't always. A lot of it is as horrifically overt as trailer hitches hurled at mothers, Indigenous boys shot for being in the wrong place at the wrong time, women raped and murdered, children stolen from their parents, and a justice system that acquits and acquits and acquits.

After more than 40 years of being a White person living among other (mostly) White people, I'm convinced that racism and White supremacy exist quietly all around us and inside of us, but we tend not to notice that racism has to do with us when we look at ourselves under the soft glow of good intentions. We tend not to see the ways that colonialism and White supremacy are served through our support of policies, governments, and institutions that enact violence, our defence of racist friends and family members, our appropriations of Indigenous cultures, our saviourism, and our denials of the lived experiences of Indigenous, Black, and non-Black people of colour. We don't think that conversations about racism are about us—*never in a million years could I be racist because I have good intentions* and *he doesn't have a racist bone in his body*. I believe that the only way that we will move forward toward meaningful reconciliation between Indigenous and non-Indigenous people is if European-descended settlers in particular are able to look at ourselves in a different light:[1] take off the beer goggles and the rose-coloured glasses, throw on the fluorescent lights of the bar at closing time, and take a closer look at who we've been, who we are, and who we're becoming.

But there are real risks to examining our ignorance, assumptions, actions, and inactions. The learning that needs to happen isn't easy. For many people, the idea that we ourselves could be racist is unthinkable. Most people would feel that "a racist" is a shameful thing to be. It's a possibility that many White settlers may never actively consider. As Robin DiAngelo describes in her article "White Fragility" (2011), most White people in North America live segregated lives, surrounded by other White people in a culture that "protects and insulates" us from racial discomfort (p. 54). We are not used to thinking critically about our racial socialization and how Whiteness operates in our society and in ourselves.

Taking a close, honest look at White supremacy and how it manifests in our actions, inactions, beliefs, and ignorance can threaten our deepest notions of ourselves as being "good people" living in "a good country"; it challenges the narratives we've created to define who we are. And recognizing that racism lives in our families can create painful cleavages in our closest relationships. There are risks to well-being, belonging, and connectedness when we question how we can love ancestors, family members, and friends whose stories, silences, and votes have nurtured historical and ongoing injustice.

Those of us who are actively engaging in "reconciliation" work are not off the hook when it comes to the necessity to examine our own complicity in ongoing settler colonial projects and the stories we tell ourselves about who we are. In their 2012 essay "Decolonization Is Not a Metaphor," Eve Tuck and K. W. Yang describe different ways that settlers try to alleviate our own discomfort and find "easier paths to reconciliation" (p. 4). As someone who has benefitted professionally from work with Indigenous communities and racialized urban youth through degrees, publications, jobs, and tenure, this description of "settler moves to innocence" hits especially close to home:

> Settler moves to innocence are those strategies or positionings that attempt to relieve the settler of feelings of guilt or responsibility without giving up land or power or privilege, without having to change much at all. In fact, settler scholars may gain professional kudos or a boost in their reputations for being so sensitive or self-aware. Yet settler moves to innocence are hollow, they only serve the settler. (Tuck & Yang, 2012, p. 10)

For those of us raised to think that White supremacists are monsters in white cloaks who have nothing to do with us, it may be nearly impossible to imagine that our work and our lives actually perpetuate and support colonialism and White supremacy or that we are the real beneficiaries of work we do under the banner of reconciliation. It feels safest to stay cocooned and avoid seeing things more clearly. But the path forward requires that we ask ourselves some hard questions like, *in what ways do I benefit, historically and in the present, from White supremacy, colonialism?* and *what people are calling reconciliation?*

These are the things I grapple with in relation to my research and my work with youth and families. These are the things I think of as I write this piece that is itself tied up with a yearning for a kind of belonging that is real and deep and built on foundations of equity, relationship, and accountability. These are things I also think about in my parenting.

A few years ago, I made a short film called *The Stories Beneath* (Breen, 2015) as part of the nIshnabek de'bwe wIn//Telling Our Truths project. Part of the methodology in this project requires that we researchers are also participants and each of us has made our own films exploring our relationship with Indigeneity and our place on these lands in which we live. The idea is that we need to centre ourselves in relationships and accountability to our co-researchers/participants before we begin our research. In my film, I explored notions of White identity from the specific vantage point of a parent raising a White son who will grow into a White man.

The film begins with an image of a little boy playing on a beach in blue pyjamas. He has curly brown hair and a very light complexion. He is busy and very focused as he builds small structures in the sand and then tears them down again. He is building a story on the beach.

My voice-over explains the story he tells me as he works: "There are two villages. One is full of bad people and the other good people. One day, the bad people come and steal the children."

The beautiful boy is my son, who has a Portuguese name because of the Brazilian (colonial) heritage he carries through his father, who is the son of a Brazilian man and a White mother of mixed Western European ancestry from Regina, Saskatchewan. The story he is telling is about residential schools. He is playing in the sand to try to understand pieces of a puzzle that doesn't make sense to him. He had learned about residential schools in the summer when we met an artist at Curve Lake First Nation near what we currently call Peterborough, Ontario. My children and I spent an afternoon watching the artist paint the feelings and dreams that he carried from his residential school experience. My kids love art and they really liked the artist. They enjoyed spending time with him and watching him paint. We went back to visit a couple more times that summer. The artist generously let my children watch while he worked, gave them candies, and told them in a gentle way about some of the pain behind the stories.

My children and I had lots of conversations after those visits with the artist. They started on the drive home and continue off and on even today. At the time, there had been other conversations that my son overheard at our dinner table with various friends and family as the grown-ups talked about the work of the Truth and Reconciliation Commission. My kids started to ask about our Anishnaabe and Inuit friends and extended Anishnaabe family members. *Did this happen to their families, too?* These conversations remind me of other difficult conversations we have with our kids. Conversations about sex, or violence, or family tragedies, topics broached carefully but honestly over and over again as we strive to get it right, questions asked and half answered, difficult silences when we don't quite know what to say because we're still figuring it all out for ourselves and are scared to say too much or too little to the little ones our hearts ache to protect.

In the voice-over on the film I describe the conversation my son and I had as he built the story on the beach. The images show him moving quickly, back and forth between imaginary villages. Knocking down. Building. Knocking down again.

*Did the children get taken away a long time ago?* he asks.

I thought of residential schools, the Sixties Scoop, today's child welfare system, and ongoing violence against First Nations, Métis, and Inuit children and their families. "Yes and no," I say. "It started a long time ago. It is still happening today."

*Did it happen far away?*

"No, sweetheart. It happened right where we live. We live on land that belonged to the First Nations."

*Will they come back for it?*

"You're safe, my love. Our home is safe."

*What did the bad guys look like?*

"They looked a lot like us."

There is tension in my voice-over. My son has lived a very good life so far. *We* live a very good life and this good life has allowed my son to believe that bad things only happen far away or long ago. I want to protect my children from knowledge of pain and suffering and I also want to raise my children to know the truth of the stories that lie beneath colonial myths that are still the master narratives of our world, the truths that lie beneath our own privileged safety. I want to raise my children to be brave and to find their own ways to strive for social justice. But there are risks and losses in this. Now my son knows that the terrible things are much closer than he thought. What does it say about where he is safe? What does it say about where he belongs? And there is something else that he is grappling with. His is a little boy's world of villains and heroes, good guys and bad guys. There is no room yet for in-between and both. If bad guys look like us, does that make him a bad guy? What does it say about who he is?

I think a lot about the stories we tell our kids. I think a lot about the kinds of stories they will need to create the lives we wish for them. For more than a decade now my research has involved studying how we make sense of ourselves by interacting with a world of stories, and I'm especially interested in how children and young adults develop a sense of identity through story-sharing. The stories we tell our children influence who they will become. Stories will help shape their values and beliefs, the way they feel about themselves, their understanding of their relationships, the paths they choose to follow throughout their lives, and their sense of belonging. It's through interacting with stories that our children develop an understanding of who and what we are accountable to, what counts as a good life, what and who matters, where "home" is. It's through listening to and telling stories that we figure out who we are. So, I have questions, more than answers, and my questions go something like this: *How do we create stories that tell the truth about who we have been and who we are, and that will offer new possibilities for who we are becoming? How do we tell stories that will end the violence of colonialism and move us toward a future that is grounded in truthfulness, accountability, respect, and love?*

For now, the protests I imagined this book making about how I don't belong have quieted. But they are not gone. I suspect that I might look back on this chapter in months or years and, perhaps, with a flash of embarrassment, wish that I wrote something different, something that reflects new awareness and understandings that I will grow into with time and in new relationships with ideas. This is the way things should be, I think. I'm pretty convinced that it's through openness, humility, striving for deep learning, and being accountable in relationships that we will get ourselves out of the terrible messes we're in. This framework for moving forward fits well with Leanne Betasamosake Simpson's description of Nishnaabeg ethical processes and Indigenous futurity: "*how* we live, *how* we organize, *how* we engage in the world—the process—not only frames the outcome, it is the transformation. *How* molds and gives birth to the present. The *how* changes us" (Simpson, 2017, p. 19). As a settler on Indigenous lands, I take these words to heart. It is the *how* that matters for all of us. Indigenous people need allies to support their work behind the scenes and White people also need to take on the burden and the risks of educating ourselves and others about colonialism, racism, and White supremacy. My commitment to allyship has evolved into something that is inclusive of allyship in both behind the scenes and more overt, out-front forms. I think my commitment keeps becoming clearer and deeper and exists somehow beyond allyship as well; I understand more fully that my activism isn't something I do for others. I am also working on my own behalf as I am striving to create the society that I want my children to belong to. The path forward isn't clear to me, but it's important to me that I keep going with the *how* always in mind and that I do my inevitably imperfect best to give my children and future generations a better story to tell and better ways of belonging with one another.

## ACKNOWLEDGEMENTS

I am deeply grateful to Lindsay DuPré, Shawn Wilson, and Hannah Fowlie for providing feedback on drafts of this chapter and, especially, to Jamie Bell for the conversations that got this whole project started.

## NOTE

1. In using the term *settler* I follow Chelsea Vowel's (2016) approach to thinking about settlers as comprising two general groups: a European-descended socio-political majority and non-Black persons of colour. As Vowel points out, "the term *settler* does not, and can never, refer to the descendants of Africans who were kidnapped and sold into chattel slavery" (p. 17).

## REFERENCES

Breen, A. V. (2015). *The stories beneath* [Digital story]. Toronto, ON.

DiAngelo, R. (2011). White fragility. *International Journal of Critical Pedagogy, 3*(3), 54–70.

Maynard, R. (2017). *Policing Black lives: State violence in Canada from slavery to the present.* Halifax: Fernwood.

Simpson, L. B. (2017). *As we have always done: Indigenous freedom through radical resistance.* Minneapolis: University of Minnesota Press.

Tuck, E., & Yang, K. W. (2012). Decolonization is not a metaphor. *Decolonization: Indigeneity, Education and Society, 1*(1), 1–40.

Vowel, C. (2016). *Indigenous writes: A guide to First Nations, Métis, and Inuit issues in Canada.* Winnipeg: HighWater Press.

## CHAPTER 5

# Distant, Invisible, Hidden Raíces. Indigenous Heritages of Central America: Renegotiation and Reconciliation

*by Paul Edward Montgomery Ramírez*

————

I'm Paul Edward Montgomery Ramírez. I'm an Indigenous Central American who grew up in the United States. I work as a decolonial heritage specialist, consulting for museums, conducting research, teaching, and doing public lectures and talks about culture. I move around a lot, making maintaining some roots difficult at times, but my spirit belongs to Nicaragua.

————

"Why is it called Masaya?" I asked as I was jolted out of the seat when the small Toyota truck hit a bump on the pathway while avoiding a skinny horse. The animal walked along the trail without a care, not even fussed by the sudden roar of a vehicle that raced along at speeds that were probably against better judgment. But that's the way you drove in Nicaragua: like you were possessed with some spirit without fear of risk to life and limb.

It was one of the few times I was ever able to sit in the front and not the bed of the truck. After a long day of picking jocotes, getting out of the heat was like a dream. Of course, it was just my luck that the fans weren't working that day, and even the rolled down windows didn't help much against the heat. "Masaya: más allá," Tío Negro responded, his attention never wavering from the road in front of him. He wiped a trail of sweat from out of his eyes, while his bald head seemed to sparkle.

Beyond. Farther. The Frontier. The middle of nowhere. And I accepted his answer.

That's what Masaya was to them, a quaint little place between two actual cities: Managua, the capital, and Granada, the colonial hub of culture. Of course, that's not what it means at all. Masaya isn't the "beyond," and its name certainly doesn't come from the Spanish. No, it comes from the Nahoa word for "deer" (másat). It means something to the effect of "the place where the deer are."

Despite this, I never saw a single deer around Masaya. But where I grew up in Ohio, there were so many that they were often a bit of a nuisance. They were fearless, and dangerous because of that; I found myself greatly disliking them. It's a bit of irony that these animals bothered me so much, all while being from "where the deer are." Well, where my family was from.

It was a place we were forced to leave shortly after the Revolution against the dictator Somoza. My mother and Tía Janina (who we simply called Tía) fled to Ohio with my father—a Yanqui (American). There, they started their new lives, and there my brother and I grew up. My mother took to being as good an American as she could. Her sister was another matter altogether. No two people could have been so different: my mother reserved and proper, Tía spirited and not infrequently crude.

Because my parents worked all the time, I spent many of my afternoons and evenings with Tía. And like any good tía, she took pleasure in telling me stories—mainly ones to horrify a child. She told me about duendes who lived near the lagoons, in caves, and in the rocks. Depending on their mood, they could do all sorts of things, from helping around the house to stealing and drowning children. I guess those were the obvious choices. She told me about the horse-faced

Cegua who lived in the woods and punished men who strayed in their faithfulness. She told me about ghostly carts—the Carretanagua—that prowled the streets at night and stole your sanity and soul. She told me about great serpents and monsters in the water and powerful man-monkeys who tormented people.

"Don't listen to your tia. Those stories are just made up," my mother would say on the way home, after I recounted what I'd been told earlier.

My mother never told me stories from Nicaragua when I was that age. I didn't see it then, but I'm certain they made her uncomfortable. And not because they had a flair for the morbid. It also wasn't entirely because of being the upstanding and wholesome Catholic that she was. She had no interest in exposing me to such things, and she had little interest in teaching me anything that went too close to a place she stopped considering home years ago.

I was around five or six when the family first came back to Nicaragua. From then on, every few years we would return—when we had the money—to see those who had stayed behind. I blended in well enough, if I didn't open my mouth too much. My mother cautioned against talking with the "market people." Not because my Spanish sounded like I'd been stung by a bunch of bees, either. They were drunks and swindlers. Still, she bought their fabrics and jewellery, their dresses and shirts and sandals. Her opinions about these people didn't stop their woodwork and weaving and pottery from filling our house. Each time we returned to our lives in the United States, we came back with more trappings of a culture my mother never spoke of.

Visiting Nicaragua was always an insightful time, whether I knew it then or not. My brother stopped going, but I always insisted on coming and staying in the house that still had holes in it from the war a decade after it had ended. And I always came back with more questions than answers; more holes, less putty.

Each visit with my family, each story from Tia, each tense conversation between her and my mother in hushed Spanish (which my mother assumed I couldn't understand) and the equally tense silences that followed made me look down at myself and see the holes. I was a branch that beetles had dug burrows through. They were the holes that you couldn't see through, yawning and dark pits without a knowable end. It was probably the accumulation of these gaps, these spaces, that made me interested in finding out about cultures—which brought me to becoming an archaeologist. Finding out about other people became more about finding out about myself.

By the last time we all returned to Nicaragua together in happiness, I was in university pursuing a degree in anthropology. I had done some research and came up with a few places that I wanted to visit while we were there. In the centre of Lago Cocibolca ("Sweet Sea") is an island made of twin volcanoes, aptly called Ometepe ("Two Mountains"). I first heard about it through research that was being carried out in the area, cataloguing petroglyphic sites.

We crammed into Tio Negro's truck, with me firmly seated in the bed as per usual, and drove to the ferry. We visited some of the easier sites, and a museum that contained artifacts from the island. A world of beautiful works was laid before me. I recognized many of the designs of pottery. That was because they looked startlingly like the ones that I had seen in the markets over the years, made by the artesanos around Masaya. Funerary urns with serpents on them reminded me of a story Tia scolded me with for trying to poke a garter snake with a stick as a child. What I saw was both new and familiar.

I left Ometepe with a fire in my stomach. It was something I could get used to. There was another set of petroglyphs in Masaya that I was set to visit and get my fix. Well, they were more appropriately in Monimbó. They were within walking distance of the house, but at the time required a guide to get to there. My lita (grandmother) shook her head when I asked about visiting them. Something always came up when I wanted to go, and my mother reminded me how we had already done my "thing." So, in the end, we all parted ways without me having had the chance to visit.

My first visit to Monimbó was the next year, to bury my grandfather. After it was done, rum and stories flowed like water. Family who had never existed to me before came to the tongues of my mother and her sisters. Memories of childhoods, sweet and sad, bubbled up. In one moment, my mother's mask dropped off. She spoke of a gentle, ancient woman she grew up with as a child. My grandmother's grandmother. For a time that passed like a breath, hidden heritages had been whispered.

The truth had finally come together in one bittersweet night. The last connecting piece fell into place and two decades of silence, distance, and denial tumbled down to leave a reality that had been hinted to me for as far as I can remember.

We were indios. Sure, I understood that whole story they tell about Latin@s being "mixed" with Spanish/Portuguese/European and Indigenous blood. That was the story we all knew: blancos, mestizos, indios (often Afro-Latin@s didn't even make it into the conversation). But my mother was always adamant that we lived on one side of that spectrum. That ancient woman, my grandmother's grandmother, whom my mother knew in her childhood secured that through her own sacrifices. She was a Bravo, her name marking her as a "wild Indian." But her children would be Aguirres, and theirs would be Robles.

For her family to survive, the indio needed to die. These parts needed to be wrapped up and shamed and hidden, never to be remembered. But this isn't just my story. It's a story that's known all too well. It's a Latin American story.

Indigeneity in Latin America has peculiarities when compared to English-speaking settler states. Genocide took shapes that were both the same and dissimilar to the experiences of Indigenous Peoples who met English-speaking settlers. And where this difference most counted is in a myth of the mestizos, of mestizaje. That is, the "mixing" of Europeans and Indigenous Peoples to create mestizos—or ladinos—while enslaving and systematically depriving Indigenous people of opportunity and social mobility: a familiar story to the Indigenous world.

As nationalist sentiments brewed and bubbled in Latin America in opposition to European and American dominance during the 19th century, the socially powerful in many areas attached to the ladino identity as a marker of uniqueness, something to lionize and unite under, as something to vindicate breaking away from imperial powers. For the sake of their cause, the "civility" of the European mixed with the "passion" of the indio to create a more perfect being. With the cultural differences of Indigenous Peoples absorbed, they could be repurposed into uniform cultural packages. And so the social undertaking of transforming the peoples in places like Nicaragua into ladinos gained new steam.

Masaya itself is considered a mestizo settlement, nestled in between two pueblos indígenas: Monimbó and Nindirí. I suppose the goal of this place, which had existed before the arrival of the Spanish, was to lure Indigenous folk into the (should I say?) trap of mestizaje. Regardless of this, the people in places like Monimbó and Sutiaba—several hours north—began to be viewed in diverging ways. First, they were "different" sorts of indios than those who lived in the mountains (either originally or to escape enslavement by settlers): they were nearly civilized. Nearly. They were also different from people like the Rama and Mískitu beyond the mountains, who fought Spanish encroachment—with the help of the United Kingdom.

They weren't even proper indios then, were they? Surely, they only needed to stop speaking their languages and wearing their traditional garb, and to let go of their communal lands and everything would be fine. Then they would be campesinos and artesanos; they would have assimilated just fine, while also not upsetting society with notions of social mobility. Ethnic differences were washed over by relabelling them as classes. Of course, these classes were still based on racial divisions.

Into the mid-19th century, it was legal for an Indigenous person to be the property of ladinos. Even after having slaves became illegal and immoral in Nicaragua, "adoptions" of children became an alternative for gaining free labour while removing their Indigenous ties. By also opening access to otherwise impossible marriages, these adoptions could serve as a path beyond the campesino. In the late 19th century, during the genocidal policies of a president named Zelaya, a woman called Bravo from Monimbó, my grandmother's grandmother, was adopted by a family in Masaya. Around this time, the Mangue-Chorotega language finally fell out of use in places like Monimbó. And around this time, the trappings of Monimboseños became an infrequent sight.

Social engineers clapped hands and congratulated themselves on the triumph of mestizaje. But even though these things that excited anthropologists (like Indigenous language and dress) were no longer as visible, Indigenous people hadn't vanished. They had been rebranded, and the goalposts of who is and who is not Indigenous were moved.

By the time my mother was growing up, class and Indigeneity in the western half of Nicaragua were impossibly intertwined. The fate that she sought to avoid was being restricted to working in the markets, to making pottery and textiles. Because that is what being indio meant. Communal lands had been stripped from pueblos and Indigenous cotton production outlawed within the first half of the 20th century. Piece by piece, the ladino society covered up Indigenous populations, and consumed their heritages as it saw fit. Indigenous performances became national and were transformed into folk "ballets." Celebration became formal and regally costumed. The Indigenous were hidden in plain sight.

My mother pitied the gentle Bravo she knew; she wept at the life this woman was forced to lead. So did Lita (this woman's granddaughter and my mother's mother). They pitied her, and feared being Indigenous, since that meant the status that her adoption bought would vanish. Tia was another matter entirely. Where my mother and Lita avoided traditional practices, Tia involved herself in them, even if it meant sneaking out to do so. But still, in those days, reconnection was something that seemed impossible. Even with Monimboseño friends, and being invited to and participating in tradition, she could never claim to be anything other than mestiza.

And that was that.

The war first came to Monimbó. The Monimboseños rebellion followed the assassination of a journalist named Chamorro. So forgotten and neglected were the Monimboseños that Somoza and Sandinistas alike were shocked by their sudden insurrection in 1978. After the rebellion in Monimbó was put down, the country was swept up in war, which saw the revolutionary socialist Sandinista party overthrow the American-supported dictatorship, and left tens of thousands of people homeless. Thousands more became refugees during the Revolution and the Contra War, which followed over the next decade.

Indigenous Peoples in the western half of the country were hailed as heroes of the Revolution, but their struggles against oppression were co-opted into the new state's vision of a struggle against imperialism. In addition to this, Indigenous uprisings in what had at times been called the Miskito Coast again moved the label of Indigenous eastwards. It was a struggle of Indigenous Peoples for autonomy against Sandinista rule. This resistance became so focal that the famous Native American rights activist Russell Means visited the region in 1985–86 to document their cause. He even went so far as to announce his intentions to recruit some 100 Native American warriors to join the Mískitu and Contras. On the other side of the country, Sutiabas and Mangue-Chorotegas people lost their Indigenous voices again. Or, rather, the voices they had always had fell once more on ears that could no longer hear them over the cacophony.

The Sandinista party lost power at the beginning of the 1990s. With that, a decade of civil war and sanction ended. And while research into the country's pasts and peoples had been carried out periodically over the previous century and a half, new interest from outside—and within—drove archaeological research. Over the next 25 years, this work brought pre-Hispanic pasts out of the shadowy realms to which they had been relegated. Early Indigenismo movements (a series of political ideologies that have sought to connect Indigenous cultures, often in the past tense, to the state) took place in modern states like Peru and Mexico, which contained powerful pre-Hispanic states and empires that had surviving chronicles about them and impressive physical remains like ruined cities and pyramids. Indigenismo movements fostered pride in pre-Hispanic characteristics but tended to do little for contemporary Indigenous groups. In places without striking monuments, like Nicaragua, study of the material remains of pre-Hispanic peoples helped to foster a sort of Indigenismo light™.

Of course, I'm not going to say that archaeology brought Indigenous pride back onto the Nicaraguan scene. It's far more complicated than that. But it did help to tease out physical evidence that could open conversations to re-evaluate the pre-Hispanic past. And in these conversations, Indigenous voices at times emerged. Naturally, other parties had their own plans for this heritage.

I visited Ometepe again in 2016, partly for my own research and partly for my work as a heritage professional. After a day of hiking with a Nahoa guide to photograph petroglyphs—and realizing how out of shape I was at the same time—we ended at a trio of statues on the church grounds of a town. A few people gathered around, not to look at the statues and their crouched bodies and animal-crowned heads. No, they were watching a couple in bright dress and feathers, with ayoyotes and drums, performing a conchero dance. I asked the guide what was going on, but the look on his face was the same as everyone else who had gathered: confusion. He hadn't the faintest clue what they were doing.

Once the pair had finished their dance, my guide and I approached them. The couple had with them a few friends with children, who stood in observation near the statues. As I spoke to the man, the woman scolded one of the children for climbing atop the eagle-headed figure. She told the children that those were their ancestors and should be respected.

As it turned out, the couple and their friends were all from Matagalpa (with the exception of the woman, who was a Breton from France), in the centre of Nicaragua. They were on a "healing mission" to bring a spiritual awakening throughout the country to reconnect to Mother Earth and tribal roots. Here, a traditional form of dance among Nahua peoples in Mexico was performed in front of Mangue-Chorotega statues, to the confusion of a crowd (some among them Nahoa), by people who said they were Matagalpinos. The whole scene was well intentioned; the dance was done out of a desire to raise the profile of Indigeneity among Spanish-speaking Nicaraguans, to reconnect people. But what they were raising had very little to do with anyone except that company of dancers. All it did was wash over cultural differences that had always existed in Nicaragua, and replace them with a foreign, exoticizing import. It became little more than self-indulgence and appropriation, while at the same time taking up space where more thoughtful dialogue could have taken place.

Actions like these continue to do the damage that communities like those in western Nicaragua have had to endure. Just as elites took dances and celebrations from pueblos and rebranded them into "ballets" and "operas" to suit a consumable Nicaraguan identity, people who try to return to seek their Indigenous roots without deep consideration do nothing more than force an image of the Indigenous, an image that can place marginal communities in a locked and unchanged past: that to be "indio" meant to wear feathers and have decidedly Classical Nahuatl names. I should say that I'm not taking issue with concheros, but simply saying that in a Nicaraguan landscape they're more a fantasy of a primordial time that probably never was. And in that, Mangue-Chorotegas and Sutiabas and Nahoas are placed as people out of time, as somehow only truly Indigenous in the far gone past.

The shocking revelation my family hid wasn't that we had an Indigenous past. That is the story of mestizaje, after all. No, it was that that past was within my mother's living memory. It wasn't something distant and shrouded in a foggy memory from half a millennium away. The lie that is mestizaje became unignorable. So did my detachment. Not only from the homeland my family was driven from, but also these roots of an Indigenous heritage that I was one generation removed from having a living attachment to. My tia bridged gaps with stories, and with her own connections, but she would have never thought it possible to consider herself an Indigenous person. But anything else for me felt like continuing a lie, a kind of betrayal.

The question becomes: Can we return? Can so-called Latinos return to communities that they have been separated from by time and kilometres? Increasingly, people who tick the little "person of Hispanic, Latino, or Spanish origin" box on censuses have also ticked "American Indian or Alaska Native," alongside—or instead of—it. The Nicaraguan census has also shown a massive upswing in people selecting the Indigenous option. Suddenly, in the 21st century, people who hadn't been allowed to consider themselves in a light other than mestizo were given the ability to identify in ways they felt more comfortable with, and the "accepted" Indigenous population in the Spanish-speaking side of the country exploded.

Changing attitudes toward the complicated heritages of Indigeneity in Latin America are giving people from backgrounds of pueblos indígenas in the Pacific, centre, and north the opportunity to become more visible. The idea that these groups are indígenas and not at the same time (or at least not "properly" Indigenous) is no longer tenable. Humanities research has been an important aspect to raising pueblos indígenas into a more prominent position. Research out of UNAN (Universidad Nacional Autónoma de Nicaragua) was recently carried out specifically with pueblos indígenas in the Pacific, centre, and north in mind. This research was used to highlight Mangue-Chorotega, Sutiaba, and Nahoa worldviews as diverse and Indigenous. Of course, the research was not for these people, but for outsiders. Among these outsiders are also people who desire to return to their heritages.

In my experience, the process of reconnecting can be difficult when you are removed by distance. Some of my cousins who remained in Nicaragua now participate in Monimboseño traditions and have come to embrace the Indigenous parts of themselves as well. I cannot do that. I don't have community so readily available to me. And this is the case for many Central Americans. We have been scattered by war, by disaster. Return for us may not be possible, or our visits infrequent and fleeting, so researching our heritages may be one of a few viable avenues of expression available to us. Access to information can be the difference between a person who remains culturally isolated and one who finds inspiration to attempt to reconnect to hidden roots. A diverse and thoughtful body of research can also combat "reconnections" that are more appropriating and marginalizing to peoples who are already under continual threat of having their Indigeneity vanished and narratives washed over or co-opted.

The existence of pueblos indígenas in the Pacific, centre, and north of Nicaragua is one of marginality in an already marginal place. Central America is a region that is subaltern to not only the Western world, but also Latin America. The concheros at Ometepe showed this all too well, placing a traditional performance from communities of Mexican backgrounds into a Nicaraguan scene like that is the way it was or should be again. Lifting voices from Central American worlds is necessary to break the cycles of reinforced, multi-layered marginalization.

Unfortunately, a staggering amount of writing is only produced in English. A book was published as a result of the project through which I had learned about Ometepe four years after its end. This monograph was written in English and cost somewhere around $50 (USD) when I eventually bought it. Many influential works on the pre-Hispanic, or even the anthropology and sociology of dozens of Nicaraguan topics, are only in the anglosphere. The problem of access within the academic world is even more exaggerated in places like Nicaragua, where the average person lives on around $2 (USD) a day and has little or no working understanding of English. This certainly isn't helping them to engage with heritages. Additionally, research that is written in Spanish can be easily ignored by much of the scholarly world. My own department doesn't have access to most works from Latin America that I make use of—so I have to get to them on my own—and while I know where to look to get a hold of these resources, that's not the case for many people. Academic resources are already difficult enough for non-academics to reach before we start to add extra sets of obstacles that can keep a Central American who speaks only Spanish resettled in Canada, or elsewhere, from engagement.

Exploring the ties we have to one another can provide us with many options. If conducted responsibly, research into decolonial pasts can help build platforms where marginal people can raise their voices clear enough to be heard over the clamour. In the case of Nicaragua, the pre-Hispanic heritages of the Pacific, centre, and north are attached to the nation building of the country, while at the same time absolutely a part of modern Indigenous Peoples' heritage. We are past the time of dismissing people of the pueblos as not being "really" Indigenous, and conversations about Indigenous roots and heritages can no longer be one-sided arguments between alleged mestizos. The talking circle is much more colourful now. Increased interest in the Indigenous and the weakening of the myth of mestizaje bring their own challenges. Still, they do bring opportunities.

I have known several Central Americans in situations similar to mine: searching for ways to reconnect to heritages that have been taken from us by wars and by genocidal policies inflicted upon our ancestors. The desire to reclaim what has been taken, hidden, is strong. But it's also bound up in many difficulties. We may not be able to physically come back to the communities our families left, or we may not have enough information about our familial pasts to even be able to know who we should be searching for. This is one thing that carrying out and making research available might help with. Researching as an archaeologist, an anthropologist, and a heritage specialist has forced me to ask difficult questions of myself over and over: Is returning to the communities our ancestors came from possible? Is it desired by those communities? Has mestizaje won?

The answers aren't simple ones, like many in life. Some people do try to return; others reconnect but keep marginal associations. The ways in which Latin@s take to interacting with their Indigenous pasts are as varied as the cultures and ethnicities they come from.

Offering people decolonial options to think and talk about Indigenous heritage is an important issue that I'm greatly invested in. Expanding on research from Indigenous pasts and presents can help to bring these options out. The uses of these options are also important. There are very few Indigenous Central American scholars, and of those only a few who work in the heritage sector. I hope that this will not be the case for much longer, but in the meantime responsibility falls on researchers to do more than just research, but to act: against stigmas and to make spaces for Indigenous voices. With over a million Nicaraguans living in other countries, humanities research can bring these people—or their children—closer to distant heritages. Without thoughtful outreach—connecting Indigenous narratives and concerns to the larger public—research can be quickly co-opted by colonizing forces like exploitative tourism that removes Indigenous people from their traditions. Even the well-intentioned can cause harm by speaking *for* others. For research to stand any chance at decoloniality and reconciling dark inheritances of Latin America, more Indigenous bodies and voices must be given platforms to renegotiate our heritages to ladino/mestizo societies in Latin America, and to Latin@s in diaspora.

I hadn't flown thousands of kilometres on a whim. The family was gathering again to celebrate, and I stopped over while waiting to pick up two of my cousins from the airport. Tia brewed us some coffee and took a bag out of the freezer. She placed it into warm water to thaw it quickly, before placing the delicious contents into a large wooden bowl.

Tia and I descended on the container of thawed jocotes, and the seeds that made up most of the tiny red fruits piled up quickly. Her house had changed since the last time I was around; then again, so much had changed. It seemed that way every time I returned to visit family. I was never the same either, so who was I to judge? But Tia never seemed to change—she even looked the same, haircut and all, in one of the few pictures we have from before she left for the United States.

Like most things, jocotes are much better from the branch than the freezer. When you get frozen ones, some of them have lost their taste or become a sickly nearly rotten mush, while the seeds in some break to the point where you have to pick the hard, cork-like pieces out of your mouth. But as Tia said while she spat a seed out to join the stack that we had created, "I'd rather have frozen than none."

And so would I.

## FURTHER READING

Consejo Pueblos Indígenas Pacífico, Centro, y Norte. (2018). *Consejo Nacional de Pueblos Indígenas del Pacífico, Centro y Norte de Nicaragua.* Retrieved from pueblosindigenaspcn.net

Field, L. (1999). *The grimace of Macho Ratón.* Durham, NC: Duke University Press.

Gould, J. (1998). *To die in this way.* Durham, NC: Duke University Press.

Lange, F., Sheets, P., Martinez, A., & Abel-Vidor, S. (1992). *The archaeology of Pacific Nicaragua.* Albuquerque: University of New Mexico Press.

Newson, L. (1987). *Indian survival in Colonial Nicaragua.* Norman: University of Oklahoma Press.

Whisnant, D. (1995). *Rascally signs in sacred places.* Chapel Hill: University of North Carolina Press.

Zambrana Lacayo, N. (Ed.). (2007–15). *Mi Museo y Vos* (Vols. 1–32). Retrieved from granadacollection.org/Revistas.htm

## CHAPTER 6

# Fish Fry as Praxis: Exploring Land as a Nexus for Reconciliation in Research

*by Lana Ray, Paul Cormier, and Leisa Desmoulins*

———

Boozhoo, Lana Ray nindizhnikaaz. Opwaaganasiniing nindoonjibaa. Oshowkinoozhe n'dodem. Anishinaabe kwe n'daaw. Waaskone Giizhigook Anishinaabe noswin.

Greetings, my name is Lana Ray. I am from Opwaaganasiniing. I am from the Muskellunge Clan. I am an Anishinaabe woman. My Anishinaabe name is the light that shines. I am also an assistant professor in the Indigenous Learning Department at Lakehead University.

Hello, Boozhoo, my name is Leisa Desmoulins. My Anishinaabe husband, children, and extended family connect me to Biigtigong Nishnaabeg, also known as Pic River First Nation, and to Thunder Bay, where I live and work as an assistant professor in the Faculty of Education at Lakehead University.

Boozhoo, Ma'iingan nindizhinikaaz. Lake Helen nindoonjibaa. Ma'iingan n'dodem.

Hi, my name is Paul Cormier and my Native name, my spirit name, is wolf. I belong to the Wolf Clan and I am a member of Lake Helen First Nation, the Red Rock Indian Band in Northern Ontario, Canada.

———

It was early morning when Lana, Leisa, and Paul, friends and colleagues at Lakehead University, drove onto the bridge at the crest of the hill, the view of the Nipigon Marina and Nipigon River now upon them. This place was familiar to Lana and Paul, as both were raised in the area, being from Opwaaganasiniing (Lake Helen First Nation), and participated in ceremony here. For Paul, this journey was almost routine, as he lived only minutes away, and for Lana, who now lived in Thunder Bay, visiting the marina and the water was part of her ritual of returning home. This moment offered something reminiscent yet new to Leisa, who was a frequent visitor to Biigtigong Nishnabeg (Pic River First Nation), along Lake Superior, the home community of her partner and a community in which she gained Indian Status through marriage. As they began their descent toward the boat launch, a gateway to the Nipigon River and the water within its reach, they could see a blanket of fog slowly residing and feel it with every breath they took. It was invigorating, a fortification of their early morning efforts and a catalyst for the full day ahead.

With the boat now launched but secured by the braided cord of rope wrapped around the dock cleat, Lana, Leisa, and Paul sought to enact the promises of their ancestors. With asemma (tobacco) in hand, Lana, Leisa and Paul spoke their honourable intentions to the water and placed them at her feet, along the shoreline. These remembered actions of Lana and Paul carried forward the treaty of the Anishinaabe and Opwaaganasiniing (the place where the pipestone comes from) until the next moment in time. For Leisa, the tobacco served as an activation of her inherited promise to acknowledge and respect Anishinaabe continuance, and a deep settling within her of the necessity to enter into her own treaty with Opwaaganasiniing. The promises of all three were received by the water, through an enduring wave that enveloped the tobacco before retreating back into the river. With the offering accepted and treaty responsibilities renewed, Lana, Leisa, and Paul embarked on their fishing trip.

**Leisa:** It is absolutely breathtaking out here—I am so glad you both invited me out on the water.

**Paul:** Sometimes we are so busy it is hard to connect, so we thought this would be a good chance to share the projects we are working on, ground the work that we are currently undertaking in the region, and discuss some potential projects for the future.

**Lana:** Yeah, we thought if there could be a trend of "walking meetings," why not "fishing meetings"! We can do a bit of fishing in the river and up toward Lake Helen, have a fire, and just chat.

**Leisa:** That's so true, isn't it? Just because we are used to doing something some way doesn't mean we have to continue. This place really is so invigorating and inspiring. So, where are all the fishing spots?

**Paul:** We used to fish all around this area, and still do for the most part. We even used to go fishing out on some islands quite a way past here in the Nipigon Bay. You may have heard of them before. They were pretty famous in the late 1970s and were petitioned to become their own nation so that they could have environmental protection. Locals in the area thought that because they weren't mentioned in the Robinson-Superior Treaty that meant they were up for grabs.

**Lana:** It is interesting how there is still the misunderstanding that our sovereignty is derived from the treaties with the British. The only treaties we derive our sovereignty from are those with the Creator and with the Land. Like today when we put down tobacco, every time we do that we are acknowledging those treaties and practising our sovereignty. (*Noticing the change of expression on Leisa's face.*) Leisa, do you have something nibbling on your line?

**Leisa:** Yes, I felt something. I thought it might be a fish, but I think it is just the currents of the water agreeing with your point!

**Lana:** Honestly, I am not much for trolling and can never tell. I am from the Muskie Clan and us muskies have a tendency to sit back and watch our surroundings. We aren't much for the current.

**Paul:** I am just going to take us a bit further out; then we can anchor the boat and cast off.

After a steady and purposeful ride, with the turn of the ignition key, the boat comes to rest, its movement now dictated by the rise and fall of the waves. Lana, Leisa, and Paul cast out their lines.

**Lana:** You know what I love the most about fishing? The humility that it brings—it is so freeing. Now don't get me wrong, there is still agency and a lot of skill involved, but just the idea of casting out your line into a blue abyss (well before fish finders anyway!) and trusting that the Land will take care of you. There is just something fundamentally different about a process rooted in trust versus control.

**Paul:** My mom shared the term *Aki Gakinoomaagewin* with me and I think it gets at what you are talking about. It means learning from the Land, and doing so within the physical and metaphysical realms of Indigenous existence. It is its own methodology (Cormier, 2016, p. 20).

**Leisa:** There is so much beauty in thinking about fishing in this way, as a methodology of care. This meaning is largely lost these days; arguably fishing has become about pride, not humility. The ability to convey these concepts often falls short, too, like in a rights-based argument, for example. But thinking about fishing as an act of care, that makes sense and it explains why it always feels so good to be out fishing!

**Lana:** Just further up the river towards Red Rock there are some pictographs that are thousands of years old. People can't fully conceive what it means to be part of a landscape but when you are in that spot and look at those pictographs you can feel it. You can feel the history and the presence of place. You come to understand that it is more than "Aboriginal and Treaty Rights." It isn't really about my right to harvest a fish, it is about knowing that my family and I have been taken care of for the whole of our existence and the gratefulness we feel and the respect that permeates from this care. People use the phrase "earth is our mother" and it is true. The Land is the mother of our Nation, of all Nations, and it is a natural act of humanity to want to protect from harm the woman who has done so much for you.

**Paul:** It's reciprocal, too. Some people from our area believe we were placed on the shores of Lake Superior at the mouth of the Nipigon River[1] by the Creator to protect the area from invaders from other lands, to protect the upper Great Lakes (Cormier, 2016, p. 26).

**Leisa:** Is this something that you both believe?

**Lana:** Yeah, I do. For me this has been one of my motivations for trying to relearn and take up our traditional teachings and practices. I wanted to better understand my responsibilities and how I can best take those up. I think that all these changes we are seeing, like climate change, are the result of broken treaties. I am trying to align the work that I am doing at the university as well and centre my work in place and construct research as an act of renewing responsibilities and collective memories to the Land.

**Leisa:** It's ethical relationality, isn't it? The idea that it's a denial of connectivity that allows violence and exploitation to occur and persist (Donald, 2012). Donald talks about it more in terms of Indigenous and non-Indigenous relations, the idea of an Indigenous métissage,[2] but it also has much broader implications, like climate change (Donald, 2009, p. 19). I have been doing a lot of my own thinking about this as well, in terms of my position in an Indigenous education department. Curricular and pedagogical enactment of ethical forms of relationality has really become a matter of survival (Donald, 2009, p. 19).

**Lana:** One of the projects that I am currently working on is looking at how we engage in curricular and pedagogical enactment at a program and institutional level at the university through the development of an Indigenous quality assurance system. On the advisement of Elders, we based our work around the term *weweni*, which means to look after something carefully and properly (Building a Strong Fire, 2018). We developed four Indigenous quality standards—Celebration and Sharing, Honour and Respect, Place and Purpose, and Relationships with Land— and we are now piloting our system to assess these standards. The project came about because there seemed to be a lot of talk about efforts of reconciliation but myself and others involved were hard-pressed to find exactly what the efforts were, whose efforts they were, how they were being carried out, and if they were having any real impact. The Place and Purpose standard is really about the development of personal relationships with Land and community and the last standard, Relationships with Land, is about institutional-level relationships. Once the standards were created and we were doing some engagement to envision what the standards would look like when they were operationalized, the last standard was by far the most challenging for people to imagine. There were some really tough questions, like how is reconciliation factored into decision-making at the institution, including allocation of resources and impacts on Indigenous Land and rights.

**Leisa:** I think it's tough because it is a new question—even though we have been talking about reconciliation for a few years now, it is still a new question. Few initiatives that I know of actually address questions of Land reclamation, reparations, Indigenous sovereignty and jurisdiction, or Canadian sovereignty on stolen Indigenous Lands (Davis et al., 2017, p. 408).

**Paul:** I think this sort of work in Indigenous studies and Indigenous education is vital because without traditional Lands, Indigenous cultures will disappear and peace will be unachievable (Ray & Cormier, 2012, p. 172). A project that Lana and I are working on is looking at how to strengthen relationships between high schools and Indigenous communities, and even looking at the possibility of building Land-based curriculum that brings back knowledges related to rites of passage. Speaking of peace and rites of passage, right over there on those banks is where Lana and I fasted. That was the first year the fast was brought back to our community. (*Lana chuckles.*)

**Lana:** I am laughing because I am remembering Paul's and my parents during the fast. Everyone was really happy and excited that fasting was happening in our community again but at the same time, even though it is a really old practice, it was really new too, because it had been so long. Paul's mom actually got someone to drive her over to this side of the bank to come check to see if he was okay. My dad was a bit subtler and took a ride over near Sawmill Point one night, where he could get a good look. He thought that he was being pretty clever and that by going at night time he would see my fire burning and then would know that I was okay. It totally backfired, though! He didn't realize that I didn't have a fire burning even though it was October. On top of that, my dog, who he had taken for the ride, wouldn't stop whining. He told me he got really worried after that! I poke fun at them, but I have to admit there was an aspect of hyper-vigilance for me too at first. I couldn't remember the last time, if ever, that I was alone in the bush, just me, as Paul was a short distance away. It's all part of a process of moving away from distant, adversarial relationships with Land toward a relationship of care. These stories of place, even the funny ones, are so important too because they are expressions of sovereignty that work to re-centre the Land as relative and citizen (Donald, 2009, p. 19).

After fishing and conversing for the good part of the morning, Leisa, hand over hand, works to pull up the anchor while Lana makes sure that all of their gear is secure in the boat. Once finished, Paul turns over the ignition and manoeuvres the boat toward Lake Helen.

**Leisa:** Is that a little church I see over there?

**Lana:** Yeah, it's St. Sylvester's Church, but it's not open anymore. It was built in the late 1800s and was a Jesuit mission (Red Rock Indian Band, 2018). I suppose there were a lot of churches like that built near Indigenous communities at the time, but I am not sure how many are left standing.

**Paul:** I was told a story about the church by George. He said that years and years ago there used to be an old trapper whose trapline was back past Second Lake, back in that area. George told me that this trapper found something back there that he showed to a bishop that used to come to the church from Montreal maybe once every six months or something. The trapper took that bishop back there, way behind the church into a cave and showed him something. I don't know what it was, but I guess it was valuable and the bishop took some of it and told the trapper not to tell anyone. This bishop took a big supply home and eventually died, and none of it was returned. The trapper had never said anything, because he was scared. See, at that time the community was really afraid of religion (Cormier, 2016, pp. 53–54).

**Lana:** That reminds me of a trip I took to the States. I went to a museum and I saw a pipe made out of red stone that was taken from this area. I still think about how it got there. Was it just taken, too? There is still so much rebuilding and reclaiming work to be done.

**Paul:** Leisa, another thing that was taken from here was a lot of fish. For over a century now, this river has been promoted as a place of pristine, untouched wilderness, available for the taking. In the 1800s and early 1900s it was aggressively promoted by the Canadian Pacific Railway and the Hudson's Bay Company. Fisherman came and, in some cases, took hundreds of kilograms of fish. When the fish population started to be depleted, the zhaaganash[3] claimed that Indigenous Peoples' subsistence was tied to the decline and tried to privatize the property to preserve it for non-Indigenous fisherman and tourism, infringing on Indigenous subsistence practices (Thoms, 1999).

**Lana:** This kind of thing still happens, too. About 10 years ago members of our community got the police called on them for fishing in a brook trout sanctuary. This is a spot where community members had fished for hundreds of years, and they don't fish the pool during spawning season. Chief and Council organized a protest and a group of about 30 people, including Chief and Council, gathered on the shores of the spot (Cormier, 2016).

**Leisa:** It is almost clichéd how textbook this story is. It is the same strategy and contentious history in which stories are told to erase Indigenous Peoples and their presence from the landscape. To make it seem that Canadians living in those places have those same connections (Donald, 2009, p. 10). There was a really great research paper that just came out that speaks about the same things that we are talking about. It looks at the decline of the caribou in the North, and particularly squashes the claim that it was Indigenous subsistence practices that led to the decline, explaining that the real reason was the mining industry (Parlee, Sandlos, & Natcher, 2018).

**Paul:** We need more research that does this, that works to challenge settler stories and delegitimize Indigenous dispossession from Lands—even if it means challenging the powers that be, including potential donors to the university.

**Lana:** Yes! It is definitely part of a settler colonial agenda to naturalize settlers to the Land while Indigenous Peoples fade into invisibility. The whole narrative of Indigenous Peoples and overfishing just works to support that idea of settler innocence instead of implicating them within the status quo (Davis et al., 2017, p. 410). Like the famous brook trout caught during the time of the fish rush here. A tourist, Dr. Cook, got credit for it, but according to our Elders it was his guide from Lake Helen who really caught the fish (Thoms, 1999). What are the odds of Anishinaaabeg fishing here for thousands of years and then a zhaaganash comes by and catches the biggest fish there ever was? I believe what our Elders said, that he didn't catch it, but even if he did, it's probably not the biggest fish, just the biggest fish ever recorded, as our ancestors wouldn't have been concerned with something like that.

**Paul:** Yeah, there are definitely some stories that get privileged over others that work to naturalize settlers and maintain their innocence. Like how many settler stories do you hear about the negative impacts of industry on the river system? A pulp-wood company used to ship logs down the river, polluting the water and affecting the fish. Then, after the tourist industry died down some, the river was dammed in the 1920s for hydro, changing the whole flow of the river forever (Thoms, 1999). My mom once told me a story that Mrs. Borg told her. She said that people from the community used to go up the river before they built the dam. They used to hear and see a woman in the falls, in the mist, and she was crying. They never knew why she was crying, but she said after they built the dam they knew she was crying because they were going to build the dam, they were going to dam it up. That's what Mrs. Borg told my mom (Cormier, 2016, p. 93).

**Lana:** I am just in awe sometimes of how this water, this place, continues to care for us even after all of this. A few years ago, my partner and I met an Elder who told us about a special gift that we would receive. We thought this was something that would come years down the road, but a few days later we were in Nipigon at my parents' house, running some errands actually, and I just walked out of the bank and something came over me. I got back in the car and told my partner that I wanted to take him to Alexander Dam, a place just further up the Nipigon River. He had never been and I just said, come on, I need to take you there. When we got there, we walked along the shoreline and sure enough that special gift was there. We put down our tobacco to say miigwetch.

Boat at rest on the shores of the Nipigon River, Lana, Leisa, and Paul begin to prepare for their fish fry. Paul works on starting a fire, first collecting some driftwood along the shore, while Leisa and Lana start to prepare the fish. It is not a big harvest, but it is enough to stave off their coming hunger and not return home empty-handed. After a few moments, the first crackle of fire is heard. Lana strong-arms the Mason jar open and pours some oil into a cast iron pan that sits atop the fire on a makeshift grill. Although tempted by her now growling stomach and smell of fresh fish, she knows that if there is to be more to come in the future the first bite cannot be hers. With spirit plate prepared and offered, the three colleagues, now joined by the ancestors, share in a meal and continue to converse.

**Leisa:** This fish is really good—is it lake trout?

**Paul:** Yeah, we have a lot of different kinds of fish around here, like pike, pickerel, lake trout, speckled trout, and salmon. The salmon wasn't always here, though; it was introduced sometime in the 1950s.

**Leisa:** I know I said this earlier, but I am so glad you brought me here. I think we are onto something in terms of how we should approach our work. There is a real need for academics to move toward concrete conversations about Land to sig-nificantly reshape settler consciousness and deep attachments that construct Canadian identities (Davis et al., 2017, p. 399). I know for me this experience has really added a layer of understanding and purpose to the work that I am doing in this region. There has been so much taken from the community to provide comforts and luxuries: sacred items, fish, power, and only the bishop knows what else! I think as researchers we need to be cognizant of all of this when we come to communities and ask for knowledge. Instead of taking it away, we need to ask ourselves, how can we use it to restore and re-story?

**Lana:** The landscape has changed so much and continues to change. Sometimes I can hardly recognize it, with the double-lane highway construction and the new cable bridge. We have made a lot of changes in the last while, like bringing back fasting, and having a lodge and fixing up the chalet, but it's like we can't keep up. Even after moving away, when I would return home for a visit I would always walk down to the water and I would look up and see the old bridge. Just when you start to make it your own, they put a new bridge up. Even the saskatoon bushes got cut down too, the ones that I used to walk by to get to the water. It's the cu-mulative impact, too. It's like imagining everything that we talked about on the fishing trip happening at one moment in time. That's what it feels like sometimes. That's something that I don't think the term *reconciliation* addresses.

**Leisa:** Does the term *reconciliation* exist or is it a foreign term for Anishinaabe peoples?

**Lana:** I am not a fluent language speaker, but when I think of reconciliation and what it means to me the closest term that we would have is *Indinawemaaganidog*—All My Relations. Intrinsic to this understanding is responsibility. So, in this way rec-onciliation can be reimagined as a process in which community responsibilities are renewed (Corntassel, 2009). And I mean community very broadly.

**Paul:** I think for me reconciliation could also be understood as "learning with each other while they are doing." Today is a good example: reconciliation is about con-tinuing with our traditional practices, like our fishing trip. By performing the ac-tivity together, we learn about ourselves, one another, and the Land. Peace is a cultural construct that, for us, comes from continuing our Land-based practices through "keeping the land" (Ariss & Cutfeet, 2012). Land is the nexus of history and culture (Cormier, 2014, p. 167), so it has to be the place to support research as reconciliation because the wisdom within Land can be accessed through multiple cultural expressions of "learning with each other while they are doing" (Ray & Cormier, 2012).

**Leisa:** I have been part of a national project that is just being wrapped up that exam-ined best practices in Indigenous education, a lot of which are Land based. What differentiates this project from other similar projects is the emphasis on relationships. Regionally, we found that understanding who you were and fostering a positive identity was important in education and was also a part of Land.

**Lana:** I heard that in the quality assurance project, too. The Elders talked about the purpose of education being to make good human beings, and that is what the Place and Purpose standard largely speaks to—how good intent and purpose comes from place.

**Paul:** Bottom line, if colonization is fundamentally about dispossessing Indigenous Peoples from Land, decolonization and reconciliation must involve forms of education that reconnect Indigenous Peoples to Land (Wildcat, McDonald, Irlbacher-Fox, & Coulthard, 2014, p. i). This happens through Land-based traditional activities and ceremony because they both bind us to our traditional homelands.

**Lana:** And we as Indigenous Peoples have to be involved in all of it—research, education, you name it. I forgot to mention this earlier, Leisa, but when we were talking about the depletion of fish in the river, the first solution the government thought of was to create a mono-population of trout, and then its other solution was to ship trout out to other areas to create a new pristine destination for fishing (Thoms, 1999); neither of these "solutions" worked for Indigenous Peoples, or took into account their needs or the deeply interconnected relationship between the people who resided there and the Land. It sounds outlandish, but this still happens today. Look at Grassy Narrows, same thing. Once the industry wasn't viable anymore, the same attitude—industry will just pick up and leave.

**Leisa:** Research and schooling in the age of reconciliation has to address this. I believe I have responsibilities in my relations with Indigenous Peoples—as a partner, mother, community member, and now with you and Paul as colleagues. To me, this means that non-Indigenous academics and educators need to understand reconciliation through a complex web of relationships, learning from Indigenous Peoples (Dion, 2009) and within communities and Land (Simpson, 2014). Wilson (2008) describes these relationships: "rather than viewing ourselves as being *in* relationship with other people or things, we *are* the relationships that we hold and are part of" (p. 80; italics in original).

**Lana:** I agree. We must also be cognizant that taking the lead from Indigenous Peoples should not be conflated with a usurping of innate responsibility, since there are spaces where non-Indigenous peoples and academics can and should take a leadership role. This was loud and clear in the Truth and Reconciliation Commission's findings, which urged that the responsibility for change be put squarely on the shoulders of all Canadians (McGregor, 2018). I think it is up to non-Indigenous

peoples to ensure that non-Indigenous peoples critically engage with their conduct and ethics, including knowledges of Whiteness and settlerness (Macoun,
2016, p. 100). Otherwise we run the risk of situating settlers at the centre of reconciliation efforts, directing Indigenous Peoples' time and energy away from resurgence. This is important work and it needs to be done. There needs to be careful
consideration of the ways that academics and educators are invested in White
innocence and are complicit in the very systems and structures that they critique
and describe (Macoun, 2016, p. 94).

**Paul:** Research is definitely a site where this needs to be reflected upon and acted
upon. Reconciliation in research must be relational, Land-centric and praxis-
focused. It must be transformational.

As the three friends drove home, each reflected on the day in their own unique
way. First, their minds wandered to the beautiful landscapes that they had experienced. For Lana it was the way the light shined on the waters; for Leisa, the
setting of the sun; and for Paul it was the sound of the waves crashing against the
rock. As the minutes went by and they began to build on and connect the landscapes, stories, movements, and words spoken throughout the day, deeper meanings began to emerge. While setting out to share in each other's company and
discuss how their work is an expression of reconciliation, they concluded that they
had actually done much more than that. Through the fish fry they had embodied
reconciliation. It became more than a thought, as they engaged in forms of doing
within a framework of connectivity—an act of ethical relationality. Reconciliation began the minute the friends agreed to partake in the fish fry. To be ready for
the activity, each party had a responsibility to show up prepared (Paul was tasked
with bringing the boat, Lana the hooks and lures, and Leisa the snacks), so that
they could begin their journey together. Once their journeys converged on the
crest of the hill overlooking the Nipigon River, they (re)initiated) shared responsibilities to the water and the Land by offerings of asemma and a listening and
storying of space. With the sun now comfortably resting in the west, the friends
and colleagues returned to their respective homes and families with their share of
the river's gifts in hand. The fish would be cooked up and shared, along with the
stories and lessons that it offered, at their dinner tables another day.

## NOTES

1. Ancestors of Lake Helen First Nation resided in what is now Red Rock, which is located
   at the mouth of the Nipigon River.

2. According to Donald (2012), "Indigenous Métissage is a research sensibility that imagines curriculum and pedagogy together as a relational, interreferential, and hermeneutic endeavour. Doing Indigenous Métissage involves the purposeful juxtaposition of mythic historical perspectives (often framed as commonsense) with Aboriginal historical perspectives" (p. 44).

3. The English translation of zhaaganash is "white" and it refers to settler(s).

## REFERENCES

Ariss, R., & Cutfeet, J. (2012). *Keeping the land: Kitchenuhmaykoosib Inninuwug, reconciliation and Canadian law.* Halifax: Fernwood.

*Building a Strong Fire: Indigenous Quality Assurance Standards in Ontario Colleges.* (2018). Retrieved from https://az184419.vo.msecnd.net/canadore-college/corporate/BuildingAStrongFire_Nov28_PrintSetup.pdf

Cormier, P. N. (2014). Aboriginal peoples in Canada and the role of religion in conflict: The ever elusive peace. In T. Matyok, M. Flaherty, H. Tuso, J. Senehi, & S. Byrne (Eds.), *Peace on earth: The role of religion in peace and conflict studies* (pp. 165–180). Lanham, MD: Lexington Books.

Cormier, P. N. (2016). *Kinoo'amaadawaad Megwaa Doodamawaad—They are learning with each other while they are doing: The Indigenous living peace methodology.* Unpublished doctoral dissertation, University of Manitoba, Winnipeg.

Corntassel, J. (2009). Indigenous storytelling, truth-telling, and community approaches to reconciliation. *English Studies in Canada, 35*(1), 137–159.

Davis, L., Hiller, C., James, C., Lloyd, K., Nasca, T., & Taylor, S. (2017). Complicated pathways: Settler Canadians learning to re/frame themselves and their relationships with Indigenous Peoples. *Settler Colonial Studies, 7*(4), 398–414. doi:10.1080/2201473X.2016.1243086

Dion, S. (2009). *Braiding histories: Learning from Aboriginal peoples' experiences and perspectives.* Vancouver: University of British Columbia Press.

Donald, D. T. (2009). Forts, curriculum, and Indigenous métissage: Imagining decolonization of Aboriginal-Canadian relations in educational contexts. *First Nations Perspectives, 2*(1), 1–24.

Donald, D. T. (2012). Forts, curriculum and ethical relationality. In N. Ng-Fook & J. Rottmann (Eds.), *Reconsidering Canadian curriculum studies: Provoking historical, present, and future perspectives* (pp. 39–46). New York: Palgrave Macmillan.

Macoun, A. (2016). Colonising White innocence: Complicity and critical encounters. In S. Maddison, T. Clark, & R. de Costa (Eds.), *The limits of settler colonial reconciliation:*

*Non-Indigenous people and the responsibility to engage* (pp. 85–102). Singapore: Springer. doi:10.1007/978-981-10-2654-6

McGregor, D. (2018). From "decolonized" to reconciliation research in Canada: Drawing from Indigenous research paradigms. *ACME: An International Journal for Critical Geographies, 17*(3), 810–831.

Parlee, B., Sandlos, J., & Natcher, D. (2018). Undermining subsistence: Barren-ground caribou in a "tragedy of open access." *Science Advances, 4*(2), e1701611. doi:10.1126/sciadv.1701611

Ray, L., & Cormier, P. (2012). Killing the weendigo with maple syrup: Anishinaabe pedagogy and post-secondary research. *Canadian Journal of Native Education, 35*(1), 163–176.

Red Rock Indian Band. (2018). Early history. Retrieved from http://rrib.ca/about-us/early-history/

Simpson, L. (2014). Land as pedagogy: Nishnaabeg intelligence and rebellious transformation. *Decolonization: Indigeneity, Education and Society, 3*(3), 1–25.

Thoms, M. (1999). An Ojibwa community, American sportsmen, and the Ontario government in the early management of the Nipigon River fishery. In D. Newell & R. Ommer (Eds.), *Fishing places, fishing people: Traditions and issues in Canadian small-scale fisheries* (pp. 170–192). Toronto: University of Toronto Press.

Wildcat, D., McDonald, M., Irlbacher-Fox, S., & Coulthard, G. (2014). Learning from the land: Indigenous land based pedagogy and decolonization. *Decolonization: Indigeneity, Education and Society, 3*(3), i–xv.

Wilson, S. (2008). *Research is ceremony: Indigenous research methods*. Halifax: Fernwood.

## Land Acknowledgement Malfunctions, Causing Land to Be Briefly Returned to First Nations

A land acknowledgement at an event in Regina malfunctioned on Tuesday, causing the city and huge parts of Saskatchewan to be briefly returned to First Nations.

Land acknowledgements are statements made by mainly non-Indigenous people before meetings and events that recognize the territories in which they occur.

The return of land occurred when a city official stated that a new school was being built on "land *belonging* to the Cree and Ojibway Peoples" instead of the required statement, "the *traditional homeland* of the Cree and Ojibway Peoples."

"After he said it the ground trembled and the lights started flickering," said Mia Delorme, a Cree woman who witnessed the event.

"Then all of a sudden the land was ours again. It was pretty awesome."

A senior official quickly evoked the correct land acknowledgement and returned the land to Saskatchewan. The province issued a statement blaming the temporary land return on "human error."

# SECTION II

# NO FUCKING THANKS-GIVING

*by Shawn Wilson*

## SO WHAT DO WE MEAN BY NO FUCKING THANKS-GIVING?

When Andrea, Lindsay, and I started in Section I to look at why reconciliation is needed, and how the colonial project has made people question their sense of being and belonging, I realized something—it's no wonder that a lot of people are really angry. Anger is an appropriate response—there are centuries of injustice that need to be addressed here.

True reconciliation with Indigenous people requires more than gluing some feathers to a headband and thanking the nobly welcoming Injuns at Thanksgiving. It requires shifting power relationships. That shift might be really scary for some people—there is a sort of power for some in staying stuck in victimhood, and another sort of power for others in denying how they've been privileged by colonialism. So, when you start talking about these things, yes, you might get people fuckin' swearing at you every once in a while.

We can't expect people to engage in real dialogue about these sensitive issues without intense feelings; it's not reasonable to expect Indigenous people to go straight to forgiveness without grieving and raging about what was taken from them. And the fear associated with acknowledging (and possibly losing!) White privilege also makes a lot of people angry. Many will never get to a place of forgiveness and many more will never overcome their fear. Emotions need to be understood and addressed as integral parts of research relationships and reconciliation. Because while there is anger and there is fear, there are other emotions that are just as powerful that can guide us in learning how to walk forward.

For many of us, there is a well-trodden pathway that we are following. Some of the steps along the way include recognizing what it is that needs to be reconciled, resistance to what got us here, and reclaiming or making space for change. We cannot move forward into planning positive change without that recognition. And that change isn't going to happen unless people stand up in resistance.

Nationally and locally in countries around the world, Truth and Reconciliation Commissions have been established that have helped to uncover and rewrite more truthful accounts of our histories. We all need to recognize that those histories do include very extreme violence and violation of other peoples, lands, and ways of being.

Just as crucially, we also need to recognize that this violence is ongoing. It is easy to point fingers at extremist groups such as Boko Haram, the KKK, the Canadian Heritage Alliance, and ISIS. But we also need to recognize the ongoing, hegemonic impact of Western scientific, cultural, and religious dogma. The increased polarization evident in our political discourse may not continually threaten our physical lives (though it often feels like it), but our minds and our spirits are definitely still under attack. And it's not just Indigenous people we're talking about here, but anyone who challenges the dogmatic norm.

## SHIFTING POWER RELATIONS

If unsettling the truth and fostering more respectful relations between one another isn't also unsettling and shifting power, then what are we really doing? On whose terms is reconciliation (and research) being based? Whose processes and values? Who has the power to decide the priorities of this work/relationship and whose language is being used? There are significant gaps in how these concepts are being taken up that need to be acknowledged and addressed. So, of course, there is also considerable resistance to the way reconciliation is often foisted upon us.

Western concepts of being objective and distanced from research/knowledge are furthered by the privileged reality that most non-Indigenous people haven't been harmed by it in the same way. They also are living in a world where their ways of knowing are viewed as superior, and because of their dominance they often aren't even aware that other knowledge systems exist. This distancing of self from research is as much a product of privilege as it is of different world-views. Similarly, Indigenous people's relationship with emotions in relation to knowledge is connected to worldview, but is also affected by historic and current experiences with research where immense harm has been done. We need to recognize that most of our institutions and systems in Western society were built on White supremacy, patriarchy, and capitalism. And if we want to change that we need to resist.

But who is leading this resistance? White fragility at the interpersonal and institutional level means that most people aren't even able to reach a point of recognizing the problem. So, there is a lot of emotional and intellectual labour placed on Indigenous people to deal with White fragility and White guilt. As you read through Section II, which deals with this resistance, it will be worthwhile to ask yourself the following questions:

What does reconciliation feel like for you?

Who is reconciliation comfortable for, and who is it uncomfortable, triggering, and even harmful for?

How are individuals demonstrating/experiencing White fragility, and how are you implicated in the greater power of Whiteness?

Some allies only rise up in resistance when it is convenient and comfortable for them. We all need to be willing to take risks and actually stand for something. This resistance takes real commitment, not just convenient tolerance. Who are we expecting to do all the work of reconciliation? Who will rise up to help shift cultural institutions and systems of power? We can honour Indigenous traditions with a feast, giving thanks every autumn while also raising a middle finger in resistance to the system that has commercialized and bastardized that feast, in a No Fucking Thanks-giving salute. Let's acknowledge that anger, face those fears, and challenge that power.

## CHAPTER 7
# Settler Apologies

*a spoken word poem by tunchai redvers*

———

ʔedlánet'e-a, sezí tunchai súlye. My given name is tunchai redvers and my spirit name is White Feather Womxn. I am a Dene/Métis two-spirit social justice warrior, writer, and wanderer born from Denendeh roots in what is now Treaty 8, Northwest Territories. I currently live in Tkaronto, where I am the co-founder and director of We Matter, a national Indigenous youth-led non-profit organization committed to Indigenous youth empowerment, hope, and life promotion. My advocacy and writing actively work to Indigenize identity, self-love, and mental health, and normalize discussions around hardship, hope, and healing. Through my connection to sacred land and blood, I often explore the personal topics of sexuality, two-spiritedness, loss, movement, resistance, reclamation, finding, and growth. I consider myself a nomad just like my ancestors.

———

i cannot count the number of times that I have said the words
"don't be sorry"
every time someone has asked me about being Indian
"but don't you get free education?" you ask
"but how brown do you have to be, to be Treaty?" you ask
"but why don't you just move to cities?" you ask
and on every single occasion I find myself apologizing on your behalf
as if your assumptions have become so normalized that
i have made a guide book on how to navigate settler colonialism
on how to shake hands with ignorance
and make peace with stereotypes
"i want to know more" you say
as my brothers abuse bottles until they drown
only a few kilometres from the comfort of your home
curtains drawn, your floorboards cover the graves of my ancestors at your feet
they say ignorance is bliss
but I cannot be afforded the same ignorance bliss as you
when I have to fight every day to heal a different pain with my tired breath
and be afraid, when I am walking home at night,
because dark alleys make me think of them
the ones that could have been me
another piece of this earth that has gone missing
has been stolen, abused, murdered, neglected
my treaty rights are not rights, they are misspelled promises
and not the promises you get to make with your pinky,
but the ones that have caused my people death
in the communities where violence was planted like a seed
that became so rotten it made rivers toxic
i don't get free education, but even if I did, I wouldn't be happy
you and i, we pay the same education
the only difference is that I am forced to sit beside you
and listen to white man lecture me about my history
the only difference is that I am forced to sit beside you,
but you are present and I am history
a textbook definition of what it is meant to be to be Indian
so let me tell you person who wants to know,
that the blood under my too light skin
is browner than the dirt in which your vegetables grow

i am this earth, not a percentage,
and if you want to talk percentage,
then let's talk about the percentage of us who live in poverty
even though we have this tag on our names that says status
status is short for second-class citizen
who doesn't have the same rights as you when it comes to demanding answers
you demand answers from me
and all I can say is I am sorry you don't know,
that if we left our communities, it would mean that you have won
but this is not a game,
i am not a settler like you
even though trauma is in my blood,
giving up is not
you are so quick to stand in front of me and hold up your hand
a quick stop Q&A when it's convenient
yet this whole time it is you
who has chosen to lock your doors when we,
we have been stuck knocking
i am done being forgiving.

## CHAPTER 8

# I Hope This Finds You Well: A Love Letter to Indigenous Youth

*by Lindsay DuPré*

———

Taanishi Lindsay DuPré dishinihkaashoon. I am a Métis woman with family roots along the Red and Assiniboine Rivers, and I carry Métis, Cree, Scottish, English, Irish, and French ancestry. My knowledge and responsibilities are connected to my relatives and ancestors from all of these parts of me, and my relationships with chosen family and friends from a range of places and nations. Having lived in the Toronto area for most of my life, I also give thanks to the Haudenosaunee and Anishinaabe peoples of this territory, whose land and knowledge has cared for me in many ways. I am a mother, daughter, sister, granddaughter, niece, cousin, auntie, friend, and partner, and my work currently places me at the intersections of social work, education, and youth mobilization.

———

February 9, 2018

Dear friend,

As I think about how to open this letter to you, the line "I hope this finds you well" keeps crossing my mind. Truthfully, I've written that sentence countless times to people, but sadly can't think of too many where I seriously meant it or followed up to see whether they were. With this letter I want you to know how much I mean it. I want you to know how much love is behind each word that I write to you here, and how expressing my hope for your wellness is not just an empty pleasantry, but a wish that I put into the world with great intention.

I know that you're probably busy and so I'll do my best to keep this short. Balancing the pressures of taking care of ourselves and our families and communities can be a lot to carry, never mind the additional weight that comes with work, school, and other commitments. Sometimes it feels like it's all up to us and, if you're like me, a lot of this pressure comes from the responsibility that we place on ourselves.

In a world that continues to be attacked and controlled through capitalism, heteropatriarchy, and White supremacy, it is easy to feel defeated. Indigenous youth face enormous barriers and carry complex traumas that can suck hope from our spirits like leeches. Recently, we have seen politicians and leaders placating people across sectors through reconciliation rhetoric, using words like *diversity, inclusion*, and *Indigenization*. Symbolic gestures are being used to mask colonialism and ongoing attacks on our lands and bodies, while calls for true justice are being met with the sound of crickets or slurs of racism. We do our best to hold on to hope, and to each other, in places that long ago decided that Indigenous freedom, love, and life are nothing more than a threat to be dealt with (Violet Lee, 2016). Through all of this we are reminded that underneath this latest packaging of Canada—decorated with feathers, medicine wheels, and land acknowledgements—many still view our lives as expendable and systems of power have largely gone unchanged.

In addition to the overt racism we have seen come to light with recent murders, jury verdicts, government treaty breaking, and White supremacist organizing, there are also more subtle forms of colonial violence threatening our Nations. In particular I am alarmed by the extent of knowledge extraction taking place on our communities and the ways in which Indigenous youth are being manipulated into this process. We are being researched, now more than ever. This research is frequently taking place without our consent and done by people who usually don't realize that they are in fact doing research. Non-Indigenous people feel entitled to our knowledge and emotional labour and are taking this from us without understanding what is at stake for us and the relational account-ability that must come with it. Where colonial exploitation once occurred pre-dominantly through control of our lands and bodies, it is now also taking place through the extraction of our knowledge (Wilson, 2008).

Don't get me wrong, sharing our stories is a central part of our cultures and identities as Indigenous young people and I do think that there is potential in some cultural exchange work to help rebuild relations in meaningful ways. Many of our ancestors and leaders fought hard for these conversations to be possible and so while I reject the ways in which reconciliation has been corrupted, I hold immense gratitude and respect for those who have dedicated so much of their lives and prayers to bring us here. It is not my place to tell you how you should be sharing your stories or cultural knowledge; however, I urge you to think carefully about when, where, and why this is taking place.

Although there are caring and committed people working alongside us to address injustices—including settlers in our own families—there are also those who are actively exploiting us and will extract our knowledge in order to main-tain power. Sometimes this looks like companies using our images and appro-priating our cultures for profit. Other times it's organizations jumping on the reconciliation bandwagon and shifting their programming to include us so that they can attract new funding. From my experience navigating the non-profit and philanthropic sectors, even when these organizations do appear to have good intentions, there is usually an underlying paternalism and saviour complex that drives the ways that they approach their work with us. People want to hear trauma stories and respond with tears and apologies, but rarely are they ready to acknowledge or make real changes to their ongoing complicity in Indigenous marginalization and oppression.

Academia has also become increasingly interested in our stories, with many universities and colleges attempting to incorporate Indigenous knowledge across educational and research practices. Indigenous scholars are contributing their expertise to replace old Western structures with new paradigms of ethical research and teaching that respect the jurisdiction of Indigenous Peoples over our knowledge and intellectual domains (Ermine & Sinclair, 2004). Indig-enous students, often young people, are also frequently pressured into doing this work with little to no acknowledgement or compensation for our time and labour. Many of us choose to do this because of the deep sense of reciprocity and responsibility that we carry to give back to our communities through the pursuit of education (Waterman, Lowe, & Shotton, 2018). This is true across a range of education, employment, and social spaces, where Indigenous youth experience the burden of educating others about Indigenous issues. We are faced with the daunting task of confronting colonial stereotypes and ignorance, while being trapped into representing not just ourselves or our Nations, but all Indigenous Peoples (DuPré et al., 2017). This is especially complicated given that many of us haven't had access to a lot of this information, and we are still in the process of figuring out who we are, where we come from, and where we are going.

This pressure to offer up our stories has also come from governments and other groups involving Indigenous youth in advisory positions and as guest speakers at events. These opportunities are usually framed as a way to have our voices heard, but rarely do they go beyond tokenism. Deciding whether or not to engage in these roles can be extremely confusing, as we are left to question whether it is better to participate and be tokenized or not to share our perspectives at all. I have love and respect for you if you decide that these places and people are deserving of your stories, but again I urge you to think carefully about the intentions behind them. Just because people say that a space is safe does not mean that it actually is. I encourage you not to be afraid to negotiate the terms of your involvement and to surround yourself with supports that can reduce the chances that you will be exploited or harmed.

*So then how can we do research in ways that honour our stories?*

The ability to learn, nurture, and mobilize our knowledge is a responsibility and beautiful gift from Creator. Every day we are given opportunities to do this work of restoring and giving testimony to spirit by telling our own stories, in our own ways, for our own purposes (Smith, 2012). In many ways our identity exploration and pathways to cultural resurgence are research, and every interaction offers entry points for expanding our understanding of the world and our place within it.

I recently spent time with a nêhiyaw Knowledge Keeper named Wes Fine-Day from Sweetgrass First Nation, who got me thinking a lot more about this. He talked to me about how there are duality in knowing, where there are always opportunities for us to learn and opportunities for us to teach. The challenge is learning to discern between the two and figuring out what to hold on to and what to leave behind. Our conversation also led me to think about self-discipline and reflection as tools for connecting to truth. We have to make intentional choices about whether we are ready to offer knowledge to others, or if we need more time to understand something in order to share it in the right way. This is an important part of being relationally accountable and protecting the integrity of Indigenous ways of knowing. The knowledge Wes carries is connected to his own teachers, and so by learning from him I am accountable not only to our relationship, but also to a greater knowledge system.

Setting boundaries around our stories can also be an empowering process. It helps us reclaim power by maintaining control over when and how knowledge is being shared. It also lets us be strategic about who and what we are gifting our energy to. Recently, I have started being much more selective about this. I continue to do outward facing work to increase understanding amongst non-Indigenous peoples, but not as much as I used to. I found myself allowing this work to consume me, where I was giving so much of myself to others that there wasn't much left to fulfill my own needs. Focusing on relationships within my own community, and with other Indigenous young people, has strengthened my sense of purpose. It has taught me that there is a delicate interconnected-ness to these relationships and power that flows from our traditions, community responsibilities, and participation in a larger Indigenous story (Ansloos, 2017). Furthermore, by shifting the focus of my energy in this way it has introduced me to new possibilities for change making.

As we look to the future, I hope to see our young people continuing to find pathways for collaborative resistance, healing, and dreaming. I hope that we will challenge the ways reconciliation has been corrupted and return to trea-ties and natural laws for direction on how to be in relation to one another. We may not agree on the exact approaches needed to do this resistance and nation building, but through an ethic of incommensurability we can understand the gaps between our perspectives while still working together toward liberation (Tuck & Yang, 2018). This work is challenging, but by committing to each other and the protection of our stories we can truly thrive and design new fu-tures for our peoples.

As I close this letter to you, I find myself again thinking about the line "I hope this finds you well." It just doesn't seem like enough. Whoever and wher-ever you are, I hope that these words don't just find you, but that they sit with you and keep you company for however long you need them.

Ki shaakiihitin—I love you,
Lindsay DuPré

## REFERENCES

Ansloos, J. (2017). *The medicine of peace*. Halifax: Fernwood.

DuPré, L., Fiddler, D., Hull, A., Komaksiutiksak, M., Kreps, P., Laroque, S., ... Strib-bell, J. (2017). *Circles of change: Indigenous Youth Leadership Forum report*. Retrieved from https://takingitglobal.uberflip.com/i/936360-circles-of-change-report/0?m4=

Ermine, W., & Sinclair, R. (2004). *The ethics of research involving Indigenous Peoples: Report of the Indigenous Peoples' Health Research Centre to the Interagency Advisory Panel on Research Ethics*. Retrieved from http://iphrc.ca/pub/documents/ethics_review_iphrc.pdf

Smith, L. T. (2012). *Decolonizing methodologies: Research and Indigenous Peoples*. London: Zed Books.

Tuck, E., & Yang, K. W. (2018). *Toward what justice? Describing diverse dreams of justice in education*. New York: Routledge.

Violet Lee, E. (2016, September 1). Indian Summer. Canadian Centre for Policy Alternatives. Retrieved from https://www.policyalternatives.ca/publications/monitor/indian-summer

Waterman, S., Lowe, S., & Shotton, H. (2018). *Beyond access: Indigenizing programs for Native American student success*. Sterling, VA: Stylus.

Wilson, S. (2008). *Research is ceremony: Indigenous research methods*. Halifax: Fernwood.

## CHAPTER 9

# Cowboy and Indian "Epigrams": An Art- and Social Media-Based Narrative

*by Kim Stewart*

_____

My name is Kim Stewart, and I am a Métis person born in Athabasca, Alberta. I have been working as a professional artist since the 1980s, earning associate degrees in fine art, illustration, and graphic design, and a master's degree in art education. My interests include investigating Métis identity through my art practice, teaching, and being outdoors doing (almost) any activity with my husband and adult kids.

_____

During this government-imposed season of reconciliation for Canada's Indigenous Peoples, I chose to clean out my mental closet. I had no idea what was expected of me or with whom I was reconciling, so I reasoned that putting things in order would prepare me for whatever might come my way. My chosen tools for the job were my art-based research and Instagram. I began posting what I call "Epigrams"—combinations of words and images that pit the 1950s, 1960s, and 1970s cowboy-and-Indian pop culture of my youth against my ever-evolving worldview.

This chapter contains 12 posts from the last 12 months of Instagramming. I like to think of them as my 12-step program to personal reconciliation. The discussions are casual, enveloped in social media syntax, hashtags, and character-limit constraints. Blend that with a little Trickster discourse and you get humour, irony, and sometimes defiance. Some posts saw deep viewer engagement, while others were more soliloquy-like, as though I'm talking to myself while the world listens. As a set, they reveal attitudes on political correctness, the public self versus the private self, and cultural stereotyping. *Reconciliation* is defined as (1) the restoration of friendly relations (fence mending, pacification, mollification…), and (2) the action of making one view or belief compatible with another. If I am reconciling with myself then perhaps I have made progress. Less obvious, however, is my relationship with others, when true feelings hide behind the safety of "likes" or are shared secretly in hallways. For some people, discussions about difficult Indigenous topics dare not extend into the social media arena, where the risk of confrontation is high. On Instagram, unlike face-to-face engagement, I can mathematically measure my relationship to viewers—90 percent of online visitors are lurkers, 9 percent will do something small, like vote, and only 1 percent will actually act (Cohen, 2012). As for my reconciliation with Canada, it will continue one post at a time @kim.art4life.

kim.art4life

kim.art4life Preserve-nation. Today's work.
#cowboysandindians #researchproject
#metisartist #canadianart #kimgullionstewart
#art4life

kim.art4life Known as 'The Resistance' or
'ē-mēyihkamikahk, (when it went wrong) to
Cree and Métis people, the events of the
1870's in Canada are a part of the past that is
ever-present.

21 likes

MARCH 23, 2017

Add a comment...

**kim.art4life**

**kim.art4life** #cowboysandindians #toyuniverse #chief #vintagetoys

**jenniferhrankowski** Nice! Is that a parsley forest?

**kim.art4life** @jenniferhrankowski carrots!

**jenniferhrankowski** @kim.art4life excellent!

**jenniferhrankowski** @jenniferhrankowski are the carrot tops significant or did you strictly use them because they make great trees?

**kgstewie** Where's the cowboy?

**kim.art4life** @jenniferhrankowski I used them because they are domesticated

**jenniferhrankowski** @kim.art4life ah. Nice!

**kim.art4life** I'm acknowledging the connection between colonizing and domesticating

**20 likes**

NOVEMBER 20, 2017

Add a comment...

**kim.art4life**

**kim.art4life** Sketching my Dad as the hero of his own comic book adventure. #westernstereotypes #cowboysandindians #whoisthatguy ?

**kim.art4life** My father, a self-declared funny guy told heroic stories about his impossible feats and in my child's mind I thought he could survive anything. I want to explore that possibility through the character of Cowboy Ken.

**20 likes**

AUGUST 24, 2017

Add a comment...

**kim.art4life**
Prince George, British Columbia

**kim.art4life** "My Home and Cowboy Land" #cowboysandindians #thislandismyland #homeandnativeland #westernstereotypes #nativecanadian #whereismyland #halfandhalf #metisresistance #courage #sohkitlehewin #creecourage #kimgullionstewart

**marykayreid** Kim I love this work.

**kim.art4life** Thank you Mary!

**boutiquetailleplus** Fantastic

**kim.art4life** Sôhkitêhêwin is the word I use here to describe my Grandfather who had low literacy until late in life. Even so, he had the courage to become a certified mechanic using his daughter as proxy to read and write on his test.

12 likes
AUGUST 30, 2017

Add a comment...

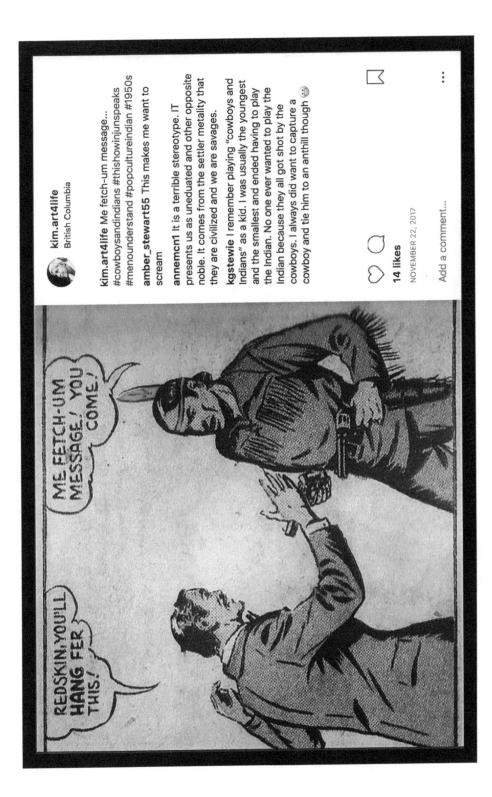

**kim.art4life**
British Columbia

**kim.art4life** Me fetch–um message...
#cowboysandindians #thishowinjunspeaks
#menounderstand #popcultureindian #1950s

**amber_stewart55** This makes me want to scream

**annemcn1** It is a terrible stereotype. IT presents us as as uneduated and other opposite noble. It comes from the settler metality that they are civilized and we are savages.

**kgstewie** I remember playing "cowboys and Indians" as a kid. I was usually the youngest and the smallest and ended having to play the Indian. No one ever wanted to play the Indian because they all got shot by the cowboys. I always did want to capture a cowboy and tie him to an anthill though 😊

14 likes
NOVEMBER 22, 2017

Add a comment...

**kim.art4life**
Prince George, British Columbia

**kim.art4life** Wild Frontier #vintagelunchbox #cowboysandindiansproject #oldwest #kitschytoys #popculture #1950s #nativestereotypes #imaginaryheros #facingthemyth

**annemcn1** The Shocking Truth about Indians in Textbooks" of the 1970s
Please read my Aunty Verna's book. Verna Jane Kirkness.

**kim.art4life** Verna Jane Kirkness was a Cree teacher who taught in residential schools during the 1950's. One day one of her students accidentally spoke the forbidden language in the classroom, then feared the worst, but Verna responded with kindness.

**kim.art4life** Creating kitsch children's toys was accepted as cultural admiration, but allowing children to speak Cree was not.

16 likes

NOVEMBER 23, 2017

Add a comment...

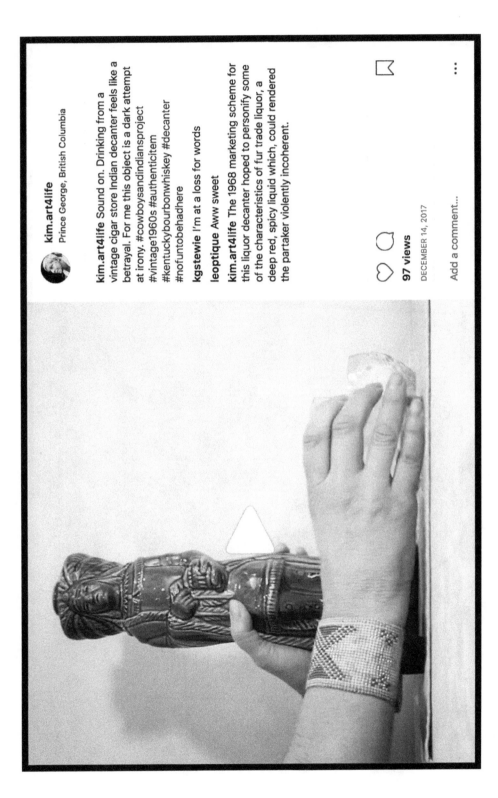

**kim.art4life**
Prince George, British Columbia

**kim.art4life** Sound on. Drinking from a vintage cigar store Indian decanter feels like a betrayal. For me this object is a dark attempt at irony. #cowboysandindiansproject #vintage1960s #authenticitem #kentuckybourbonwhiskey #decanter #nofuntobehadhere

**kgstewie** I'm at a loss for words

**leoptique** Aww sweet

**kim.art4life** The 1968 marketing scheme for this liquor decanter hoped to personify some of the characteristics of fur trade liquor, a deep red, spicy liquid which, could rendered the partaker violently incoherent.

97 views

DECEMBER 14, 2017

Add a comment...

**kim.art4life**
Prince George, British Columbia

**kim.art4life** Comic book shred. So satisfying. #cowboysandindiansproject #oldcomicbooks #stampoutstereotypes #ifeelconflicted

**kim.art4life** In an attempt to contain the damage caused by stereotypes found in comics and history books, I shredded this paper and gave it new life providing support and protection for fragile objects.

19 likes

JANUARY 22

Add a comment...

**kim.art4life**
British Columbia

**kim.art4life** Sound on. Can one make the savage more palatable? #cowboysandindiansproject #1970svintage #exposingthetruth #kitschdecor #westernstereotypes #commentsappreciated

**gfpet** 😂😂😂😂

**mcbchanna** Is this in the show? Cause it's fucking good.

**kim.art4life** While serving myself tea, I think metaphorically about what it would take to make a halfbreed like me more palatable.

72 views
JANUARY 16

Add a comment...

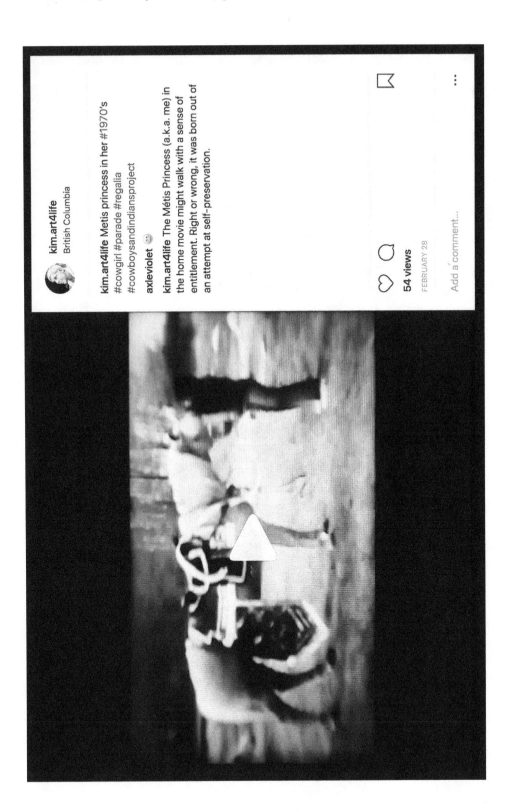

**kim.art4life**
British Columbia

**kim.art4life** It's a conclusion of sorts. I have been thinking how my Dad's childhood experiences with exclusion due to race compare with mine. Being #halfbreed means we are not half bad. #halfbreed #metis #childrenare #nothalfbad

**otipemisiwak_artist** I love this piece Kim. I so relate to your thoughts. I am so glad our pride can shine as the blankets of shame are removed.

**kim.art4life** Hiy Hiy

**kgstewie** Great play on the double negatives!

**kim.art4life** Word play and humour are my tools to defuse tension in the face of difficult topics.

13 likes

MARCH 9

Add a comment...

not half bad

# REFERENCES

Carreiro, D. (2015, June 15). Manitoba residential school survivor, teacher reunite after 50 years. *CBC News*. Retrieved from www.cbc.ca/news/canada/manitoba/manitoba-residential-school-survivor-teacher-reunite-after-50-years-1.3113270

Cohen, H. (2012, May 29). *How does your target audience engage on social media?* [Blog post]. Actionable marketing guide. Retrieved from heidicohen.com/social-media-personas-what-you-need-to-know

Reconciliation. (2018). *Google dictionary*. Retrieved from www.google.com

Stewart, K. [kim.art4life] (2017–18). Selected posts. Retrieved from www.instagram.com/kim.art4life

## CHAPTER 10

# Indigenizing the Academy: Listen to the Stories

*by Anna-Leah King, Dustin Brass, and Patrick Lewis*

––––––––––

The stories and the storytellers in this chapter appear to stand apart in this iteration you hold in your hands. However, that is really just the result of the artifice of the printed word trying to take up oral storytelling. The three voices in this chapter travel together across the landscape of narrative—the story and the storyteller. It is the spirit of story that moves through the world of being and the world of story. In the world of being we are Anna-Leah King, Anishnaabekwe from Wikwemikong Unceded Reserve Nidoo Minissing (Manitoulin Island), Ontario; Dustin Brass, Anihšināpēk, inini, nitoncī ōtahpēkākaw; and Patrick Lewis, Irish settler. In the world of story/ies we are what follows…

––––––––––

Hello. My name is Patrick Lewis. I am the son of Ronald Lewis and Jacquelyn Donnelly. I am descended from Irish White settlers and I now live on Treaty 4 land, which is the territory of the Cree, Saulteaux, Dakota, Lakota, and Nakota. It is also the homeland of the Métis. I am a storyteller-teacher-researcher in early childhood education at the University of Regina. Speaking of storytelling, I have a story about indigenization to share from my experience at the University of Regina.

One day not too long ago at oskana kâ-asastêki (Cree: "the place by the pile of bones"), the leader of the university there initiated the creation of a circle, an Indigenous Advisory Circle. Not to be outdone, the leadership of the Faculty of Education in the university also created an Indigenous Advisory Circle. Now, it is said that the circle is very important to Indigenous people of Turtle Island, but that is usually the extent of non-Indigenous people's knowledge of the circle. So, it made sense to make the circle to show that the university and settler society are trying to move toward reconciliation with Indigenous Peoples. And, to be fair, in some small way that's true, but when the leader of the university and the leadership of education called out to the people in the university to join the circles they were perplexed by the hesitation amongst some folks to do so. So, they decided to talk to people and suggest to certain people that it might be a good idea for them to join the circle. The leader of the university had hired an executive lead of indigenization and made sure that person was part of the big university circle and also made sure that the circle had all Indigenous representation, so that on October 20, 2011, the leader of the university announced,

> A new chapter began this week at the University of Regina when the University's Aboriginal Advisory Circle met for the first time. The Advisory Circle was established this fall to help address the challenges Aboriginal students face while pursuing post-secondary education, and identify solutions to help ensure the campus is dedicated to and focused on meeting Aboriginal student needs. The Advisory Circle is comprised of Aboriginal faculty and staff who will provide recommendations directly to the President. (University of Regina External Relations, 2011)

But the Faculty of Education circle was not all Indigenous; in fact, it had a lot of different people around it. All of the Indigenous education faculty at the time were asked to join the circle and so too were others, which made some folks think differently about othering. An email announcement went out about the new circle in the Faculty of Education and when the first meeting would take place. But before that first meeting a reply-all email came from someone, it might have been Nanabush, saying they were "nominating" Reynard to be part of the circle. The leadership of education said, "Mais bien sur!" But Reynard wasn't sure why he had been asked to join the circle and he knew Wisakedjak and Nanabush, maybe even Coyote might be there. He also knew that some folks said they might be distant cousins, but he really wasn't sure about that. Besides, the last time he saw Wisakedjak he had said, "Hey Reynard, maybe you should bring Humility with you when you go out into the world instead of leaving it home under your bed. You might learn something about yourself." Reynard decided to go to the circle and brought Humility with him and listened like his friend Verna said: "Just try listening for a change, and keep your mouth shut." When everyone was sitting in the circle Reynard asked, "Where's Coyote?" Everyone said, "He's busy!"

The meeting started, but as hard as he tried Reynard couldn't help himself in spite of Humility trying to stop him by pulling his tail and twisting his ears, and he shouted out, "What's this circle for anyway?"

The leadership of education said, "That's a very good question so we have written that down."

> The Faculty of Education Aboriginal Advisory Circle provides recommenda-
> tions, guidance and support to the Associate Dean, Faculty Development and
> Human Resources, pertaining to indigenization of all academic and admin-
> istrative areas within the Faculty. The Circle is a space in which issues, ideas
> and perspectives are constructively shared/explored so a place of understanding
> may be reached. (University of Regina Faculty of Education, 2016, p. 25)

Reynard nodded his head thoughtfully, glancing around the circle trying
to see if any faces might convey their feelings about the purpose of the circle.
Some faces are really difficult to read so Reynard said, "I see, indigenization of
the academy?"

"Yes. It is important that we write things down," said the leadership of
education,

> [and] in keeping with the Faculty of Education Criteria document and its
> intentions toward social change (page 3), the Circle recognizes the need to
> engage with knowledge and pedagogical practices that might challenge and
> disrupt the ongoing legacy of Canada's colonial history. (University of Regina
> Faculty of Education, 2016, p. 25)

Heads rapidly nodded around the circle to this and Humility took the opportunity and stomped on Reynard's foot extra hard til he yelped and spent
the next while licking his sore foot while the meeting carried on. People in the
circle talked and talked about indigenization all through the meeting—in fact,
they talked about indigenization through most of the subsequent meetings, but
Reynard just kept sucking his sore paw from meeting to meeting, which also
helped him keep his mouth shut so he had to listen. After many meetings, it was
clear folks had lots of different ideas or no idea what indigenization might mean
or look like. Reynard was certain that at the very least what Nanabush and Wisakedjak thought of as indigenization was often very different from what he and
the others thought. So, after many more meetings the university's big Indigenous
Advisory Circle said,

> The Aboriginal Advisory Circle to the President (AAC) defines Indigeniza-
> tion as "the transformation of the existing academy by including Indigenous
> knowledges, voices, critiques, scholars, students and materials as well as the
> establishment of physical and epistemic spaces that facilitate the ethical stew-
> ardship of a plurality of Indigenous knowledges and practices so thoroughly

as to constitute an essential element of the university. It is not limited to Indigenous people, but encompasses all students and faculty, for the benefit of our academic integrity and our social viability. (Indigenous Advisory Circle, University of Regina, 2015)

The education circle folks seemed to like that a somewhat clear delineation of what is meant by indigenization was provided, but most of them were teachers and most of them were not Indigenous and they looked around the circle at each other, nodding their heads in a pleased way. Reynard, who was still sucking his foot, was trying to say something so Humility yanked it out of his mouth and he blurted, "That's a good definition, but what does indigenization look like?"

Humility thrust Reynard's foot back in his mouth before he could say anything else.

Heads stopped nodding and everyone started talking animatedly about what indigenization might look like; and how that might work with reconciliation; and maybe a subcommittee could work on a list of ways to indigenize; and perhaps there should be some funding so folks could research indigenization—everyone got really excited about funding (which meant another subcommittee); and maybe create some workshops on indigenization; and…

The associate dean suggested that subcommittees be formed and people took on assignments and then people were asked to join committees and subcommittees. It was all very exciting, if not efficient, the way they were taking up indigenization.

The associate dean said, "Reynard, can you please join the indigenization funding subcommittee?"

Reynard's head snapped up from sucking his paw and he said, "What about Coyote?"

"She's busy!" said everyone.

Reynard acquiesced and joined the committee. They had to come up with an application and process for faculty to apply for the indigenization funding. Reynard thought it would be a lot of work. But then he remembered that the big university circle had already done that work for their indigenization fund. So, he said, "Why don't we just use the university's circle application and process as a template?"

"Maybe not a good idea—that kind of taking has historical echoes," said Nanabush.

Reynard said, "Nah, it is us honouring them by using what they made, it's all good."

Nanabush just smiled and shook their head.

Then Reynard said, "Okay, that's done. Let's think about some other things to indigenize."

Reynard was pretty sure he had a couple of really good ideas. He was thinking of a list of things that they could work through to make sure they were doing this right. Reynard and all his people really liked lists, especially top 10 lists. So, he started thinking of the top 10 ways to indigenize the academy.

"Perhaps we should think about having an Elder in our faculty, like an Elder in Residence!"

Everyone around the circle started nodding their heads because they were all pretty certain that would be a good thing to do.

"Maybe we can get all our signage changed so it is also in Cree."

Someone said, "What about Saulteaux?"

"What about applying for a Canada Research Chair in indigenization? Or wait, better still, one in reconciliation?"

Everyone really liked that idea and heads were nodding as fast as those bobbleheads.

"Oh, what about a chair of indigenization in our faculty, kind of like program chairs?"

"Maybe we could make a MOOC about indigenization of education."

Reynard was enjoying this; they were doing a lot of indigenizing and making great plans for more indigenizing. He looked around and noticed that Wisakedjak was gone and Nanabush was smiling at him shaking their head slowly then said, "Reynard, you seem to be enjoying yourself. Remember, you shouldn't take yourself too seriously." Then they proceeded to hop out of the room. Reynard wasn't sure what to make of that. Everyone in the room was quite excited and they were thinking up more ways to indigenize and adding them to the list.

Then Reynard said, "Has anyone seen Coyote?"

"He's busy!" came the chorus.

ᘓ ᘔ

Anin. My name is Anna-Leah King, I am Anishnaabe kwe from Wikwemikong Unceded Reserve, Manitoulin Island, Ontario. I am a professor in education core studies, covering anti-racist courses and, currently, critical issues in language acquisition. In addition to teaching I am finding my way in my new role

coyote

as chair of Indigenization, where the discussion for this paper really begins. I am also vice-chair of the Indigenous Advisory Circle (IAC) for the University of Regina (UR) and the chair of IAC-Education. In this leadership role promoting the importance of Indigenous education I am faced with the challenges of making that happen in a Western institution with settler students and predominantly mainstream colleagues.

Hmmm … there goes Coyote racing clear across the field from the highway. I wonder what your message is for me today. It is crazy to you that I'm cruising down this highway as an Indigenous person to help a community save their Indigenous language as a Faculty of Education representative. Strange to be in this position, isn't it. I know the Elders wonder what we do and they do not always think we do any good—for the people anyway. Making up terms in academe like *Indigenization*, for example.

As the now chair of Indigenization for the Faculty of Education and vice-chair of the Indigenous Advisory Council for the university, I am attempting to lead us in an onward projection and grappling with how Indigenization is being interpreted in a mainstream institution. I have inquired with my colleagues since I began working here a year ago. Some say it is about weaving anti-racist literature into all the courses. Others direct me to a list on ways to Decolonize. No one seems to want to offer their own definition. And now, the recent court verdicts for Stanley (2018) and Cormier (2018), which bring to mind the multiple cases that have come before that clearly remind Indigenous people that there is still no justice for us. They raise questions about the circumstances in which we teach with regard to the great Canadian racial divide.

Nanabosho hides behind tall grasses and peers into the university. Of every 400 people that go by, he sees one of us. He stomps his feet, leaping in the air excited and almost giving himself away. Hey, did you see that rabbit? Awesome jump! I remember clearly the first time I saw Nanabosho on campus. He appeared as the tiniest bunny, even smaller than my hand. Just sitting there, eyes closed, soaking up the sun, occasionally twitching his nose. That waboosense is pretty confident, I thought to myself, as hundreds of students trudge along the pathway, including myself just inches away from him. Unless ... is it Nanabosho? Hmmm, he is supposed to return and live among us. He said he would come back to help us. Well, Nanboshoense, I think I need your help.

*Indigenization.* Well it's not easy to step into someone else's vision. I do have a list: 100 Ways to Indigenize and Decolonize (Pete, 2015) on our university website. Although I have learned that Indigenizing is not the same as Decolonizing and that you have to Decolonize first before Indigenizing can take place. *Indigenization* at the University of Regina is understood as

> the transformation of the existing academy by including Indigenous knowledges, voices, critiques, scholars, students and materials as well as the establishment of physical and epistemic spaces that facilitate the ethical stewardship of a plurality of Indigenous knowledges and practices so thoroughly as to constitute an essential element of the university. It is not limited to Indigenous people, but encompasses all students and faculty, for the benefit of our academic integrity and our social viability. (Indigenous Advisory Circle, University of Regina, 2015)

In our education faculty I have been informed that anti-oppressive or anti-racist education is the main focal point for certain courses and this discourse is understood as being woven into all courses. There have been treaty education courses developed and taught, Treaty Camp, OTC (Office of the Treaty Commissioner) treaty teaching, and treaty tours to the Fort Qu'Appelle Treaty Centre. There is also an annual treaty conference that tends to centre the narrative of the settler without much mention of the impact on Indigenous people of the territory. And everyone across the entire university introduces themselves by acknowledging that the land they're standing on is Treaty 4 Territory. The professors in education, in one way or another, invest time and energy Indigenizing course work by adding Indigenous scholarship and literature, or in doing service work with Indigenous people, as well as through research and so much more.

Building on the discussion from the university's Indigenizing and Decolonizing plan,

> the UR Strategic Plan, Peyak Aski Kikawinaw (2015–2020) identifies three key priority areas that include Student Success, Community Engagement and Research Impact. Indigenization and sustainability are over-arching themes for this plan. Each key priority identifies particular objectives. Indigenization is embedded in our collective work at the University of Regina and the Federated Colleges. (University of Regina, 2015)

Therefore, university-wide we are making valiant efforts toward Indigenizing and Decolonizing. This does not come without challenges considering this is a predominantly mainstream institution full of mainstream academics and students.

Upon arrival at the university I wondered about where my colleagues were positioned in terms of Indigenizing and Decolonizing. When I left 10 years ago this province seemed more progressive with regard to Indigenous education. There was an established Indigenous Advisory Council to the Minister of Education for over 20 years, and graduates of the Indian Teacher Education and Indian and Northern Education Graduate Studies Programs at the University of Saskatchewan were working in leadership roles in education around the province. There were changes to the curriculum being written and teachers piloting these changes in classrooms. Simply adding on to the mainstream curriculum or creating a unit of study or "Indigenous Days" in the schools was not enough. A team of Indigenous writers was created by Saskatchewan Learning to work on these Indigenous curricular changes. Treaty teachers were being trained by the OTC. There were many settler people willing to make this effort who were already working in allyship with Indigenous people.

*Enter Nanabosho.*

All good but again there are challenges.

"Wepton!" said Nanabosho.

"Pardon me?" I questioned.

"Get to the challenges. I need a good laugh!"

"In theory everything is progressing nicely but then again we're dealing with settler people. They often misinterpret what you are saying."

"How so?" said Nanabosho.

"Well, for example, I spent time with this professor talking about smudge and the medicines. And he asked if he could write down our conversation. I was fine with that but in his writing he termed the smudge as 'smoke ceremony.' I never used that turn of phrase."

"Ah hah hah hah!" exclaimed Nanabosho.

"They don't know how to listen. They lack the training. Elders speak at a slower cadence, they're ponderous thinkers. They think before they speak. And most importantly they are translating for you, in words that you can understand, in a language that misses the spiritual imbuement of the language when translated to basic English. They need more training in listening. Elders also teach in analogous ways. They use story to teach you. You might think they're speaking about something completely different and wonder 'well how does this relate to my question?' You need to think about what their message is to you. My father, who is Anishnaabe, would say this is a deliberate indirect approach to teaching that is part of our social discourse, which is built on respect and a whole worldview. Which brings to mind that English language tends to prefer the interrogative, which often makes the listener feel under attack. It is a good lesson in the need for more reflection and listening at the intersection of two ways of being."

## CHALLENGES

### First Meeting Interrogation

"Unfortunately, there are those who want to peg you down, label you, put you in their category of organization for efficiency's sake right away."

"Efficiency's sake! How so?" asked Nanabosho.

"Well first they drill you:

Where you from?
Are you Treaty?

Are you Status?

How long have you lived off the reserve?

Do you speak your language?

Are you fluent?

Do you know about your culture?...

"I think they can predict the answers because part of the questioning is about showing how much they know and then they rate you as an Indigenous person in some category in their head for future reference....

"That leads me to another thing. White people like to show you what they know. I suppose this is okay although it does not follow our way of humility and they can kind of come across as a 'know it all.' Once you have been interrogated and they have the facts straight: language, knowledge, identity, cultural knowledge. Check."

"Hey! What about blood quantum?" laughed Nanabosho.

"The language deficit is hardly our fault and it is heartbreaking to fathom the realization of potentially losing our languages. The time, effort, financing are all on us. Without funding, we are madly scrambling to save languages in crisis in meagre ways with limited funding. Since Harper, who clawed back millions, initial bilingual and immersion programming has never been restored and who is to say that funding was enough in the first place? And blood quantum? No! No measuring of blood quantum that I have detected....

"To be drilled with this invasive line of questioning that attacks straight at your heart is bad enough. In addition, we are also judged by the White cultural measuring stick, which is abhorrent, leaving you feeling rejected."

"Absurd!" shouted Nanabosho. "None of that matters. Nothing strips you of who you are or makes you less. Did the Elders not teach you this? Where is the empathy or compassion? This sounds like the White fire of the fast race."

"What is that?" I asked.

"It is the competitive nature of White people," said Nanabosho. "Even when they say they are not—they are. They cannot see themselves for this competitive nature that is built into their language, and belief and education systems. In fact, education has slowly absorbed a corporate model. Put simply, it is about getting to the top first. And having significance over everyone else. We walk a double-edged sword: are you Indian enough by your Indians and then you get further measured by White people—so insulting. Gehgit sa nah maba! Who do they think they are even thinking they have the right to quantify but, then again, they have always thought this way. Remember cranial capacity as a measure of intelligence. Competitive blindness that can never see the forest for the trees when you're in a hurry to get to the top. The same characters spend an afternoon with an Elder and, before you know it, they are lead Indigenous cultural guru to their mainstream colleagues. I've been watching," said Nanabosho.

"'I need smudge ties for 120, please. Is this something that you do?'" I recalled being asked in one instance. "Pretty soon I'll be reduced to the resident bannock maker."

"Wah ha!!" Nanabosho laughed as he hopped off to chew some grass.

It seems we're on a slippery slope between sharing and appropriation.

## Well-Meaning White People

"I have heard this phrase many times. To walk in someone's moccasins is a tremendous fathoming for some."

"What do you mean?" demanded Nanabosho.

"Well some White people in their position of superiority feel they are entitled to everything because they have never been challenged about their White privilege, which puts them there. Like the school systems perpetuating the status quo without being challenged, like the people who write the textbooks who have all the power and the say and profit from them, too."

"Sounds like a guised way to keep people down?" concluded Nanabosho.

"You mean oppressed. Yes, if a person does not wake up and become conscientized to the issues of the oppressed they just continue to walk on their heads."

"What?!" cried Nanabosho.

"In a manner of speaking. It is like operating deaf, mute, and blind. Deaf as in always assuming we want them to be the cultural promulgators. You can give a lecture on truths in history, accurate depictions by Indigenous scholarship, and they hear culture and think, 'we have to teach culture?' That's not quite it. I, as an Anishnaabe scholar, would never take Tai chi quan classes and then decide I'm the expert after a few years of lessons to write a book and establish myself as world expert on Tai chi and Chinese culture. Cultural teaching would never be an expectation but they always seem to hear it this way. Mute is witnessing racism play out but not speaking up against it. Blind is the competitive edge driven by speed, going too fast and missing the point."

"Or what the Elder was trying to teach you!" exclaimed Nanabosho.

"Precisely. We do not appreciate mainstream colleagues competing against us as they jockey for power and world lead on Indigenizing. They like to befriend and take. The worst thing is they expect a pat on the back and a handshake from us as if they did us a big favour! Have we not already been abused enough? By their very nature, it's still a race to be to the top first in education!"

"What do you mean by this?" asked Nanabosho.

"I mean if a mainstream learns something from an Elder, they consider it theirs. They don't know the cultural protocols and nuances of our culture. They are still operating by their competitive culture. They are being taught but not freely given to act as a ceremonialist. After a very short time spent with an Elder some of them believe they're straight on the path to cultural guru for Indigenous people."

"Not!" said Nanabosho.

"Yes! And when you dig a little deeper, you come to find one copies the other like the blind leading the blind who are mimicking culture, not aware that this is never an expectation of them. Culture. It's ours. The teachings are not even freely given amongst ourselves. Their competition with each other in the spirit of Indigenizing gets in the way. They look sideways at each other but ignore the Elders that we put there for them to give them guidance on this very thing."

## WHERE TO FROM HERE...

"Well Indigenizing can be about many things depending on individual interpretation. When I questioned my colleagues, what is Indigenization, they gave me blank stares. From what I have witnessed, some view it as curricular change or inclusion. Others see it as an inclusion of anti-racist theory embedded in the course menu and stand-alone courses. Some see it as treaty education, while others see it as implementing Indigenous literatures into the courses as a focal point. I see it as language initiatives, literatures written in the language, language courses, Elders' teachings, stories, ceremonies, songs, and dancing. The re-enactment of our culture in every way is not harmful to the learner, namely the settler. It is teaching and an enculturation. In this context, they understand quickly and are more respectful as they learn the protocol and are a part of ceremony.

"I could sure use your help toward Indigenizing, Nanabosho."

"Elders are waiting for us to seek their wisdom," he said.

Some believe the prophecies foretold a time when the Elders would fall asleep and it would be many years before the youth would seek their wisdom. I know I cannot move forward without Elders' guidance. They are the ones with wisdom. They have more value than books. Our knowledge is long-standing. It is here with them and beyond the here and now. *Indigenizing* and *Decolonizing* are terms of academe and it will not work to use those words with Elders. The university can only be on a good trajectory when the voice of the Elder comes through it.

I am cognizant that we are all making efforts here and a lot of them are good. Sharing from our Indigenous perspective (not that I represent anyone but myself) might help the settlers see themselves when they are indeed part of this "Indigenizing and Decolonizing story."

In the words of one settler colleague, when asked to reflect on what Indigenization means to her, "There is an urgent need to transform our institutions, learning spaces and curriculum. This is a collective and shared responsibility. Many people are speaking of the importance of relationships. When we are focused on relationships, we may learn in meaningful ways from one another by listening. I invite my students to listen and engage with works created by Indigenous authors, artists, and filmmakers. We still have much learning and work to do to address the inequities. Engaging with story is a powerful entry point" (Heather Phipps, personal communication, May 16, 2018). And, I would add, this is the humble entry point to traverse the written grounds of Indigenous experience and thought by Indigenous authors, which will take you into our world to places you have never been. A way of learning that will make you cry, make you laugh, make you stand with us, and, most importantly, make you understand. It is a way of riding the wave of thunderous storms with us and then you are ready for discussion.

"Mino gishigad! It's a good day!" Nanabosho exclaimed excitedly.

"How so?" I asked.

"The future looks brighter for us. Brighter than it has in 500 years!" stated Nanabosho. He did a twirl in the snow and created a snow powder cloud that caught the sun's light like he was enveloped in a cloud of sparkles.

"We'll be looking brightly ahead! N'ahow!" Nanabosho scampered off to play and frolic among the trees.

&#8270; &#8450;

Anīn nitišinihkas Dustin Brass, nīn Nahkwē šikwa from the Pisiw Clan, nitōnči Key First Nations. I completed a bachelor of education in the Secondary Indian Education Program at the First Nations University of Canada (FNUniv). I am currently completing a master's of education in curriculum and instruction at the University of Regina. After I graduated from FNUniv, I became the first employee in the Regina Public School Division to serve as a school's

Nanabosho

Aboriginal advocate and set precedent on many initiatives with the School Division. Since 2013, I have been an instructor in the Faculty of Indigenous Education at FNUniv, and I joined the Indigenous Peoples' Health Research Centre (IPHRC) as a community research associate in the same year.

While employed with IPHRC I used a variety of arts-based research methods and activities to support wellness with Indigenous youth. I delivered arts-based and holistic learning methods in a number of First Nations communities in the File Hills Qu'Appelle area. In 2017, I was the chair for the Indigenous Advisory Circle to the president at the University of Regina.

It was the evening before the warmest New Moon of the year. It was one of the evenings in the year when the sun hangs in eternity and it nearly seeps from night to next morning's daylight. Nanabosho walked down a long gravel road, walking as he morphed himself into the image of a two-legged; he did this slightly out of travel economics, as he'd be able to hitchhike, and because he always felt two-legged were the easiest beings to live as. Two-legged are the ones that walk earth believing in the constructs that they build instead of the reverberating interactions of life. Nanabosho always spoke in bigger, more grand words, dressed a little more expensive, sometimes in tailored garments, or conveyed the image of masculinity, as many times this gave Nanabosho the best opportunity to be in the position of envy and adornment by other two-legged.

Nanabosho walked down the gravel road, but stopped along the side of the road at a slough surrounded in long grass as the wind continually twirled it. In a cup formation, he dipped his right hand and pulled from the slough a nice cool drink of mineral-rich water; pressing it to his lips he tilted back his hand so the water could steadily run in to fulfill his thirst deep in his belly. Gulp! Gulp! Gulp! Each handful more replenishing than the last.

In the near distance a half-ton truck was headed toward Nanabosho, so he quickly leapt from the slough onto the side of the gravel road. If the driver saw him drinking from the water in the slough they may find something askew. The red truck drove closer and Nanabosho could begin to make out the driver's facial features from their previous simple silhouette. Quickly then, Nanabosho flipped up his right-hand thumb to get a ride; the truck drove past without even so much as a fake-courteous slow. As the truck passed, Nanabosho saw on the back bumper a yellow bumper sticker that read, "Increase rides for people walking on gravel roads." The dust and rocks from the truck spit as the tires spun off into the distance.

Good thing for all the water he drank because the next car didn't come for another few miles of walking. Even faster than the red truck that dusted Nanabosho, so did this little blue car; it too had the same bumper sticker: "Increase rides for people walking on gravel roads." After this time Nanabosho was perturbed at the vehicles driving by him on the gravel road, especially when they proclaimed such a claim, so publicly and widespread—every place that vehicle travelled that bumper sticker was displayed across it for everyone to read. Nanabosho is always so curious, and because he can become whatever he desires, he quickly morphed from a human into a hawk because he wanted to fly fast and watch the vehicles that passed him because, surely, they must not pick up people walking anywhere, not just gravel roads. His wings flapped as he drew closer to the blue car that previously passed him by; soon he was completely caught up so he had time to periodically fly in a mid-size circle in the sky. The blue car pulled onto the blacktop highway just as Nanabosho was about to quit following it, as he felt he had confirmed that the blue car simply did not pick up people walking on roads, period. Flying so high in the air afforded the ability to look down the road, and Nanabosho noticed a middle-aged human walking, hitchhiking;

would the blue car stop? No sooner did this question cross his mind than he saw the back brake lights illuminate. The blue car pulled over and picked up its passenger.

Now the perplexity grew. Why say you want to "increase rides for people walking on gravel roads," when you only pick up people on the blacktop highway?

Why have the bumper sticker? Just continue to drive past people walking on gravel roads and pick up people who walk on the blacktop.

"Isolated incident," Nanabosho thought.

"This must be a one-off, a one-time phenomenon," said Nanabosho.

No sooner did the last words leave his mouth than he began to fly as fast as he could to the first red truck that passed him by on the gravel road. Nanabosho flew for an extended amount of time in the human world searching for the red truck, and he flew over top the gravel roads a second time to make sure he didn't just miss it. Over in the distance the red truck glistened as the near mid-evening sun glimmered a far-stretching reflection against its shiny side. As Nanabosho got close to approaching the truck he noticed that it was pulled over on the side of the two-lane, divided blacktop; a few feet behind was a human with a leather overnight bag jogging toward the passenger door of the red truck. In jumped the human into the passenger side and they slammed shut the door as they sat comfortably in the red truck.

Nanabosho had to ground himself as his mind began to spin with the reality of these two incidents, so he flew down from the sky and landed in an open farmer's field of wheat and morphed from a hawk into a badger. He dug into the earth to create a well-rounded hole, one where he could feel secure, but more importantly he dug it so he could reflect on what had just happened, as he would lay burrowed against the cooling soil as it calmed the belly of a badger as its stomach and the soil lay in unison, with nothing except the slow breaths of Nanabosho's expanded lungs making noise. It was in this state that Nanabosho reflected on watching both vehicles race past him on the gravel road, only to find each vehicle pick up a person walking on the blacktop highway. Nanabosho thought, "This is fine and all, but don't have the bumper sticker for everyone to read, then intentionally not comply with the very sticker the person pressed across their bumper."

It was tough in these moments of tension to see the good, to feel like it was a disconnect between action and words. This was no state of mind to remain in as Nanabosho knew of many other vehicles with that same bumper sticker that did "increase rides for people walking on gravel roads," so he decided the next time he picked a gravel road to walk down he'd make sure it was a road those vehicles drove down.

The time had come for a quick rest in the secure confines of the deep badger hole. A dream will bring positivity and the opportunity for inspiration, so Nanabosho lowered his head onto the ground and quickly and peacefully fell asleep.

Small pieces of dirt from the top of the badger hole shook down onto Nanabosho and brought him awake into consciousness. He dreamed of a bush of trees, he knew that that is where he needed to walk to; he came out of the badger hole and morphed back into a two-legged and began to walk to the edge of the wheat field to the narrow gravel road.

Five steps onto the road and the noise of a loud truck roared. As the noise descended on Nanabosho's ears he turned and stuck out his right thumb. Pulling to a stop was a big green truck; the tires were oversized and the sound that came from under the hood through to the exit of the exhaust was near deafening. Nanabosho hurried toward the passenger door and tried to quit thinking about all the things the truck "was not," so he jumped into the tattered cloth seat of the passenger side and slammed shut the door. The driver talked a mile a minute, using words that Nanabosho knew the man wasn't supposed to be using, but each time he finished by saying, "I mean don't get me wrong, I like badgers, I just wish they wouldn't …" A few miles down the road Nanabosho couldn't take it anymore: the loud sound of the truck, the springs protruding through the foam of the tattered passenger seat, but mainly the driver's hurtful words about badgers.

Nanabosho pretended he had reached his destination as he turned to his left and said, "Right here, this is where I was headed to."

As the truck pulled over and he opened the passenger door to let himself out, he stepped one step out and turned back to the driver and said, "You know, I'm a badger."

The driver chuckled and said, "If you're a badger, how come your hair is so sparse? And your nails so short? And most importantly, why are you walking on two legs? I mean, you don't really look like a badger!"

Feeling defeated by the driver's words and improper categorization, Nanabosho lowered his head and stepped out of the truck and, as he closed the door, he softly said in a volume that maybe only he could hear, "Well, I am a badger."

As Nanabosho turned from the truck he noticed a heavily populated bush of trees. He knew through his dream that this is where he was supposed to go, so he did.

After entering Nanabosho began to look further into the trees; there were so many living together, some standing tall, others lying on the cool comfort of the soil, even a few propped up against each other. How nice it was to see the trees supporting the trees that didn't have the support to stand on their own. The first time Nanabosho saw a tree leaning against another it was two birch trees; one birch was supporting another, but as he walked farther he saw a birch tree leaning against a clump of maple trees, a maple tree lying across the top of a thick arrangement of willows.

Four steps, each step crunching with the interaction of Nanabosho's feet pressing into the layers of life living before that day. Each sound of each step reminded Nanabosho about all the living that had happened before the day he was there. He began to wonder why his dream had taken him here, but he realized that when he thought too hard about what was supposed to be, rather than taking in what is, at times this left him over thinking, over analyzing, but isn't this what "they" want? To make you think deeper, think further than the next being?

Nanabosho shook his head as that question left his lips. "Why pretend better? Why believe in 'better' than another as though it's one big competition? What about collaboration and co-operation instead of competition? How can two-legged think they are better—more prominent—than the other? I mean they are all just two-legged."

Nanabosho paused and quit walking for a moment and remembered, "Right! That's because they believe in things they created. And 'if they created it, then it was probably made to benefit those who created it.' And then they operate on actions of ego and hierarchy, as the path leads to the power of one."

Nanabosho grabbed his belly as he laughed. "They've always liked their ways of organizing, that's why it's called organizing, so it defines their interpretation of what it is to be organized."

Nanabosho realized that these were just his own thoughts, but surely his dream didn't take him to this bush of trees just for him to hear his own thoughts, so he began to walk farther into the trees. Thirty more steps and he came over a knoll, down around the bottom he noticed a deer drinking from the water, feet pressed into the soft soil that surrounded the water, the wind sent light ripples into the water and kept the flying insects working hard as they pressed against it, trees shaded the deer from the final strength of the day's sun, gaps amongst the trees allowed the light and warmth to penetrate the deer as its lips, tongue, and suction drew in deep gulps of water, the water passed from lips to tongue, to mouth, to throat, to the deer's thirst harboured inside its belly.

On top of the knoll Nanabosho stood tall so the deer would see him. The deer did, and it ran off into the trees until it disappeared from sight. Carrying on with his walk, Nanabosho took 50 more steps and he became tired so he leaned against a thick birch tree. Leaning against the tree, he let out an exasperated breath. All of a sudden, a voice came from the tree: "Finally, took you long enough!"

Nanabosho stepped back. Where was the voice coming from?

He looked around. Staring back at him was the thick birch tree he leaned against.

"I said, 'Took you long enough to get here.' I've been here waiting for 526 years, and I know you were here long before I was even a young sapling, sprouting from the intertwined leaves of past years."

In from the south flew a prairie chicken, landing on the lower branch of the thick birch tree. Shortly after the bird landed, it turned to the tree and asked, "Where am I? Where is this located?"

The thick birch tree cleared its voice and said, "This is Treaty 4, the territory of the maple tree and willow, and homeland of the aspen."

The prairie chicken stood tall and thought. "This sounds so good, thank you."

The thick birch tree puffed up and said, "You're welcome, that's the way it has always been since the beginning, it's been 144 years."

Nanabosho listened and thought, "Well that's tree-centric."

The prairie chicken flew from the thick birch tree to a rock that stood half out of the ground. Maybe it was the energy from the sun against the top of the rock that made the rock grumble, but he said to the prairie chicken, "I'm tired, please don't stand on me. I've been here since time immemorial, I don't need another birdbrain standing on me. Haven't you asked enough of me?"

The prairie chicken looked at the rock and said, "Well I was going to ask you where we are since I thought you've been here the longest, but if you're going to be like that then I'll just talk and work with the birch tree. He's been around you for a few days, he should know everything that you do!"

The birch tree felt pride and stood straight as the prairie chicken flew back to his limbs and he said to the bird, "*Peyak Aski Kikawinaw* (2015–2020), we identify three key priority areas that include Student Success, Community Engagement, and Research for here in this bush."

The rock piped up, "You aren't even pronouncing it correctly, birch, and you definitely haven't spelt it right!"

In unison prairie chicken and birch looked to rock. "Why are you so angry? At least we tried to learn.… At least we tried to spell it and say it in rock and not birch, so ungrateful you are, rock."

Nanabosho had learned enough for one evening, his head was full. He saw in action, not just words upon his ears. He encountered interactions throughout his evening journey about success, engagement, and research. He quickly turned and began running from the bush of trees. As he ran through the trees, he thought to be safe is to be accepted and embraced by acknowledging what is and was. When Nanabosho exited, he heard the wind blow through the trees and the wind pressed words out of the trees:

"Decolonization, indigenization, reconciliation, tough conversations, helping them heal, anti-oppressive, lateral violence, they don't know how to act, and that's a good one of them."

Each step Nanabosho took was quicker than the last. Wanting to escape the passing of windblown words because he knew that tomorrow there will be hardly any wind and we won't hear the same gust of words.

Nanabosho ran

Faster

And

Faster

Until he found a nice rock to lie on for the night to rest his mind from all the day's learnings and interactions. The light breeze of the night wind blew across Nanabosho's back as he drifted off to sleep.

## REFERENCES

Indigenous Advisory Circle, University of Regina. (2015). Indigenization; Indigenization definition. Retrieved from https://www.uregina.ca/strategic-plan/priorities/indigenization.html

Pete, S. (2015). *100 ways to Indigenize and decolonize academic programs and courses.* Retrieved from https://www.uregina.ca/president/assets/docs/president-docs/indigenization/indigenize-decolonize-university-courses.pdf

University of Regina. (2015). *Peyak aski kikawinaw: Together we are stronger: Strategic plan 2015–2020.* Retrieved from https://www.uregina.ca/strategic-plan/assets/docs/pdf/sp-2015-20-together-we-are-stronger.pdf

University of Regina External Relations. (2011). Release: University of Regina taking new steps to support Aboriginal student success. Retrieved from http://hdl.handle.net/10294/5080

University of Regina Faculty of Education. (2016). *University of Regina, Faculty of Education Structure Document.* Retrieved from https://www.uregina.ca/education/assets/Faculty-Structure-Document-July-2016.pdf

# The Trickiness of Storytelling with Indigenous Social Workers: Implications for Research in the Era of Reconciliation

*by Nicole Penak*

————

Kwe, my name is Nicole Penak. I am a member of the Eagle Clan, and I am a First Nations woman of mixed Mi'kmaw, Maliseet, Acadian, and Ukrainian heritage. My family is from the territory stretching through what is now known as the Gaspé Region in Quebec in through the province of New Brunswick, but I was born, live, and work in the vibrant Indigenous community of Toronto. I'm also a mom to my fierce toddler, Raven, and I don't know what's more of a Trickster tale—parenthood or my work as a social worker and social work educator here in the city. My traditional name translates to "cedar woman," reflecting some of the healing work I am involved with here in the community, but I have found that stories are my chosen medicine. It's an honour to be here and to share in all these medicine stories.

————

It's about two o'clock in the afternoon. I'm off work early today, trying to make it to afternoon classes. *Hnnnnng*, I manage to squeeze into a seat between two others on a bench in the TTC shelter, waiting for my streetcar. It's a hot day in the city, almost 30 degrees. I can feel the heat off the bodies surrounding me at the stop and hear the pavement sizzle under the tires of cars stopped at the intersection. *Phew.* I pull out a notebook, partly to fan myself, partly to review my work. *Boop. Boop. Boop. Boop.* My foot starts tapping at the concrete under me, and my reading begins to follow a new rhythm. I notice that I am bobbing along to someone's music. *Haaay, yaaa, boom, boom.* I look up and see him. Trickster. Unapologetically himself. Sporting a new pair of sweet sneakers, skinny jeans, and an ironic t-shirt with a portrait of Sitting Bull wearing neon sunglasses. From his bright red headphones pours the sound of powwow tunes mixed with electronic beats. He is squealing and dancing as he moves through the crowd of people. *Click.* We make eye contact. I try to make myself look busy but he comes right over to me. "Ah ho, my sister! What are you reading?" he says as he grabs the book from my hands, flipping quickly through the pages like you shuffle a deck of cards. "Wooh, that's a lot of English words!" Trickster says, handing the book back. He looks over at the bag on my lap. "Have any snacks in there, too?" I pull out a granola bar and hand it over. *Crunch. Crunch.* "What's this all for anyways?" Trickster asks, pointing with his half-eaten bar. "My research," I tell him. "Well what are you researching, you know, I am very clever." I don't doubt it. I have heard many stories of this Trickster before. In most of them he gets into trouble (and a lot of it). "The stories of Indigenous social workers here in Toronto," I tell him. "Social workers!?! Yikes!" proclaims Trickster with mocking laughter. "Don't steal my granola bar!" he continues, gripping his snack dramatically. Trickster has keeled over laughing. I'm annoyed. But I get it. I stop and think to myself, dropping my face into my hands. Trickster stories really do reinforce the principal motive of my research project: the importance of relationship. *Plink!* I feel something smack me in the nose. I crinkle my face and lift my head—I'm still sitting in the TTC shelter, no Trickster, and strangers are staring at me cockeyed. In my lap there's a scrunched up granola bar wrapper. I rub my nose and look around.

Storytelling can be tricky. *Snicker.* "Shhh, just let me get through this intro." *Sigh.* "Sorry, jeez!" *Shrug.* As I was saying, storytelling can be tricky, I'm never clear on where to begin, I mean, is there even really a beginning? Should we launch right into it? Maybe d

r

o

p

readers somewhere in the middle … mid dle … mid [*] dle…. Apologies. Having to translate an oral and often performative version of storytelling into text always takes some getting used to. The written word has transformed the process of storytelling, as "text was supposedly complete, self-contained, a thing to dissect rather than to have a relationship with" (Archibald, 2008, p. 33). However, storytelling, like Indigenous research, is an innately relational activity. So the rules on grammar are going to have to bend here, to allow for these words to have some LIFE! Well, this story arises from my research with Indigenous social workers in Toronto. Reflections about my time sharing and creating stories with other Indigenous – social – workers – in – Toronto. When I see those words all together the story is already so >crammed< … narratives about social work, accounts of Indigenous folks, anecdotes about this city—and yet these stories cut right through all those narratives, intersections of various tales, so many different layers

layers

layers

layers of stories. I guess that's where we can start. As Vine Deloria Jr. states, "the contrast between Christianity and its interpretation of history—the temporal dimension—and the American Indian tribal religions—basically spatially located—is clearly illustrated when we understand the nature of sacred mountains, sacred hills, sacred rivers, and other geographical features sacred to Indian tribes" (1973, p. 120). A renowned Indigenous scholar, philosopher, and writer, Deloria Jr.'s work on the centring of space for Indigenous Peoples, versus time, confirms teachings I have been told about past, present, and future all existing in the same moment. Teachings of stories layered on    top    Top    TOP of stories. Making room for multiple realities being experienced in the same space. "Wow, that sounds pretty sci-fi, sister!" Trickster says with a snicker. *Sigh.* "I promise we will come to you soon. How about you take a little walk or something?" I say to him, attempting to soften a forced smile. "Fine. I'm bored anyways," he says, running off through the next paragraph. *Whew.* That will give us a minute alone. With all of Trickster's interrupting I forgot to mention that Canada is in an era of reconciliation, not sure if that's a layer per se, or an EXPLOSION, a s-p-l-a-t-t-e-r, a BuMp, or a foooog hooooorn. A government-sponsored initiative laid out by the Truth and Reconciliation Commission of Canada (TRC), where "'reconciliation' is about establishing and maintaining a mutually respectful relationship between Aboriginal and non-Aboriginal peoples in this country" (TRC, 2015b, p. 113). Interestingly, it was never central to my research, not even in the plans! But somehow it infiltrated the stories in a lot of different ways. In some places it took over entirely, kind of ironic. *Wink.*

Well one thing about this time of reconciliation—I have never heard so many land acknowledgements in my entire life! It brings to mind again the significance of place in my research process. These reconciliation-era acknowledgements, some kind of an effort to capture the Indigeneity of this space in a pronouncement, bound by the strict confines of the past tense. Though they are being tediously worked over by committees of expert consultants, the story they tell still seems to place Indigenous people outside of this time and outside of this space. When people talk about connecting to the land, they often point outside of the city. That Indigenous lives, culture, stories live somewhere separate from here. These *land* acknowledgements do little to correct this, as they fail to talk about the land but centre people involved in political dealings. As Indigenous Peoples our connection to land is somewhat dialectic. The trickery that removes the land—the landness—from the city's story appears to take Indigenous Peoples and our stories with it.

"Trickery indeed!" Trickster shouts. Arms outstretched, bowing to some silent applause only he can hear. "Ah yes, welcome back." You see, the reconciliation era is absolutely brimming with trickery. "Really, it's hard to imagine you have any time to spend with us at all, Trickster," I say, looking over. "Ah well." *Blush.* Social work, too, has found itself part of the calls for reconciliation. In fact, of the 94 Calls to Action published by the TRC, the social work profession is the first to be called to task (TRC, 2015a, p. 1). You see, the history of social work and that of Indigenous Peoples in North America are intimately connected, growing out of a long history of treaty building between Indigenous and European Nations. Though the history of treaty making is fraught with trickery, violence, and tension, it is from these original relations that social work itself has developed, and from which its working relationship with Indigenous Peoples has formed. Social assistance, of some kind, is cited as a condition in many treaty negotiations, most notably in the Robinson-Superior and Robinson-Huron Treaties (1850), the Numbered Treaties (1871–1921), and today's modern treaties (1975–present). However, when examining the impact of such "assistance," the contradictory role in which social workers have long found themselves in their work with Indigenous Peoples becomes overwhelmingly clear. On the one hand, treaty relationships have pushed Indigenous communities into desperate poverty, removed from traditional territories and subsistence practices, causing a scourge of social and health problems to sweep through our Nations like never before. On the other hand, the Canadian state, through social workers, seeks to rectify the very problems its interference in Indigenous communities has caused, absurdly, with even more interference! *Huh?* Even Trickster's scratching his head about that one.

After the Second World War, the Canadian state sought to rearrange its interactions with Indigenous Peoples. Faced with the devastating impacts of its oppressive relationship with Indigenous Nations, there emerged a "different kind of state paternalism ... more associated with planned programs, positivism, the promise of professionalism and applied social science. The state was determined to become a friend of the Indian but an enemy of the 'Indian Problem'" (Shewell, 2004, p. 172). The Canadian government called for an organized effort to address this very issue, which became the Special Joint Committee of the Senate and the House of Commons Appointed to Consider and Examine the Indian Act, 1946–1948. The committee, formed in May 1946, was set up primarily to make recommendations for revising the 1876 Indian Act—an Act infamously recognized as a piece of violent colonial legislation. A number of professional organizations provided briefs, the most significant of which may have been the joint submission of the Canadian Welfare Council and the Canadian Association of Social Workers (Shewell, 2004, p. 190). This was largely due to the importance of state social welfare, and to the emergence of social work as one of the first professions in "applied" social science (Shewell, 2004, p. 190). They advocated for universal welfare programs to extend to reserve communities, because in their view, the challenges faced by Indigenous Peoples were the result of the absence of their universality with other Canadians. The submission advocated for a new federal-provincial relations plan for developing professional social services on reserves (Shewell, 2004, p. 190). This resulted in the introduction of Section 87 (now Section 88) of the Indian Act of 1951, which opened Indigenous well-being to provincial interventions, allowing provincial authority on reserves. This has had an everlasting impact on Indigenous self-determination, both at the level of state sovereignty—distorting the Nation-to-Nation relationship set up by our treaties—and at the level of families and individuals. There was a mass hiring of social workers by the state to accompany and slowly replace the long-standing colonial position that Indian agents held in Indigenous communities. From this point, "social workers were tasked to accompany Indian agents onto reserves to remove children to residential schools and later, in the 1960s and 1970s, to apprehend children deemed to be in need of protection" (Sinclair, 2009, p. 20). At the same time, the number of Indigenous children made legal wards of the state quickly ballooned from 1 percent of all children in care in 1959 to 30 to 40 percent of all legal wards being Indigenous children in 1960 (Fournier & Crey, 1997, p. 83). This period of social work intervention was coined the "Sixties Scoop" by Patrick Johnston (1983). He acknowledged that Indigenous children were apprehended from their homes and communities, often without the knowledge or consent of families and Bands (Sinclair, 2007, p. 66). These harmful interventions by social workers have not slowed over time, but rather have increased with the proliferation of the profession. As Cindy Blackstock, fierce advocate for Indigenous children and executive director of the First Nations Child and Family Caring Society of Canada, has stated, "Overall, we estimate that there may be as many as three times more Aboriginal children in the care of child welfare authorities now than were placed in residential schools at the height of those operations in the 1940s" (Blackstock & Trocmé, 2005, p. 13). This continues to contribute to the reasons why "social work has negative connotations to many Indigenous people and is often synonymous with the theft of children, the destruction of families, and the deliberate oppression of Aboriginal communities" (Sinclair, 2009, pp. 20–21).

"What a mess!" Trickster remarks, observing the carnage of this social work narrative. "Indeed it is," I say sorrowfully, kicking at the scattered ellipses in the middle of the story.......... You can see why Indigenous social workers have a complicated and nuanced relationship to their profession, myself included. A First Nations woman born right here in the city, a practising social worker for over 10 years, I live, am raising my own family, and work in the vibrant Indigenous community of Toronto. The fact that my profession lends itself to me being able to spend my days with community is a complicated gift that I am both grateful for and yet greatly cautious about. In all my years as part of this community I have come to know some truly remarkable people, such as the 10 people who were part of my research with Indigenous social workers in Toronto. Professionally, these are people I have worked for, worked beside, or even those I helped to train. There are now generations of Indigenous social workers in the city who have found their way into this profession, attempting to navigate its contradictions. It makes one keenly aware that there is a legacy of experiences here, of stories that can be passed down, of important lessons to be learned, and cautions to heed. Current and future Indigenous social workers in Toronto could look to these stories as they navigate their own complex relationships with the profession. A storied pathway through the city as an Indigenous social worker. "Aye. Not more walking!" sighs Trickster. He's such a complainer. "Fine with me, Trickster," I say, feigning concern. "You can stay here and I'll go on ahead!"

In *Indigenous Storywork* (2008), Jo-ann Archibald highlights the significance of story pathways for Indigenous Peoples. She interviews some significant people who have lived their lives by the teachings found within Indigenous stories. Archibald borrows from Gregory Cajete's Navajo understanding of pathways: "'path' symbolizes a journey and a process; 'way' is a cultural, philosophical framework" (2008, p. 12). Though some may see Archibald's use of *pathway* as figurative, a literary device much like metaphor, I am over-taken by these words, and believe they are far more material, as in "like *literally*,"    really,    actually,    physically,    story pathways. Listening and creating stories with Indigenous social workers in this city reminds me that "stories serve as signs or marks of our presence, functioning much like landmarks on a map" (Doerfler, Sinclair, & Stark, 2013, p. 1). This is similar to Deloria Jr.'s description of a "sacred geography" (1973, p. 121) where "every location within their original homeland has a multitude of stories … that cumulatively produced the tribe in its current tradition" (p. 121). Participants' stories help to make fa-miliar this landscape of Indigenous social workers in Toronto. Ojibwe scholar Heid E. Erdrich describes landmarks, the marks or signs that we leave behind that help us to understand place and connect us across time. She points out that the marks can be literary, that they can be stories (2013, p. 14). It's important to point out that this is not an effort to toil with colonial geography, or to engage in Western practices of mapping. These stories exist somewhere between the func-tion of petroglyphs and carving your name into wet cement. They can be found in parks, buildings, intersections, and neighbourhoods of Toronto. Working to restore the landness of this city, and placing ourselves and our stories inside it. Our stories LIVE here. Not bound by the Western restraints of time. Walking through the city, you may see them if you look openly, you may hear them if you listen carefully.

"Aho! Sister, wait up!" You've got to be kidding me. I continue to walk for-ward, hoping it's all in my head. "You just left me back there next to an ex-clamation mark! … Umm, wait. Can I include an exclamation mark after I've said *exclamation mark*?" Nope. It's happening. Trickster runs up alongside me. "Where are you headed, Trickster?" I inquire. "Well, with you, of course." *Eye roll.* Great. "You did mention you had stories, didn't you? Well I am a master storyteller, perhaps I could be of some assistance?" he says, plucking a hat out of the air and *tipping* it toward me. A part of me hates to admit it, but he's right. Though I believe Indigenous storytelling has the power to restore the relation-ships in our lives, it's not prescriptive in nature, with an index to follow to appli-cable solutions to life's challenges. In many cases, rather, "our teachers help us to see 'the upside down, the opposite, and the other balances of things around us'" (Graveline, 1998, p. 11). Among many First Nations these stories take up the Trickster character whom you have already met, in their/her/his/its many mani-festations, such as Coyote, Raven, Wesakejac, Glooscap, and Nanabozho, which have been part of Indigenous storytelling since time immemorial. The English word *trickster* does not portray the diverse range of roles and ideas First Nations associate with the Trickster,

> who sometimes is like a magician, an enchanter, an absurd prankster ... a shape shifter, and who often takes on human characteristics, ... one whose transformations often use humour, satire, self-mocking, and absurdity to carry good lessons.... Trickster seems to learn lessons the hard way and sometimes not at all. At the same time, Trickster has the ability to do good things for others and is sometimes like a powerful spiritual being and given much respect. (Archibald, 2008, p. 5)

As I have explored in previous work (Penak, 2018), Archibald puts forward the notion that Trickster can be as much a "doing" as a "being," and can be understood as a process that we interact with, as much as a person (2008, p. 6). Various expressions of Trickster have been applied in academic works by Indigenous scholars to explore diverse imbalances, from the "white man as Trickster" (Graveline, 1998, p. 11) in educational pedagogy, to Weesageechak as the tension between Canadian high schools and Aboriginal students (Bazylak, 2002), to a journey with Coyote and Raven through Canadian educational institutions (Cole, 2006). This notion of Trickster is useful in reframing the idea of a "research problem" as an imbalance or disharmony that participants or the researcher is engaging with. The disharmony of interest to my project being, what is the relationship like between Toronto's Indigenous social workers and their profession? You see, our friend Trickster gets into trouble when *disconnected* from traditional teachings, family, community, Nation, culture, and land (Archibald, 2008, p. i). And so his stories carry the principal motive of this knowledge-gathering project, the importance of relationships. Journeying with Indigenous social workers through their stories, as they encounter what has historically been an oppressive grand narrative of social work, has proven itself to be a series of Trickster tales. And where these stories intersect with efforts of reconciliation, they seem to get trickier and trickier. *Cackle.*

It's much later in the day now and there's a refreshing coolness to the air that wasn't there a few hours ago. *Shuffle. Shuffle. Shuffle.* I'm walking through the park at Allan Gardens. Moving slowly. On my way home. This park has long been part of my life as an Indigenous person and social worker in the city. It is bordered by Indigenous organizations: Anishnawbe Health, the Native Women's Resource Centre, and Miziwe Biik. It has also been the site of many gatherings, from organized vigils honouring missing and murdered Indigenous women, girls, and two-spirit people, to the Idle No More food and clothing drive, to casual meet-ups with friends and community members. It's no wonder the park features prominently as one of the landmarks on the pathway of Indigenous social work stories. I see there's a spot on the stairs leading up to the greenhouse, I wander over and take a seat. Looking out into the park, its stories COME ALIVE! *Wooooow*. All those past, present, and future, moving through the space at the same time. I can see the efforts the Indigenous social workers shared with me playing out right before my eyes! Decades of grassroots organizing from within Indigenous homeless communities, the movement to reclaim Indigenous healing practices in an urban context, and infinite moments of presence from counsellors supporting individuals and families through unspeakable trauma and incredible resiliency. *Whistling*. Wait a minute—what's that sound? *Hwee, hwee, hwee, hwoo, hwoo.* Where's that whistling coming from? I scan the park. *Aha!* There he is. I should have known. It's Trickster. *Gasp!* I can see the southeast corner of our story is disappearing! I jump off the steps and run over. I find Trickster with a giant bucket of whiteout correction fluid! "What in the world are you doing?!" I yell. "Who me?" says Trickster casually, paintbrush in hand. I throw my hands up in shock and confusion. "Relax, I'm restructuring," he tells me. "Restructuring, what the heck do you mean?!" I say, my mouth gaping open, horrified. "You know, switching things up, shifting the narrative." He continues at his task. "There must be a mistake, I was just telling these fine readers about the story landmarks for that research project." "Ya, the one with Indigenous social workers, I know. Well there's another story I'm making space for here too." *Huh?* I think for a minute and it comes to me. "Reconciliation!?!" I shout out, pulling at my hair. "Hey, don't shoot the messenger." Trickster shrugs.

*Facepalm.* Just like land acknowledgements can simultaneously work to disappear landness, it seems reconciliation can also disappear other important relationships in my research project. I've seen this in social work before, when race was disappeared from social work education in exchange for the concept of anti-oppressive practice (AOP). Based on semi-structured interviews of social work educators and archival research of the Canadian Association of Schools of Social Work (CASSW), Jeffery explains how the "Educational Policy Committee was opposed to the shopping list ... of 'isms'" (2007, p. 444), and did not feel it could privilege race, and so there has been a shift in preference for anti-oppression language over that of anti-racism. This same shift can be seen in much of the social work literature, as there is a "redefining [of] anti-racism as something less threatening, for example, anti-discrimination or anti-oppressive practice" (Heron, 2004, p. 290), where instead, "'differences' are now spoken everywhere in the academy" (Crosby, 1992, p. 131) and there are "texts on research in social work … in which 'race' is not even indexed" (Boushel, 2000, p. 75).

McLaughlin takes up the shift from anti-racism to AOP as having "allowed the problems of society to be recast as due to the moral failings of individuals who need censure and correction from the anti-oppressive social worker" (2005, p. 300). The question of who holds power over knowledge is particularly interesting in the case of the disappearance of race in favour of AOP language in social work. As illuminated by Jeffery's study, fees paid by member schools finance the CASSW, and to be an accredited school one must be a member of the association. To restrict accreditation on the basis of lack of content pertaining to race is to restrict association funding. As one participant stated, "They see how much it will cost to implement. There is that calculation that comes into effect for people" (Jeffery, 2007, p. 448). Another participant notes: "Can you block an accreditation or re-accreditation on that race issue alone? … We're dealing with a rather fragile association so do you create a major crisis someplace that could blow the whole thing apart?" (p. 449). Therefore, rather than threatening to destabilize the status quo, CASSW members have sought to preserve the existing governing structures at the sacrifice of meaningful discussions and content pertaining to race in social work. I would argue that this shift mirrors the disappearance of race in the larger society, where decades of efforts of anti-racist organizing—think civil rights movement and beyond—have been taken up by the Canadian state again and again and recast to society as an important part of Canada's commitment to multiculturalism and diversity. This new narrative distorts the Canadian state's role in maintaining systems that cause racial inequities and shifts attention to moral attitudes about acceptance of difference.

As race was recast as AOP in social work, efforts of Indigenous resistance and community healing are now being cast as "reconciliation." Somehow the work of Indigenous social workers to address the very gap caused by the ongoing oppressive relationship between the Canadian state and their communities is be re-storied as proof that social work can repair its relationship with Indigenous Peoples. It's worth mentioning that participants in this research project are acutely aware that they have specialized training in an applied social science with an ongoing colonial heritage. Many shared that this very choice is a response to the ongoing divisive colonialism that has in many ways severed informal support systems, as many in the city have limited connection to family or community, making formal Indigenous supports a stand-in as community heals and rebuilds its connections.

As race discourse in social work can be found reformed into discussions of history and Whiteness, reconciliation too has worked to re-centre settler desires, power, and identity. Indigenous social workers shared stories of being pulled from the work they are doing within community to discuss things like land acknowledgements, staff training, smudging policies, and ventilation systems— all of which carry an important theme: consideration for non-Indigenous social work bodies. Similar to what we saw with the disappearance of race in social work, reconciliation has disappeared conversations of Indigenous self-determination. Though there are now explicit attempts to include Indigenous content in social work education and workplaces, it is more often the case today that Indigenous content is placed in a separate course, or training for a sole Indigenous worker, or one Indigenous-themed service, rather than entire programs or workplaces working toward their decolonization. Reconciliation efforts largely resist the restructuring of the profession, keeping oppressive systems intact, and favour instead the moral development of non-Indigenous workers.

*Splatter.* "Hey, what are you doing now?" I say, wiping the corrective fluid from my face. "Collateral damage." Trickster shrugs, taking his paintbrush to my arm. "Holaaay," I say, exacerbated, pushing him away and plopping down on the half-disappeared park lawn. I need to pull myself together here. *Cringe.* I glance over at my right hand and wiggle my fingers to make sure they are still there. *Whew.* You see, reconciliation has attempted to distort this story in quite a few ways. But one relationship it threatens to disappear is really central to this research project: the relationship between Indigenous social workers and their profession. I hadn't quite thought about it before, until participants in this study articulated it so clearly, that reconciliation is a deeply personal journey for Indigenous social workers. Though some actively resist participating in the profession's call for reconciliation with Indigenous Peoples, who they are, both as Indigenous people and social workers, is a relationship at the core of their stories. It became necessary to re-centre reconciliation as it was taken up by Indigenous social workers' stories, namely reconciling with their own identity as Indigenous, and who they are in their relationship to community.

I stop for a moment and take in the scenery. I think of the story pathways we have travelled in this research and the landmarks where important lessons live. From here I can almost see the ghosts of social work past gathering at the intersection of Yonge and College, and hear the powwow drum from the stories living in Regent Park. The wolf pack from Vaughan and St. Clair run through, knocking over Trickster on their way south to Queen and Bathurst. *Hehehe.* I laugh at the mess. Bucket over his head. Trickster appears to have resigned himself for the moment. Thinking of these stories, I am reminded of Trickster, where trouble and imbalance follow from a disjuncture in relationships. These stories, like Trickster tales, can carry good lessons in their disorder. This journey has taught me that research on reconciliation needs to repair and uphold relationships, and re-centre those relationships that the reconciliation process continues to distort. Trickster stories have helped me to do this: to restore landness, to re-centre Indigenous narratives, and to explore some challenging relationships. For myself, these stories represent a rich and powerful challenge, not just to social work, but to the hegemony of traditional research methodologies. As these stories reflect not solely on content but also on process, they can demonstrate the strength of Indigenous research that brings relationships to the forefront of the research process.

*Bang! Clunk! Thud!* "A little help here, please?" strains Trickster, tangled in his painting provisions. "Oh Trickster." I take a cloth from his supplies and help to clear his eyes, and then remove his limbs from the clutter. "What do I do now?" he says, tears in his eyes, looking over his broken gear. "Perhaps you should join me on a stroll through the rest of these stories. Maybe we can *both* learn something," I say, extending a hand. As we walk together through the story pathway of Indigenous social workers in Toronto, moving from landmark to landmark, I am reminded of what Heid E. Erdrich shared: "We want to know who has gone before us, who now guide us. We take comfort in their signs of presence along our way" (2013, p. 14). I look to Trickster and smile. With reconciliation I have a feeling there are a lot of tricky stories awaiting us. *Chuckle.* I am grateful to have an old friend in Trickster. He helps to navigate this path, showing me it's more familiar than I had once expected. *Wink.*

## REFERENCES

Archibald, J. (2008). *Indigenous storywork: Educating the heart, mind, body, and spirit.* Vancouver: University of British Columbia Press.

Bazylak, D. (2002). Journeys to success: Perceptions of five female Aboriginal high school graduates. *Canadian Journal of Native Education, 26*(2), 134–151.

Blackstock, C., & Trocmé, N. (2005). Community-based child welfare for Aboriginal children: Supporting resilience through structural change. *Social Policy Journal of New Zealand, 24*, 12–33.

Boushel, M. (2000). What kind of people are we? "Race," anti-racism and social welfare research. *British Journal of Social Work, 30*(1), 71–89.

Cole, P. (2006). *Coyote and Raven go canoeing: Coming home to the village.* Kingston, ON: McGill-Queen's University Press.

Crosby, C. (1992). Dealing with differences. In J. Butler & J. W. Scott (Eds.), *Feminists theorize the political* (pp. 130–143). New York: Routledge.

Deloria, V., Jr. (1973). *God is red: A Native view of religion.* New York: Putnam.

Doerfler, J., Sinclair, N. J., & Stark, H. K. (Eds.). (2013). *Centering Anishnaabeg studies: Understanding the world through stories.* East Lansing: Michigan State University Press.

Erdrich, H. E. (2013). Name': Literary Ancestry as Presence. In J. Doerfler, N. J. Sinclair, & H. K. Stark (Eds.), *Centering Anishnaabeg studies: Understanding the world through stories* (pp. 13–34). East Lansing: Michigan State University Press.

Fournier, S., & Crey, E. (1997). *Stolen from our embrace: The abduction of First Nations children and the restoration of Aboriginal communities.* Toronto: Douglas and McIntyre.

Graveline, F. J. (1998). *Circle works: Transforming Eurocentric consciousness.* Halifax: Fernwood.

Heron, G. (2004). Evidencing anti-racism in student assignments: Where has all the racism gone? *Qualitative Social Work, 3*(3), 277–295.

Jeffery, D. (2007). Managing race in social work education policy. *Journal of Education Policy, 22*(4), 429–454.

Johnston, P. (1983). *Aboriginal children and the child welfare system.* Toronto: Canadian Council on Social Development.

McLaughlin, K. (2005). From ridicule to institutionalization: Anti-oppression, the state and social work. *Critical Social Policy, 25*(3), 283–305.

Penak, N. (2018). A story pathway: Restoring wholeness in the research process. In D. McGregor, J.-P. Restoule, & R. Johnston (Eds.), *Indigenous research: Theories, practices, and relationships* (pp. 257–270). Toronto: Canadian Scholars.

Shewell, H. (2004). *"Enough to keep them alive": Indian welfare in Canada, 1873–1965.* Toronto: University of Toronto Press.

Sinclair, R. (2007). Identity lost and found: Lessons from the Sixties Scoop. *First Peoples Child & Family Review, 3*(1), 65–82.

Sinclair, R. (2009). Bridging the past and future: An introduction to Indigenous social work issues. In R. Sinclair, M. A. Hart, & G. Bruyere (Eds.), *Wicihitowin: Aboriginal social work in Canada* (pp. 19–24). Halifax: Fernwood.

Truth and Reconciliation Commission of Canada. (2015a). *Calls to action.* Winnipeg: Truth and Reconciliation Commission of Canada.

Truth and Reconciliation Commission of Canada. (2015b). *What we have learned: Principles of Truth and Reconciliation.* Winnipeg: Truth and Reconciliation Commission of Canada.

# Health Canada Issues Massive Recall of Liberal Tears

Health Canada has issued a massive recall of tears shed by senior Liberal government officials over Indigenous issues, including those from Prime Minister Justin Trudeau.

The wide-ranging recall, the largest of its kind in recent history, includes tears shed since the party took power in the 2015 federal election over everything from residential schools to Indigenous child welfare and reconcili-ACTION.

"Should you come into contact with any of these Liberal tears, it's important to bottle them and return them to the federal government at once," said a spokesperson from the Public Health Agency of Canada.

"We're working with our partners in the First Nations Inuit Health Branch to come up with a solution now."

The agency issued the recall over fears the tears could be contaminated with E. coli and Insincerity. Recalled brands include Carolyn Bennett Eyewells and Justin Trudeau Waterworks, among many others.

# SECTION III

# LEARNING TO WALK

*by Andrea V. Breen*

The chapters in this final section represent the closing of this book, but we also see this section as a beginning. As we've worked together, Shawn, Lindsay, and I have had many conversations about the various topics and themes in this book—Indigenous research, settler colonialism, reconciliation, White supremacy, violence, injustice, relationship, accountability—and their shifting meanings in each of our lives. If you listened in on our conversations, you might think that we've talked a lot in circles.

This is probably as it should be.

Usually when non-Indigenous people say "they talk in circles," it's meant to be a bad thing, like the conversation isn't really leading anywhere. Indigenous ways of knowing offer a better way of understanding circles. It's through engaging in circles of questioning, learning, searching, reflecting, and participating in life and ceremony that knowledge and understanding grow (Absolon, 2011; Simpson, 2017; Wilson, 2008). Unlearning is also an important part of learning. Often, before we can move forward we need to take a few steps backwards, to rethink what we've learned, recognize and shed unexamined assumptions, to see things in the new light of a changed perspective.

That's how we walk forward in a good way. But we need to pause here and look a little closer at what this means. We've noticed that the phrase "walk in a good way" is used a lot by Indigenous people and, increasingly, by settlers. Like other terms (*reconciliation, Indigenization, decolonization*), it can be tossed around without much thought being given to what it means in practice. There are variations in where each of us is on the path to walking in a good way, from those who engage in tokenistic attempts that are disconnected from Indigenous people and community, to those who fully embody with their words and actions deep accountability to relationships with the human and non-human world, land, spirit, and ideas. And there are many places in between. We are each at different points on different paths and we have different understandings of what it means to walk in a good way. Each of us will likely take our own journeys, make our own meanings, and carry our own maps and other tools.

Indigenous research methods are among the tools and maps that can be used to walk in a good way. As Strega and Brown (2015) point out in the edited collection *Research as Resistance*, Indigenous methods exist alongside feminist approaches, critical approaches, and other anti-oppressive research methodologies in providing tools that researchers can use to engage in research that illuminates and challenges the status quo and works toward creating conditions for social justice to flourish. And over the past two decades, Indigenous scholars such as Shawn Wilson (2008), Margaret Kovach (2010), Kathleen Absolon (2011), and indeed the authors in this collection have contributed to creating new spaces and possibilities for Indigenous methods to be used to gain knowledge and improve people's lives. As Absolon (2011) points out, Indigenous methodologies provide tools for re-membering that which has been dis-membered. This is essential to a meaningful project of reconciliation.

But it's important to recognize that sovereignty is also fundamental to reconciliation. As researchers, we need to be reflective about our relationships with Indigenous methodologies and the possibilities and limitations of these relationships. Reconciliation requires that we non-Indigenous people move forward with humility, recognizing that there need to be Indigenous spaces that are protected for Indigenous people; spaces that are not for us. We should not expect to have access to every aspect of knowledge, every tool, and every ceremony.

As we hope will be pretty clear by now, reconciliation is complicated and it's not about an end point: it's about processes and deep accountability to past, present, and future relationships. There are no quick fixes or how-to guides to follow. But we do have stories to help guide us toward new understandings, stories that have been handed down to us and those we are creating now as we live. Each of the chapters in this final section tells stories about moving forward. While the authors each speak about a different journey in a different place, there are some common questions that draw these chapters together: What does it mean to you at this point in time to walk in a good way? Has the meaning of this changed for you over time? How does your own path forward relate to processes of reconciliation in your own community and/or Nation? What sources of support and guidance will you carry with you as you move forward?

## REFERENCES

Absolon, K. E. (2011). *Kaandossiwin: How we come to know.* Winnipeg: Fernwood.

Kovach, M. E. (2010). *Indigenous methodologies: Characteristics, conversations, and contexts.* Toronto: University of Toronto Press.

Simpson, L. B. (2017). *As we have always done: Indigenous freedom through radical resistance.* Minneapolis: University of Minnesota Press.

Strega, S., & Brown, L. (Eds.). (2015). *Research as resistance: Revisiting critical, Indigenous and anti-oppressive approaches* (2nd ed.). Toronto: Canadian Scholars' Press.

Wilson, S. (2008). *Research is ceremony: Indigenous research methods.* Halifax: Fernwood.

## CHAPTER 12

# Experiencing Resonance as a Practice of Ritual Engagement

*by Manulani Aluli-Meyer, Delphine Armstrong, Mariel Belanger, Jill Carter, Cori Derickson, Claire Fogal, Vicki Kelly, Carolyn Kenny, Virginie Magnat, Joseph Naytowhow, Julia Ulehla, and Winston Wuttunee*

———

In loving memory of Carolyn Kenny

I am Virginie Magnat and I have been collaborating with a group of seven Indigenous artist-scholars and Elders/Traditional Knowledge Keepers, as well as two Indigenous and two non-Indigenous graduate students. We each introduce ourselves in our own voices in the pages that follow.

———

## CAROLYN

I often think of my Choctaw mother and her advice to me while I was growing up. She always said, "Be a human being first. The rest comes later."

Raven teased the humans into existence through his playful song. The myth goes that tiny humans were hiding in a giant clamshell on the beach, afraid to come into being. Raven was flying around and flying around. Then he saw the clamshell and heard their sighs. He landed on top of the shell and began to sing to these little creatures. Gradually, they emerged from their hiding place in the clamshell to become human beings.

After my mother died, I was adopted by a Haida Elder. The Haida Gwaii is a magnificent group of islands just off the coast of British Columbia near Alaska. Because our traditional territory was one of the only areas of land in North America not touched by the ice age, we have magnificent old growth trees in our rain forests.

As a Native American, I had a wealth of traditional knowledge to access in my discovery process. Traditional knowledge is filled with intuitive science that has been passed down through the generations in a different way than Western science. For example, in my Native education, I learned that music is an energy system.

## DELPHINE

I heard songs as a very young child. The first song that I heard about our culture was the Winter Ceremony. I never went to residential school, I'm one of the lucky ones, I didn't go, so I never lost my language, I grew up knowing the songs. I spent a lot of time with my grandmother, she taught me that we're connected to the land, our language comes from the land. My grandma told us captikʷəł, our historical stories to which landmarks are connected throughout our territory, the stories about when there were plants and animals only, and then the people finally came. She would say: "The song that I'm going to sing or the story that I'm going to tell is captikʷəł, before there were humans." In every story, captikʷəł, there's a song.

## VIRGINIE

As a European performance practitioner, researcher, and educator working at a public Canadian university located on the unceded traditional territories of First Nations communities that comprise the province of British Columbia, I am deeply inspired by the powerful cultural revitalization movement for self-determination and sovereignty in which Indigenous Elders, Traditional Knowledge Keepers, artist-scholars, educators, and activists have been engaged for generations.

The braiding methodology employed in this polyphonic chapter entails searching for echoes and resonances between voices while leaving space for dissonances. Jill Carter's reflections about the challenges of working toward reconciliation point to something other than unanimity, unison, or perfect harmony. What I learned from my vocal training, my work with traditional songs, and my experience with my research collaborators for this project is that polyphony or plurivocality requires listening very attentively to other voices, which are all unique within the group, so that something can emerge from their relationships. Manulani Aluli-Meyer's contribution provides a testimony of this collective experience of resonance, which is also deeply personal.

## JILL

I was born and raised in Tkaronto—part of the territory that was shared for centuries by the Seneca of the Haudenosaunee Confederacy with the Michi Saagig Anishinaabeg under the Dish with One Spoon (Haudenosaunee) or Our (collectively shared) Dish (Anishinaabe) Treaty. Within these territories—whether approached over water or across land—protocols around an announcement of presence, a request to enter, and profferings of consent and welcome have been maintained and continue to be observed. The Haudenosaunee continue to practice, as part of their cycle of Condolence, an "Edge of the Woods" ceremony (Smith, 2016, n.p.). And we Anishinaabeg have a like ceremony. Traditionally, we did not just enter another's territory. Instead we waited at the outskirts—"at the edge of the woods" or in our canoes some distance from shore—announcing our presence in song and waiting to be welcomed *con* verse with an answering song and a series of actions devised to cleanse us and prepare us for entry into the host community (Simpson, 2008, p. 36). The announcement of self; the welcome; the exchange of song, story, and gifts; the sharing of food—this is all part

of the treaty process between humans. They constitute a resonant Speech Act—
or as Manulani Aluli-Meyer terms it, a "resonance performance"—witnessed by
the Creation, *settling* each into his own accountability, making kin of us all.

## MANULANI

Ulu a'e ke welina a ke aloha.

Here is the mele Hawaii we chanted together in Kelowna within Native lands
and diverse cultures. It is a statement of our commitment to loving and its mana
is expressed within one breath. Inhale. Exhale. It is where I understood what
research was and can be—to explore difference until resonance fills our shared
knowing; a synergy reaching inward toward the heart to strengthen faith in collective purpose. Here was the sound of our trans-historic present the world is
working toward. How indeed do we go forward to engage in what is best about
the coherence of principles, individual excellence, and collective aspirations
within the cacophony of our harmonic potential? How do we occupy universal
truth with our own specificity? How can sound help research find the resonance
within society?

## VIRGINIE

When I discussed my plans to use my Social Sciences and Humanities Research
Council (SSHRC) grant for the Performative Power of Vocality project to support two Syilx/Okanagan graduate students, my colleagues of the Indigenous
Inquiries Circle, a group that meets annually at the International Congress of
Qualitative Inquiry, recommended that I form an Indigenous Advisory Com-
mittee that would provide the research team with advice, guidance, and men-
torship throughout the development of the project. I later obtained a SSHRC
Connection Grant to bring the members of the Advisory Committee and the
graduate students together for the practice-based project Honoring Cultural
Diversity through Collective Vocal Practice.

Drawing on my 25 years of experience as a performance practitioner and educator,
which includes (re-)learning traditional songs in Occitan, the critically endangered
language of my Mediterranean cultural legacy, I have been working in close consultation with the Advisory Committee, composed of seven established Indigenous
artist-scholars and Elders/Traditional Knowledge Keepers, and in collaboration

with two Indigenous and two non-Indigenous graduate research assistants pursu-ing MFA and PhD degrees in theatre/performance studies, Indigenous studies, and ethnomusicology at the University of British Columbia. In 2016–17, we co-facilitated community gatherings hinging on the Indigenous ethical principles of respect, reciprocity, and relationality (Wilson, 2008). These encounters took place in British Columbia and consisted of three singing circles hosted in two Okanagan traditional winter homes (kekuli) and at the UBC First Nations Longhouse in Vancouver; two open workshops at Simon Fraser University and UBC's Okanagan Campus; and two performative presentations for the International Congress of Qualitative Inquiry and for the Canadian Association for Theatre Research Con-ference; as well as a three-day retreat/closed meeting in the Okanagan.

## JOSEPH

A few weeks prior to my departure for kʷunkʷancin, lulum chet, 'tiləm ct ("We Sing" in the Syilx, Squamish, and Musqueam languages), this beautiful encoun-ter with other Indigenous singer/musicians from Canada, I was trying to recall the west coast anthem, but for some reason I couldn't remember how it was sung. I arrived at the UBC First Nations House of Learning and as soon as I walked into this magnificent building, I remembered the west coast anthem. This an-them came from the west coast and, energetically, I would definitely be able to sing it where it felt like home.

The introduction of west coast traditional drummers and singers is what I'd ex-pected. I felt welcomed. The west coast not being my traditional territory, it was important to receive an invitation from the ones who've lived there for many generations. It's an honour to have the acceptance and appreciation of other In-digenous Nations when traversing this planet. Ultimately, we need to respect one another in our respective lands. It's what I have been taught by my Elders back in Saskatchewan. Whenever I am in another Indigenous Nation's land study-ing, medicine picking, or exchanging cultural information, I connect and ask for consent to do so. This is paramount in building good relations.

## CLAIRE

On Saturday, February 18, 2017, on the path to the UBC Longhouse I met Carolyn, a long-time family friend and renowned music therapist. She too was coming for the planning part of the singing circle that day, and she shared with me that she was seriously ill. We hugged out in the cold air and entered the space together. Full of Carolyn's news, I breathed in the height and natural wood and light of the central hall and felt awed and soothed all at once.... Participants began to fill the Great Hall of the Longhouse, and as the circle progressed, I was more and more moved. Amanda, a young Musqueam woman who was pregnant, stood and spoke with confidence, then danced a story sung by her mother, Madeline, and their relative Ian Campbell, the Squamish Nation Chief. At one point, several women of European origin sang traditional songs, one after the other: Julia in the Moravian dialect of Czech, Ana Elia in Catalan, and Jocelyn in Scottish Gaelic.... Sung a cappella from open throats under the roof of the Longhouse, these songs had a similar raw unadorned power. I felt like a tuning fork vibrating with each offering, or some kind of song barrel, with all the resonance collecting inside me. Then Gary Oker, a traditional song keeper from Doig River First Nation, talked about how he found his song in a dream, and he sang and played it on both his drum ("Dene, so with that snare drum–like resonance," he explained as he played) and then on his spirit gong-drum. I felt this song splinter the wood of my barrel-chest open and give my heart a rigorous cleansing. It was such a relief.

## CAROLYN

The seasons come and go. The day turns to night. We wake. Then we sleep. We breathe. We follow the natural rhythms and textures of the Earth. As human beings, we are bioregions, just as the earth we inhabit. Our beings are in a state of dynamic flux. Elements of our being are dying and being reborn constantly. Music is one of the sensory elements that permeates our consciousness to ground us in this ecology. It is important to remember that all people have tribal roots. Modern Indigenous Peoples represent this tribal identity. But is there a possibility of re-membering the essential spiritual principle of the interdependence of all things embedded in our ancient tribal memory? The essential question is how do we come to a greater awareness of just being? And in an ecology of being, our second question must be how do we come to a greater awareness of the principle of the interconnectivity between all things?

## JILL

Currently, in the wake of the Truth and Reconciliation Commission's final report, a rush to reconcile is occurring. Partnerships are proposed, workshops are requested, Indigenous scholars are consulted, Indigenous artists are invited to perform, and Indigenous Elders are invited to open events and offer Land Acknowledgements. Circles are formed and smudge bowls make their way around these circles, as our settler-allies listen to stories, research historical events, and labour to pronounce original names. Such initiatives signal good intent, I believe, but the task for all Canadians goes beyond education; it goes beyond learning historical events, names, or geography. It requires those who have settled on Indigenous lands to *re-imagine* themselves in light of this learning (Saul, 2009, p. 317).

The work to which we have committed ourselves with the singing circles, facilitated by Virginie Magnat, concerns itself with the project of re-worlding—the re-imagination of right relationships and the invitation to articulate *con* verse a deepening understanding of ancient commitments and kinship ties. Embodied practices such as these, it seems to me, chart a processual pathway upon which we might negotiate a difficult journey (through a challenging landscape that teems with the verdant overgrowth of frustration, hardship, deception, mourning, and danger) toward a place of "reconciliation with the natural world" and conciliation between our peoples (Crowshoe, as cited in Truth and Reconciliation Commission, 2015, p. 123).

## JULIA

Like many people in North America, I am a hybrid. My father escaped communist Czechoslovakia in 1968 and eventually made his way to North America, where he fell in love with my American mother. They created a family and made a home. I am ostensibly one of the three non-Indigenous voices contributing to this chapter, although in fact, my maternal great-grandfather was a Cherokee named Jackson Lister. His mother, Helen Self, died when he was a boy, and he was adopted by a White family. My mother met him only once. Any kind of living family connection to his heritage has long since disappeared.

On my father's side, generations of my family (who all still live in the Czech Republic) have been deeply involved with a particular land-based folk song tradition that is rooted in the alluvial lowlands and foothills of the White Carpathian Mountains. The tradition didn't really make the trip with my father when he came to America. Over the last eight years, I have been working to recover this

Moravian (Czech) cultural heritage from my living grandmother, from others in her extended community, and by singing these songs as much as I can, in as many situations as I can.

## DELPHINE

I wanted to be a professional singer, like Hank Williams, like Elvis Presley, and others, like all the singers in my day, but I was tricked one time, and that's how I got started singing Native songs. I got hired at a very young age at the Friendship Centre in the seventies because they wanted me to present our culture, our songs, and our history. There was this program director who was Mi'kmaq, and the first week I was hired he asked me to accompany him to do a presentation at a school. After he had drummed and sang a song from his culture on stage, he said, "I'm going to ask Delphine to come up here, she can sing her song and speak in her language." I had never sung and played the drum in my life but I had heard songs so I went up on the stage, because I was taught by my grandma never to say you can't do it: when you're asked, you do it. So, I took the drum and I hit it, and guess what song came? The Winter Dance ceremonial song that I heard when I was around three or five years old, that's the first song that came, and I couldn't believe it because I never ever sang Native songs. I drummed and I sang this song right through. On our way home, I asked the program director, "What if I didn't have a song? You're lucky that song came to me because I heard it when I was little." So, that's how I got started singing Native songs.

## JILL

As an Anishinaabe visitor, walking upon these lands for the first time in my life, I was first welcomed in song at the En'owkin Centre in Penticton by Delphine Armstrong and Cori Derickson (sister and niece, respectively, of En'owkin founder Jeannette Armstrong). How fitting is it that it was in this place of story, which has mentored, trained, and disseminated the works of Indigenous artists for nearly five decades, that we were first invited into relationship with our beautiful Syilx hosts and the biota to which they attribute their beauty. Gifted with such beauty, we visitors (Indigenous and non-Indigenous) were impelled to return the gift, sharing the beauty of our personal histories, families, and Nations in song and story. This was my first encounter at the "edge of the woods." And as the days went on, this process of welcoming continued, carrying us—Indigenous and non-Indigenous culture workers—deeper and deeper into relationship with our hosts, with their lands, and with each other, as we regaled each other *con* verse, imagining together what our world (on these shores) reconciled might look like.

## VICKI

I have been journeying with the Native flute for a while now, and have come to understand that on this pathway or through this way I am "in the discipline of wind" and, more importantly, "in the discipline of song on the wind." It has been a deep learning journey, actively exploring the co-created acoustic ecologies between my flute and the community of life present on the land. The tradition was and is playing in the canyons or places of profound resonance, and actively listening into sacred sites of acoustic ecology.

It has required another way of knowing, a deep listening and participating in an acoustic pedagogy. This leaning into the polyphonic reality of place has allowed me to become more resonant to what is collectively sounding. So, when I joined the gathering in Kelowna that December day in the kekuli, I was deeply grateful to be singing and sounding within a traditional house, resonating with the power of traditional songs. Since then, these sonic experiences have echoed and lingered, much like the drum that lies vibrating long after the beating of the drumstick has stopped. The drum has many teachings but perhaps its greatest gift is the offering of the pedagogy of resonance as it has sounded over the lands of Indigenous Peoples for millennia. What role does the drum and the pedagogy of resonance play today? What role can the reawakening of the drum and traditional song play in creating moments of ceremony that actively heal and reconcile our broken relationships with family, community, the land, and all our relations? What can this sonic inquiry into resonance reveal for our collective well-being and future generations?

## DELPHINE

I told my father how I was tricked, well, how I felt I was tricked, and he laughed. He thought I knew songs because I knew my culture, and he thought I sang songs—I did, but not those. So, my father gave me six songs, and I still have them, like the bear song, which is a ceremonial song, and the Okanagan song, and the morning prayer song. In our culture we have all kinds of songs. I didn't really pay attention because this was all around me, I thought everybody knew all this, but then I found out that not everybody grew up like I did. So, I started learning about all these different songs, and I went back and I thanked my mother and my father for the way I grew up, and the way they didn't let me go to residential school, they didn't send me, my dad wouldn't let us go. I thanked my parents and my grandmother, who also was a very strong influence on my life, because I know my culture, I know the language so well.

## WINSTON

Our people were always outdoors and learned to live in balance with nature. For instance, on the Prairies in the fall we camped in sheltered places that could break the cold furies of winter. We had corrals that were shelter for our horses, where water and good prairie wool was available. We were aware of every wind and every ray of sunshine and all our food sources. We camped in the fall beside great stands of chokecherries, pin cherries, saskatoon berries, buffalo berries, cranberries, strawberries, and blueberries. We learned to live for every season and consequently saw the drama of every season—good and bad. We were learning our whole lives and our old people told us what Joseph told us: "When the Creator put us here on the earth he told us to do the best we can wherever we are." I try to remember that every day in all that I do. I remember being younger and doing the best I could wherever I was. Because of knowledge like this, I go anywhere in the world and am always comfortable in my own skin; I have been taught good common sense by the old people.

## MARIEL

When I was younger, I heard my grandmother singing a song without any words. It had sounds but they were a series of vocables that made a catchy tune. I sang it to Richard Armstrong, a Syilx traditional Knowledge Keeper from Penticton Indian Band, and he said he hadn't heard it before but it sounded like a lullaby: you would insert words of endearment or parts of the body, like hands, feet, eyes, ears, to sing to a baby.

Kwan na ta

Na kook alum sa

An-a-yo a-hooo oh

Toonstin sa ha ahh yah

Na kook alum sa

Na kwan na ta

I carried this song with me to our first Honoring Cultural Diversity through Collective Vocal Practice singing circle in the kekuli at Summerhill Pyramid winery in Kelowna. To be honest, I have held on to shame that expresses itself as anxious tears and wavers in my voice as it did that day by the fire. I am not sure where the shame came from, considering I come from a long line of singers. In the late 1970s to early 1980s, anthropology student Wendy Wickwire spent summers with my family specifically recording my grandmother and great-grandfather's songs. My grandmother Mary Abel told Wickwire about her practices of cultural identity, which were embodied through dreams, designs, song, and dance.

## JULIA

When I entered the kekuli—the beautiful structure that Elder Delphine Armstrong and Cori Derickson's family laboured to build with their own hands, that Vicki Kelly warmed that night with logs she carefully split, and that we entered, one by one, along with that which we carry in the world—I asked my ancestors to come too. I asked them to be with me while I sang their song in the sharing circle, with my great-grandmother Marta's shawl—gifted to me by my grandmother Blanka—hung on my shoulders. I felt them there, and others told me they felt them too. As a doctoral student writing about her experiences with song heritage within the Western academy, I have been advised to consider a series of inexplicable phenomena—certain events and situations that I have come to associate with the presence of spirit and appearance of my ancestors—with critical skepticism, and to approach them with scholarly distance. But to sing the songs of my ancestors within the ceremonial gatherings of this project, to have them received with generosity and openness, and to have the presence of spirit named and acknowledged has been a tremendous teaching and a different kind of advice or encouragement from that which has come from within the Western academy.

## CORI

I am a sqilxʷ singer.... The songs choose me. To sing is to be a keeper of the songs. It is a responsibility not only to your family, but also to your community and your Nation. The songs are sacred and alive. Within the songs live a power of past generations and knowledge embedded in the lands, the trees, the birds, and the wind. Songs have been used in our Nation for healing, prayers, education, and enjoyment.

Most of the songs I learned from listening to my mother sing. The songs can be traced back to my maternal family lineage to my great-grandmother Christine Joseph. The songs then passed to my grandfather, to my mother, and then to me. The songs then made their way to my children and now grandchildren. Living through six generations, the songs have travelled through our family that I have known in my lifetime. This is the way of our people; this is how the songs stay alive. I love to hear my grandson sing now. It warms my heart.

## WINSTON

All my senses were wide awakened, starting from the smudge outside by the bushes to the traditional prayer song Mariel sang to the spirits of the land, air, and water. This smudge ceremony permitted us to go ahead and participate fully in brotherhood and music. I was aware of the ancestral spirits who previously lived daily in the kekuli. What a beautiful family experience that must have been for them, conversing and thinking in their own language. The old kekulis were alive every day, mentally and spiritually, with language, food, and life. It was good for all of us in our special group to experience this even for just a day. We are better people for it!

## JILL

In May 2017, the annual conference of the Canadian Association for Theatre Research (CATR) brought me together with Mariel Belanger, Cori Derickson, Vicki Kelly, and Virginie Magnat to share our questions and pursuits and to consider how our work might inform and be transformed by the resonances emerging from our collaboration within an embodied, relational practice. In anticipation of the conference presentation we would deliver, we had shared ourselves through our papers, our poetry, and our reflections. So, from Tkaronto, I stood at the "edge of the woods" to reveal myself and seek entry. At the same time, these women were planning a journey to the biota in which I live and with which I have a historical relationship. They too waited at the edge of the woods, revealing themselves, as I prepared myself to welcome them.

## DELPHINE

My grandmother always said that in our culture there were songs or prayer for any time we gather, for any time we do anything. We have songs for picking the first roots, the first berries, still today, and that's what I teach. We have songs for every ceremony that we do, that's what we have to do, it goes back to the captikʷəł. We were given laws in our captikʷəł, and that was taken away by the residential schools, and a lot of the people have forgotten that, forgotten their language. So few of us still remember the stories, the songs, and the ceremonies, so we do them and teach them today, which is really good, because we bring them back.

## CORI

At one point in our history we were not allowed to sing our songs. It was against the law to even gather in numbers more than four. Why? Because the federal government of Canada made it unlawful. The songs were connected to our ceremonies, to our language, and to our culture. Canada's goal was to assimilate us into Catholic patrons following the ways of Jesus instead of Kʷuləncutən (The Great Spirit).

The songs, along with the drum, have become my best friend. The songs have comforted me and others. Together we have travelled both locally and internationally to Peru and France. Wherever the songs and the drum call me I am there, and wherever I am called I go.… I do not own the songs. The songs and drum own me from a place that is from time immemorial. As long as I am living and breathing, I will sing. I will sing for those past that could sing or couldn't sing; I will sing for those present … for the ones who do not know the songs; I will sing for the future … for the ones coming … for those that will learn the songs. The circle will continue because I sing.

## JILL

When we sat together in Tkaronto to prepare our CATR presentation, Mariel shared a poem that she wrote. Its first stanza revolved in my head, colouring my reception of everything that my colleagues were sharing: "I am in a box/That surrounds me/And makes me stumble/When I Walk." "Where," she asks later, at the apex of the poem, "do I belong?"

## MARIEL

> Where do I belong?
> The white indian holding

Her granny's song
Oh God, Oh Creator
Why rip me in half?
Why do I suffer
While others laugh?
The song in me implores
Protect your mother earth
She needs your care
But my soul yearns for more
And begs to explore
The future
Wings spread
Waiting to soar

## JILL

"In the circle," I wanted to tell her. But in which circle? And when is a circle not a circle—but just a cleverly disguised "box" in which most speak at cross-purposes, while some never get to speak at all? As we talked, other questions presented themselves: How would we open? How might we most affectively braid our voices, so that the resultant reverberations might transform a polite audience of interested researchers who had come to observe and learn into a fully invested community of active witnesses? How might we affectively curate an encounter that would locate us all (presenters and witnesses) in space and time, deepening our relationships with place and with each other? How might we curate the space so as to defamiliarize the ubiquitous "circle" and architect an intermediary space through which presenter (host) and witness (visitor) might transit to meet each other in a relational hoop—wrought through affect and not through the arrangement of furniture in a room?

## DELPHINE

I tell the children that I teach, and my grandchildren, and my great-grand-children, "You know, all you have to do is listen." I remember that back then there were so many birds. My dad used to get up early in the morning and he'd say in the language, "You can hear the birds singing, and that's beauti-ful," so I used to love getting up early. I'd go outside just to hear the birds sing, and the frogs, it was like an orchestra, the small voices, the loud voices, there's rhythm to it, harmony. We had three or four types of grouse, and I would hear these wings flapping in the bush, and my dad would say, "That's the winter grouse." We used to hear coyotes and wolves, but after we grew up they kind of disappeared, no more wolves. We used to hear bears growl in the bush, and my dad would say, "That's a black bear." There was a little bird, a little grey one, I don't know the name of it and I don't even see those birds anymore, but anyway, this bird would make a nest every year in the spring and it would sing and sing and sing. I believe that's where songs come from. It was really, really nice hearing those animals, seeing them, and growing up with them. I believe that when you listen to everything, everything has a song, you can hear the song, you can hear the music, and I always think, "Is it because I'm musical?" Maybe, I don't know, but I can hear it, I can hear the rhythm, and that's beautiful.

## JILL

Resisting the arrangement of chairs in a circle, which has become a common-place choice for any gathering that includes Indigenous bodies or that alludes to Indigenous knowledge systems, we stood apart from our colleague-witnesses, facing the small island of chairs upon which they patiently awaited our CATR conference presentation. Moving through and around them, we called out and responded to each other (in words, in song, with flute, and with drum) from the cardinal directions, locating ourselves within the space and locating our audi-ence within a medicine wheel that we were physically mapping and vocally in-scribing. This opening ultimately expressed a key issue with which this research question concerns itself.

Mariel Belanger's poem unfolds within seven stanzas and speaks powerfully to the *dis-ease* experienced by so many Indigenous people as a consequence of a sus-tained, historic campaign of dislocation (ontological, epistemological, relational, and geographical). And throughout our opening, as Mariel delivered each stanza from the north (behind our audience), we responded from the south, from the east, from the west, from above, from below, and from the place where she/we stood, locating ourselves and our witnesses directionally and seasonally as we reflected, through spoken word and ancestral music, on the stages of life and the seasons of ceremony that govern the human condition.

## JOSEPH

For our workshop held at Simon Fraser University, I suggested using the "hand drum stick" tradition of inviting people to sing for the community. It's what we do at piciciwin (stepping into) dances back home in Treaty Six territory/kiskaciwan (Saskatchewan). The hand drum stick passing is a time-honoured ritual; I'm not aware of its beginning. What happens is that a designated co-ordinator referred to as an oskapewis (young apprentice) brings a hand drum stick and passes it on to the singing leader of the first group of invited piciciwin singers. This first group will sing four songs, then the stick will be passed on all night until all singing groups have been invited to sing.

I wasn't sure how this passing on of the hand drum stick ritual would be received. Participants responded and sang to their heart's content. That's a good sign. It means that the invited singers were open. And that's what Indigenous people who come from communal societies regard as there being a "spirit" or "ancestor" in the ceremonial gathering. It was definitely not about holding back. The stick went from person to person, perhaps with some anticipation and excitement. Maybe the participants didn't expect to be lead singers or to sing a song from their family or community. Yet, here we were in downtown Vancouver, awakening to the challenge of a time-honoured tradition practiced by all Indigenous Peoples from all over the world.

When my turn came, I took charge like you're supposed to because you know your songs and drum rhythms. You know how to ignite the fire in the circle. The "spirit" is with you whether you choose to know it or not. You're lifted and carried from the first song to the last. I don't even remember if I completed my four songs. I was on fire. Well, my energy was anyway. I was ready to be part of this ceremony and research into Indigenous sound.

## JILL

In introducing this project through an étude in seven directions, we managed, I believe, to craft a container within which to protect the work and through which to invite our auditors to actively join us in this endeavour. At the same time, we recognized that our settler colleagues are also struggling with the disease that comes from being "out of place," of being connected to *no* land. What profound mourning must reside in the settler psyche? This uninvited "guest" has never been condoled, never sought welcome at "the edge of the woods," and, therefore, never been properly welcomed. She has undergone no ceremony to establish kinship. And her grief (unrecognized by she herself and unaddressed) continues, as it has since contact, to fuel incalculable destruction. To locate and orientate this settler and to intervene upon a dis-ease that cuts across Indigenous and non-Indigenous experience, we applied the first fruits of our research, utilizing ancestral mechanisms to inscribe a healing circle with the resonance produced by our own instruments. Within this circle, we intended to re-*place* our witnesses in mindful relationship to the biota we share, to each other, and to the calling we all share as researchers in this historical moment.

## MANULANI

Ulu aʻe ke welina a ke aloha.

Here is what I learned with chanting this Hawaiian proverb within a diverse world of cultural sounds waiting to understand itself through trust, faith, and its own excellence. I now feel the mystic function of vowels and their purpose within my being, my heart, and within a transpatial space of sound shared with others. *Loving is the practice of an awake mind.* Who can say if it was the meaning of the words or the frequency of sound that electrified my heart? Are they not simultaneous? Is not *aloha* the centre of all ideas?

Chanting, singing, expressing sound in this unusual way changed everything for me, and for the first time I could feel, really feel, *resonance*—a touching of shared meaning with strangers because that is what we could all offer: our own excellence and faith that it would be brought forth for something useful. We became vowels in expansion, reaching from an inside-out knowing, to bring each other to the shores of our own shared *purpose.*

He imi naʻauao—this search for collective wisdom was an unexpected gift with sound practitioners from different continents, islands, and dispositions.

## JOSEPH

nêhiyawêwin-pîkiskwêwin (Cree language) is deliberately non-capitalized because it does not come from a hierarchical culture. "kakwi tâpawi" was a phrase the old men used with young people when I began singing the old songs from the Cree tradition. In nêhiyawêwin-pîkiskwêwin, this phrase means "sing in the way the song was introduced." At the time, I didn't know exactly what those two words meant.

I was attending university back in 1973 in Regina, Saskatchewan, when the nikamowin atayohkan (singing spirit) and this principle of singing and drumming with precision led me to understand the critical nature of paying attention. Songs were passed on from one generation to the next and often these songs would have been dreamt about or heard during sleep. The spirit of songs being passed on told me that someone no longer here on the earth had sung the song that I refer to as "old." My wanting to sing in the old Cree way was very strong. I didn't deny myself the opportunity to learn how to sing in the way my ancestors did long before I came into this world. I had to sing. I wanted to sing. In retrospect I now know that the nikamowin atayohkan had arrived as my guide and motivator. After 13 years of residential school and not hearing these old songs, I was in heaven. In my experience with the nikamowin atayohkan, it will enter into your life when you're ready to sing. At 20 years of age I needed an outlet, a method to express myself that would lift my mind, body, and spirit. I had experienced extreme pain and trauma at the hands of the residential school. Thank you, nikamowin atayohkan. You saved my life. Today, when I sit quietly, all the songs I have sung over the last 40 years come visiting in my mind now and then, and they still sound the same as I'd first heard them. This is how I understand and appreciate nikamowin atayohkan. kahkiyo niwahkomakanik! (For All My Relations)

## MANULANI

Ulu a'e ke welina a ke aloha.
Loving is the practice of an awake mind.
—Hawaiian proverb

Singing one line over and over and over to find resonance felt like swimming in my favourite stream and pond along Hilo Paliku. I had to catch my breath—it was that kind of beauty. Nurturing, delightful, rejuvenating. A secluded process filled with joy and secrets found in harmony. All of it unusual and familiar at the same time. To know myself through sound. Now, how to express that in ways that engage the fullness of Other to bring us to Self again, and again, and again.

Radical insight of mystical union experienced through vibrational correlations is indeed something to repeat, to know, to joy in!

I ka 'ōlelo no ke ola, I ka 'ōlelo no ka make.
In language there is life. In language there is death.
—Hawaiian proverb

Language is sound shaped by intentionality and all that entails with regard to context, continuity, and culture. Thus begin the lessons of place-based knowing and its linkages with the world of perception and the quality of depth found in vowel vibrations. All sounds shaped by the priorities of culture—*best practices of a group of people specific to place, over time.* It is found in our *practices*: dance, song, food, colour, oration, *sound.*

## VIRGINIE

Jill Carter shared with us the notion of "deep time," which I came to associate with the collective toning experience that Carolyn Kenny so generously guided us through on the first day of our retreat, and that later enabled us to delve into the depths of Manulani Aluli-Meyer's chant to embody what she named "practice of ritual engagement." I felt that we entered a sacred space and experienced deep time. Manu told us that infinity is encompassed in the vibratory quality of the sound "A" in Hawaiian culture, and Winston Wuttunee spoke about singing as a way of calling for our ancestors and asking them to join us so that we may experience the connection between the living past and the living present. This reminded me of Shawn Wilson's statement in *Research Is Ceremony*: "Bringing things together so that they share the same space is what ceremony is all about" (2008, p. 87). In the kekuli, Winston invited us to take a stick from the firewood and use it to drum on the large rocks lining the fire—he called these rocks the Grandfathers—to create rhythm as he sang. Through this simple but profound collective action emerging from our sitting together around the fire, we asked the Grandfathers to help us renew our commitment to honour and respect each other through transformative cultural practice holding the potential for reconciliation.

## JULIA

I don't have a prescription for how reconciliation can be achieved through cross-cultural, collective vocal practice, but I can testify to the profoundly *creative* environment that emerged, especially during the days of our retreat together. It was *creative* in the sense that new life was being generated. In our song sharing and sound making, there was a great variety of contours, textures, timbres, and densities. I am reminded of the overtones and harmonics that spontaneously rang out on top of the intervals we sang during collective toning at the retreat—led with warmth and grace by dear Carolyn Kenny. I am reminded of the presence of something (a sound, but is it something else too?) that was not issued from any *one* body, but rather emerged when one person's utterance interacted with those of all the others, an act achievable only through the concerted participation of a group of human beings. And I am reminded of another kind of polyphony that we created, not by voices sounded simultaneously, but rather by voices that were spun out over time, accumulating in the slow movement of the sharing circle. Voices that didn't disappear when their sound decayed, threads of utterance issued dialogically, as each individual spoke or sang not for him or herself, but in order to weave a new composite story, a resulting polyphony, out of all the different fibres we brought.

## WINSTON

I am a singer-nikamouyan. In Cree, nikamoun or nika-mo literally means to sing or eat. nika (neegan) refers to the one in front and mo means to eat. We feed you spiritually with song/food by the one in front, who leads us. Today in our UBC Okanagan workshop, I felt important and welcomed the chance when I was asked to add to the flow. It is good to work together to make something for the good of our brothers and sisters. To be with similar spirits is a gift I cherish. It was so fulfilling to be in a workshop where we breathed and talked and sang in an atmosphere that was totally safe, fun, educational, and reassuring. Music is my life and I see it is the life of many others, too.

## VICKI

This past summer our research community gathered again, and this time we spent many hours carefully co-creating acoustic ecologies in various localities and topographies. What a gift it was to play within landscapes of acoustic resonance moving from dissonance, to resonance, to harmonies inclusive of each and every voice. What astonished me most was that through this inquiry into the pedagogies of sound we drew near to the ancestors, or perhaps they drew near to us. Through our co-learning we were collectively cultivating the capacity to dwell within an acoustemology that is Indigenous to us all.

Recently I attended a ceremony for the passing of a Tsleil-Waututh Chief. What I witnessed throughout the ceremony was an acoustic enactment of the final canoe journey involving preparation, transformation, and the crossing over, followed by release, and finally being embraced by the ancestors, all this through the power of song. Various First Nations delegations stood with drums thundering, a mighty chorus singing their traditional songs, each creating their own unique acoustic ecology echoing within the longhouse. Some were songs of prayer, some were songs of celebration, some were songs for eagles to dance, soar, and ascend to. Lastly, the petals of multicoloured flowers were scattered over the sacred ground of our ancestors. It was a day of few words, rich in acoustic resonance, a sounding ceremony that offered songs of dignity and healing to all.

## MARIEL

I had a personal experience with song after being with the Elders of the Advisory Committee during our retreat this summer. I sang as I "paddled home" to an ancestral gathering place on the Spokane River. I heard my own voice return. I first felt it singing Manulani Aluli-Meyer's oli in the earth-covered winter home with Carolyn Kenny. On the Spokane River, I paddled across to the main village site where the community and guests gathered and visited, almost like we did at Komasket. I saw the shore and waited, lying in the canoe listening to the echoes reverberate around me, through the air, across the water, in my soul, and through my voice. Since time immemorial we have been engaging and embodying the ancestors as the story of our lives intertwines in concert with those around us. From these places on the Okanagan Trail I gathered the pieces of my spirit that were carried away downriver, forgotten and lost by old loves. Broken pieces put back in place. Sealed with new intentions, meant for new love.

## CAROLYN

If we choose to join the river on its journey, we understand that the river embraces all things. Does the river know the end point of its journey? Does it know what joys and sorrows it will meet along the way to its destination? We feel the animation of the world and our place in it. We know that we are all connected and related.

## AUTHORS' NOTES

Carolyn Kenny's words are from her 2014 article "The Field of Play: Ecology of Being in Music Therapy," featured in *Voices: A World Forum for Music Therapy*. We would like to thank Rune Rolvsjord, the journal's managing editor, for granting us permission to feature excerpts of this article in our co-authored chapter.

Our companion documentary film, edited by Mariel Belanger, can be found on the Institute for Community Engaged Research website: https://icer.ok.ubc.ca/research/.

## REFERENCES

Kenny, C. (2014). The field of play: Ecology of being in music therapy. *Voices*, *14*(1). doi. org/10.15845/voices.v14i1.737

Saul, J. R. (2009). Reconciliation: Four barriers to paradigm shifting. In *Response, responsibility, and renewal: Canada's truth and reconciliation journey* (pp. 309–320). Ottawa: Aboriginal Healing Foundation.

Simpson, L. (2008). Looking after Gdoo-naaganinaa: Precolonial Nishnaabeg diplomatic and treaty relationships. *Wicazo Sa Review*, *23*(2), 29–42.

Smith, S. (2016). Edge of the woods [Workshop]. Indigenous directors' initiative, Stratford Festival, September 1 to 6, 2016.

The Truth and Reconciliation Commission of Canada. (2015). *The final report of the Truth and Reconciliation Commission of Canada: Canada's residential schools; The legacy*. Ottawa: Author.

Wilson, S. (2008). *Research is ceremony: Indigenous research methods*. Halifax: Fernwood.

## CHAPTER 13

# How Did I Get Here? Retracing Steps to Enlighten an Obscured Research Journey

*by Anjali Helferty*

———

My name is Anjali Helferty. I am a mixed race woman of Indian and Irish descent. I am a climate activist, an academic, a partner and friend and sister and daughter, a doula, a baker, an activist drummer, and a cellist (of sorts). I currently live in Tkaronto/ Toronto, but have moved 12 times around Canada and the United States.

———

This chapter is an invitation to walk alongside a research process that was un-expected for me, but that I suspect tells an entirely ordinary story from its well-intentioned beginning to perplexed end. I began writing the chapter from a place of discomfort, with the goal of figuring out how I had made the decisions I had made and taken the steps I had taken. Now that I have finished this (round of) exploration, I am simultaneously glad to have this knowledge of my own processes and disturbed by how default modes of operating directed my actions throughout this research. I am left reflecting about the importance of building islands of support for Indigenist and decolonizing work within the vast ocean of settler colonial research institutions.[1]

I am a (sometimes) White-passing mixed race woman currently nearing the end of my PhD program. My mother grew up in Mombasa, Kenya, with her extended family and my father grew up in a farming community in the Ottawa Valley in Canada, where Irish roots are strong. I began identifying as an environmental activist as a child via a love of animals learned from my mother, who sends me anti-poaching petitions (and cat videos) to this day. My interest in climate change and fossil fuels most likely comes from my father, who spent his career in the oil industry. As a result of this work, my family moved from city to city every few years throughout my childhood. The past five years working on my PhD in Toronto are the longest that I have ever stayed in one place. My education has nearly exclusively taught me Western constructions of knowledge, although, like many mixed and diasporic people, my life experiences have included multiple cultures and worldviews. In my activist work, I was particularly drawn to coalition building between different communities; however, in retrospect, I can see that my ways of operational-izing this interest were most easily aligned with the White culture dominant in environmentalism.

Today, I am researching Indigenous-settler collaborative anti-pipeline campaign work in Canada.[2] I came to this topic after working in youth cli-mate change activist coalitions in Canada and the United States. The coalitions brought together organizations from environmental, environmental justice, and Indigenous movements to organize collective campaigns. It was work that I loved but that left me with many unanswered questions about why smart, thoughtful, dedicated young people sometimes found it so difficult to disrupt the racist and colonial dynamics prevalent in environmental activism (Gelobter et al., 2005). I entered the PhD program ready to explore these issues from a kind but critical perspective.

## BOOKENDS OF THE JOURNEY

I start this exploration with an excerpt from a paper I submitted for a course taught by Wanda Nanibush, an Anishinaabe-kwe from Beausoleil First Nation, in the fall of 2013 (my first semester in the program):

> As a non-Indigenous/settler activist researcher proposing to conduct research with Indigenous peoples in Canada, a colonial country, it is important to me to participate in decolonization through the process of this research and to ensure that I am in no way replicating colonial, hegemonic practices, as has been so common with research in the past and in the present day. (Helferty, 2013)

At the other end of this path is the following excerpt from my research proposal, submitted to my committee in September 2016:

> I will conduct this research primarily through unstructured, in-depth interviews, an appropriate choice when the research questions call for understanding participants' lived experiences (Hesse-Biber, 2007). An interview method is also a practical choice, because the research participants are geographically dispersed throughout central and eastern Canada. (Helferty, 2016b)

The contrast in content and tone between these two pieces of writing jumps out at me. I knew at the beginning of planning my research that I wanted to do decolonizing, participatory work that would be useful to participants while they were involved with it, not just as a result of the findings. How did I end up conducting almost entirely interview-based work in which I extracted information from participants and then walked away? At what junctures did this shift occur?

## DECOLONIZING RESEARCH?

Reflecting on this process makes me wonder what I thought "decolonizing" research meant in the first place. My introduction to Indigenist research methodologies was *Decolonizing Methodologies* (Smith, 2012), which informed my initial use of the language of decolonization. As I moved through my PhD, I learned about more perspectives on Indigenist research methodologies (including Hampton, 1995; Kovach, 2009; Simpson, 2011; Wilson, 2008) and engaged with questions of what it meant for research to be decolonizing. What I found most disruptive to my developing understanding of Indigenist research methodologies and decolonizing research was Tuck and Yang's (2012) article "Decolonization Is Not a Metaphor." This article turned on its head my previous perceptions of whether or not the research I was doing could be decolonizing when it was not directly supporting "repatriation of Indigenous land and life" (p. 21).[3]

I also learned a great deal about Indigenist methodologies from my supervisor, Dr. Jean-Paul Restoule, who is Anishinaabe from the Dokis First Nation. At the beginning of each class in our course on Indigenist research methodologies, Dr. Restoule would smudge to help us start the class in a good way. He encouraged us to locate ourselves within the research and reflect on how who we are and what we have experienced brought us to our current path. We talked a great deal in that class about what makes a methodology an Indigenist methodology, since there can be significant overlap in actual methods with, for example, participatory or feminist research.

Nearing the end of the semester, the course turned to discussions of spirit in relation to Indigenist research. As a result of these conversations, I learned that crucial to Indigenist methodologies is that they are coming from an Indigenous paradigm and that they are connected to spirit. The following excerpt from a response journal submitted to Dr. Restoule during the course illustrates this:

> I see in this article (Wilson & Restoule, 2010) two points—one that tobacco is about spirit (which leads me to think I maybe shouldn't mess around with tobacco until I have a better understanding of spirit),[4] and another that suggests a protocol of offering tobacco when you are "visiting." Perhaps, since I would be visiting in a way, it does make sense to offer tobacco even if I don't totally understand spirit. (A. Helferty, personal communication, March 1, 2015)

With only a glimpse of an understanding of the complexities involved, I concluded that it would not be right to say that I was using Indigenist methodologies, because I did not connect to spirit through an Indigenist paradigm. Reflecting on this decision many months later, I have a sense that I was backing away from making the effort to engage with Indigenist methodologies because they seemed to require too much of me to be able to do justice to in the limited context of PhD research. Sticking with the paradigm I had spent decades operating within was the easier path. I was inspired by people who had invested the time in learning and relationship building to use Indigenist methodologies, whether or not they felt that they were very familiar with them from the beginning of their research processes. However, I did not see how I could do this myself without giving up the few elements of research planning that I had together at the time (which, in retrospect, is perhaps part of the point).

At the time of proposal development, and with a strong desire to move forward with the project, I had taken the position that I was not conducting decolonizing research or using Indigenist methodologies. However, I thought I could still conduct an activist research project that would be useful for the participants involved, and that I could still do it in a way that was informed by Indigenous scholars. The following excerpt from my original research proposal, submitted in July 2016, illustrates my perspective at the time:

> The problem of documenting, textualizing, and stealing Indigenous knowledge is articulated by many Indigenous scholars (Simpson, 1999), and Indigenous peoples have been researched more than any other group in history (Smith, 2012). The research I propose is not "on" Indigenous peoples and does not ask about Indigenous knowledge; however, it does involve Indigenous people.... It is therefore important that I undertake this research with some knowledge of Indigenous research methodologies. (Helferty, 2016a)

I then listed a number of what I felt were guiding principles learned from Indigenous scholars that I could apply to my research. These included, for example, the importance of relationship and relational accountability (Wilson, 2008), that Indigenous knowledge is not generalizable but is particular to the place in which it is known (Restoule, 2004), and the need to be clear about personal and academic motivations for the research (Kovach, 2009). These works have much more complexity and depth than I just identified, and I look back at lists I made in my proposal with some discomfort. I also know that decades of Western education have taught me to extract key points and write them in lists, and this is what I did here.

Having decided that I was not using Indigenist methodologies, I turned to participatory action research (PAR) in order to investigate its potential fit for my research. It seemed an approach to research with a mix of settler and Indigenous participants that was respectful and appropriate, given areas of alignment between participatory and Indigenist methodologies (Kovach, 2009); however, I did not ultimately use participatory methods. Working to continue to understand how this happened, I will now describe three unexpected detours I took as I walked along this research path.

## DETOUR ONE: DOUBT

> Would I be okay with this if I wrote my dissertation and it turned into a book, and that was it? No, I don't think so. But do I think that the process of doing this research and turning over these questions with other people will result in them learning something that they can apply to their work? Yes. So maybe I can design a project that has a learning component but it's through examining questions together.... I wonder if there's anyone who would want to do this with me? (A. Helferty, personal communication, October 14, 2015)

As this excerpt from a research journal illustrates, I was invested in doing research where the process would be collaborative and useful for the participants while they were doing it. My focus on research that was useful during the process itself stemmed from my experience of the lack of conversation between activism and academia; I had a perhaps overly developed skepticism about the usefulness of research findings for the participants. At the same time, I was concerned about my ability to recruit participants for a participatory research project, given the time and effort involved. The contradiction I was facing was that I could not envision a scenario in which paid activists would commit to a participatory research project. My interest in the project was connected to paid activists in funded social movement organizations because of my own experiences and challenges in these environments. However, I knew that when I was a paid activist, I definitely would not have had the time or energy to add a research project to my already overtaxed schedule.

What I can reflect on now is that I never seriously considered changing the research participants to activists involved in primarily grassroots-based or volunteer organizations in Toronto, where it is possible I would have had more success gathering a small group to engage in a participatory research project.[5] I had also never thought through how difficult my interest in researching funded organizations would make it to have any kind of balance in terms of Indigenous and settler participation in the research, given the scarcity of Indigenous paid activists in anti-pipeline work as a result of current funding models and organizational priorities. Instead, I felt that a participatory approach was not practical, and that I needed to find a more sensible way to undertake the research.

I will take a minute here to reflect on how I was understanding and enacting "practical" and "sensible." My determination of what was or was not an available approach for this research was dependent on the context I was in, a doctoral program with deadlines and limited funding, and my worldview, which is informed by my

Western upbringing and experience in academic and activist settings. Although I was learning how to work from an Indigenist perspective, when in a time crunch, my default was to fall back on hunches or gut feelings about the right path forward.

Looking back at response journals I wrote for Dr. Restoule's class, I can see that I was thinking about how to do this research in a way that was respectful and appropriate as a settler, and theorizing about differences in where hunches might lead as a result of different worldviews:

> What if a non-Indigenous person wanted to do research with an Indigenous community, and was willing to spend so much time with that community (that the person presumably already had some connection to) that it's sort of as if the person is "adopted in." Is one of the differences between Indigenous and non-Indigenous researchers that a non-Indigenous person is so much less likely to take this kind of step? (A. Helferty, personal communication, February 2, 2015)

> I can't just follow my gut about what feels right or not. I have to notice the gut and then think it all through, and it's very confusing. (A. Helferty, personal communication, February 1, 2015)

Looking back at these research journals, I see that what limited me was not the ability to learn and see where differences in worldviews and associated priorities between Indigenous and settler researchers might lead us. It was the ability to apply this knowledge and critically interrogate my decisions when experiencing external pressures.

Instead, I created what felt like a workable compromise. In order to maintain at least some of the participatory elements of the work while engaging with paid activists, I decided to see if I could find one organization to collaborate with. I thought that if I received official approval from an organization to do this work, I could at least engage in conversations with staff to ensure relevant research questions and get feedback on the analysis. It would not be an entirely participatory project, but it would maintain some participatory elements and would meet my interest in working with paid activists. It seemed like an ideal plan.

## DETOUR TWO: DISAPPOINTMENT

I had an organization in mind that was ideally suited to work with for this project. I was able to connect with them through my networks, and submitted a short proposal to them. The proposal was approved much more quickly than

I anticipated and my contact person with the organization, whom I had briefly worked with in the past, was supportive of the project. In the proposal, I included elements about meeting with organizational staff members to plan the research together and ensure it aligned with their priorities, and to conduct a four- to eight-hour collective analysis process with a group of staff members using arts-based methods. I was excited about the project, and was surprised and relieved to find a research site so quickly.

I was planning to work on my research proposal over the subsequent six months, which would have resulted in its completion right at the end of my third year in the program. I thought this provided plenty of opportunity to meet with the organization two or three times to ensure that the proposal was developing in a way that worked well for them. However, as I worked on the proposal, I was unable to connect with key members of the organization. Coming up against academic deadlines, I put the proposal together with little organizational input and submitted it to my supervisory committee. I continued to try to meet with members of the organization's leadership team to confirm that what I had proposed was appropriate and to make any needed adjustments, but was never able to get on their calendars. I began to wonder if they were really ready to participate in the project; I believed they had the interest, but I began to think they may not have capacity or it may not be a priority.

After a few months of little communication, and only one meeting where no one able to make decisions was present, I asked my contact if they really thought the organization was willing to participate in the project. The next week, they told me they were not able to participate.

I am not blaming the organization for backing out of the project, and I am glad they did so before we had begun to conduct the research. That said, I was very disappointed when they decided not to participate. That they approved the short proposal so quickly and without any clarifying questions may have been an indication that they were not clear on the extent of what I was asking and offering. I was trying to work in a way that was relational and would support their work, but perhaps something failed in the translation to organizational language. What was clear, however, was that I had a vision of their level of involvement in the project that was either not aligned with what they anticipated and/or not aligned with what they ultimately found feasible.[6]

## DETOUR THREE: URGENCY

On the whole, I've been lucky during my PhD program that the factors that delayed my PhD work have been nearly entirely within what are considered "normal" ups and downs of doctoral progress, perhaps with the exception of four frigid and exhausting weeks on strike (and the unanticipated months of recovery/attempts to find work and leave the degree) in the winter of my second year. I had thought I was just managing to get by when I completed my proposal at the very end of my third year in the program. However, when the organization decided not to participate, I found myself in fourth year without any research plan, and missed the departmental deadline to have my proposal approved and achieve candidacy. Funding for my program was going to run out and I hadn't even started my research. I didn't even know what my research was going to be.

Once again at a turning point, I had decisions to make. I could have reached out to other organizations to work with and started to develop a proposal with them. I could have prioritized the relational and participatory elements of the research and started from there to determine next steps. In that moment, however, these felt like risky paths. I could easily, once again, find myself without a research site. I quickly wrote up a new proposal in which, looking back, it is clear that I decided to prioritize getting started with the research over any of the principles I had learned about or goals I had established.

In my new proposal, I removed any attempt to do participatory work that asked more of participants, but I would also offer more to them in the process. My new project was focused on individuals rather than organizations, and my plan was to travel around the country interviewing Indigenous and settler anti-pipeline activists and land defenders.[7] I was determined to get started with the research and get on with the degree.

## LOST

In early 2016, I took a few trips to conduct interviews. I had decided to focus the research on the Energy East pipeline, so I selected locations accordingly: Montreal, Ottawa, Saint John, Fredericton, Regina, Winnipeg, and Kenora. I conducted interviews with thoughtful and brilliant people working to stop the pipelines, most of whom I had never met before. While I had learned that it was important to conduct research that was mutually beneficial (Absolon, 2011), I was not clear how to act on this. I only met with people once, or occasionally twice, and they were geographically dispersed, so I was not able to participate in their work on an ongoing basis. Instead, during the interviews I offered to stay in touch, to support their strategic planning, to participate in an upcoming event. I really felt like I was back with my community, which I had lost connection to since burning out of activism in 2011. The trips were sometimes exhausting, and timelines were rushed due to travel grant restrictions, but I also found them energizing and restoring.

It was when I was back home at my desk that I suddenly felt the contradiction of having implemented a research method that was misaligned with the theory I had learned about good ways to do research. I had attempted to incorporate a partial approach to Indigenist methodologies that, on reflection, did not really serve the participants. I had made offers of support in an attempt to be in relationship, but they were not offers of support that participants were likely to take me up on because they did not really know me. Even though I felt we were part of the same community, and perhaps they did as well, we did not have a common current context. The following excerpt is from this time of uncertainty. It is not comfortable to reflect on this experience and I feel vulnerable sharing it, but it shows an important moment in this process:

> I've been reviewing interview transcripts to send out to research participants and I feel sad. This is hard to write because I'm wondering if I've done something wrong—if I've promised or implied something I don't know how to deliver, or that maybe I know how to deliver but am unwilling to spend the time and energy and money to do it. I know this research is grounded in my movement experiences and the relationships I built with people during activist work. I think about those people all the time, and feel connected to them even if I haven't been in touch for years. Those relationships are complicated, but they have a long foundation and I don't worry about them. But what about my new relationships? These new relationships that I'm building with people now— people who I'm asking to trust me, to give me their time, to tell me stories. If I see them once and say I'll be back, I'll follow up, what does that mean if I live across the country? Is there a way to ground research in relationships if the people these relationships are with are in many different places? Is there a way to ground the research in relationships with land when I don't feel connected to land, and don't spend enough time in any place to feel connected? (A. Helferty, personal communication, August 14, 2017)

Intent on moving forward despite my discomfort, I began to analyze the data and formulated follow-up questions for several participants. They generously offered additional thoughts, often quite extensively. The follow-up emails and conversations were incredibly interesting, but I realized that my timing was wrong—I needed to analyze the data to find a clearer focus before I followed up. In an effort to alleviate my own anxiety about not being in relationship with the participants, I had unnecessarily asked more of them. I got back in touch with some other participants to see if I could visit again or could support their work in another way, and received positive but vague responses that did not result in any action.

In my attempt to feel like I was doing this research in a way that was reciprocal, I ended up asking the participants to do more work and give me more time. I have twice been interviewed for other gradute student research, and when I participated in these projects I was not offered longer-term support and I did not feel that there was a problem with the relationship. I had been asked to do something (give an interview), had agreed to do it, and had done it. While I would have preferred to hear back from them about the outcomes of the research, I was not expecting them to suddenly be involved in other aspects of my work or life. Neither were the participants of my research—because it was neither Indigenist nor participatory. Fortunately, I fairly quickly realized that I was attempting to stay in touch to make myself feel better, not for the research or for the participants, and ended the outreach.

I experienced another significant cause for concern when reflecting on my research process. I found it fairly easy to schedule interviews with settler environmentalists and fairly difficult to schedule them with Indigenous land defenders and activists. Even after removing my criteria of paid activists, I was unable to get anywhere close to approximately equal numbers of Indigenous and settler research participants. In my first round of research, I interviewed three Indigenous and twenty settler participants. This presented a significant issue for me: How could I say I was doing research on Indigenous and settler relationships without having more Indigenous participants? This sounds like a rhetorical question, but I was genuinely asking myself whether this could be done. With the guidance of my committee, I concluded it could not.

In this moment, I was left with a dilemma that was different from those experienced during my planning. I had already conducted a significant amount of research and had learned a lot from the participants. I wanted to do something that would serve them in their work, and that was appropriate for who I am and who they are. Rather than try to answer research questions about relationships that would have required more Indigenous participants in the study, I realized that I could answer questions about settler experiences in their efforts to work in collaboration with Indigenous Peoples and communities. The desire to do good work together was incredibly present in the interviews with settlers, and I felt that centring my research on settler efforts to change their individual and organizational actions, as someone who had struggled with this myself, was an appropriate path forward. This approach also enabled me respond to calls for settlers to support each other to be in better relationship with Indigenous Peoples.

## AN IMPERFECT BUT WORKABLE PATH FORWARD

It continues to confound me that I could plan so intensively for a project focused on relationships and collaboration, and undertake research largely disconnected from these very processes. The path that I thought would extend "naturally" from good intentions to aligned actions was much more obscure than I anticipated. As much as I think of myself as a participatory-oriented person, it seems that ultimately my default mode (likely learned from years of working in activist organizations) is Get It Done. Now.

While there are moments when I really regret the decisions I've made (or, perhaps, the lack of thoughtful decision-making), I believe that I have found an imperfect but workable path forward. Rather than research relationships between Indigenous and settler anti-pipeline activists, I can research the settler experience of engaging in these relationships. Much of the problematic behaviour in the context of attempts to collaborate comes from settlers, and many settler activists are striving to make changes and are enthusiastic to learn what comes of the project.

There are a few other lessons I've learned in this project that seem obvious after the fact, but were not clear to me until I began to reflect from a place of discomfort. First, I have realized that I am thinking about my participants much more than they are thinking about me.[8] I give a passing thought to the studies for which I was interviewed, but they hardly keep me up at night. I think it is safe to assume that there is a similar dynamic at play with the participants in my research—that they thought I was a decent enough person and were happy to meet me, but that they then quite quickly got on with their own busy lives. No need to have an overblown sense of my own importance in their day-to-day lives!

Second, I have realized the value in getting this project done so I can return something useful back to the participants, and now understand that this is a valid way to be in a reciprocal relationship. Analyzing this research and communicating findings is difficult work. When the participants tell me they want to see the results and appreciate that I am doing this study, I can believe them. So, I will finish this, and make it readable, and write a summary, and organize webinars or meetings or conversations or whatever would be helpful to bring the results back to the participants in a way that works for them.

Finally, I have realized that I do not need to invent a reason to be in touch with the participants, like asking a follow-up question or offering to support their strategic planning. I am re-entering this community after some time away, and I can be in touch with people as a fellow activist and human. We can have relationships outside and adjacent to the research.

## REFLECTING ON THOUGHTFULNESS

As PhD students, our professors are constantly reminding us that the PhD cannot be everything we ever wanted to research, that this is a starting place. This is difficult to internalize when it seems they are reflecting on their own experiences, whereas most of us currently in PhD programs will never become faculty. That said, whether this PhD is the first or the only research project I undertake, the time I have taken to reflect on this experience will inform my future work in activism, research, or both. I will be more conscious, moving forward, to identify and question my ways of operating in the world, and to be aware of what I am letting slip when I am in a rush.

Revisiting the work of Indigenous scholars, I am reminded that key to whether or not this is relational, reciprocal research doesn't depend on whether I support participants' strategic planning or travel across the country to show up to one of their meetings. It depends on whether the research comes back to participants in a way that is useful to them, and whether they are able to apply and use the research in ways that are relevant for their own work and lives (Kovach, 2009). These attributes do not necessarily make this decolonizing research, but it is research that was appropriate for me to do in this time and in these places. The importance of research that is useful to participants was always foundational to this process, and continues to be today. It is in this circling back and connecting with participants about the outcomes of the research, and in our future work as fellow activists, that I can continue to be in relationship with them.

## ACKNOWLEDGEMENTS

I would like to thank Velta Douglas and Lauren Spring for their feedback on earlier drafts of this chapter, the editors for bringing these stories together, and my supervisor, Dr. Jean-Paul Restoule, for his kindness, generosity, and support throughout this research process. I would also like to thank the members of the Indigenous Inquiries Circle at the International Congress of Qualitative Inquiry, from whom I have learned a great deal over the past few years.

## NOTES

1. In this paper, I use the term *Indigenist research* to mean research stemming from Indigenous paradigms, and to delink research methodologies from researcher identities (Simpson, 2004; Wilson, 2007).

2. I use the terms *Indigenous* and *settler* throughout this chapter in a way that can seem like a binary: that people are either Indigenous or settlers, and that all non-Indigenous people are settlers. As a mixed race woman whose presence on Turtle Island is the result of various colonial systems working on and through my ancestors, I know that identities are complicated and that the ways different people or groups of people arrived to this land are divergent.

3. Many of the other scholars I mention here talk about decolonizing research through methods and methodologies, and what *decolonizing* means in this context continues to be a topic of discussion. In highlighting Tuck and Yang's (2012) assertions about decolonization, I am not intending to contradict the use of the term in various other ways.

4. I left this phrasing as I originally wrote it, but am finding the flippant tone of "mess around with" quite uncomfortable to read as I write this chapter. I want to offer apologies for this lack of respect for tobacco and ceremony.

5. This is not to suggest that unpaid activists are not busy! I am primarily reflecting that activists not in paid positions in funded social movement organizations may sometimes have more flexibility with how they choose to spend the time they have available for activist work.

6. Staff members from this organization and I are on good terms, and they have remained supportive of the study.

7. Most settler people and some Indigenous people working to stop pipelines call themselves activists, but not all. Some Indigenous people call themselves land defenders or water protectors to foreground relationship to land. In this chapter, I use terms to reflect these preferences, while knowing that none of the terms perfectly represents all members of the groups I am referencing.

8. I realized months after writing this that a research participant said this to me in an interview when reflecting on her collaborative experiences—so thanks to Teika Newton for this wisdom.

## REFERENCES

Absolon, K. E. (2011). *Kaandossiwin: How we come to know*. Winnipeg: Fernwood.

Gelobter, M., Dorsey, M., Fields, L., Goldtooth, T., Mendiratta, A., Moore, R., ... Torres, G. (2005). *The soul of environmentalism: Rediscovering transformational politics in the 21st century*. Oakland, CA: Redefining Progress.

Hampton, E. (1995). Memory comes before knowledge: Research may improve if research-ers remember their motives. *Canadian Journal of Native Education, 21,* 46–54.

Helferty, A. (2013). *Treading unsteady ground: Conducting activist research with Indigenous Peoples as a settler researcher.* Unpublished manuscript, Ontario Institute for Studies in Education, University of Toronto.

Helferty, A. (2016a). *A new kind of environmentalism: Unlearning colonial practices in environ-mental activism.* Unpublished manuscript, Ontario Institute for Studies in Education, University of Toronto.

Helferty, A. (2016b). *Untitled research proposal.* Unpublished manuscript, Ontario Institute for Studies in Education, University of Toronto.

Hesse-Biber, S. N. (2007). The practice of feminist in-depth interviewing. In S. N. Hesse-Biber (Ed.), *Feminist research practice: A primer* (pp. 111–148). Thousand Oaks, CA: Sage.

Kovach, M. (2009). *Indigenous methodologies: Characteristics, conversations, and contexts.* To-ronto: University of Toronto Press.

Restoule, J.-P. (2004). *Male Aboriginal identity formation in urban areas: A focus on process and context.* Doctoral dissertation, Ontario Institute for Studies in Education, University of Toronto.

Simpson, L. (2011). *Dancing on our turtle's back: Stories of Nishnaabeg re-creation, resurgence and a new emergence.* Winnipeg: Arbeiter Ring.

Simpson, L. R. (1999). *The construction of traditional ecological knowledge: Issues, implications and insights.* Winnipeg: University of Manitoba.

Simpson, L. R. (2004). Anticolonial strategies for the recovery and maintenance of Indig-enous knowledge. *American Indian Quarterly, 28*(3), 373–384.

Smith, L. T. (2012). *Decolonizing methodologies: Research and Indigenous Peoples* (2nd ed.). London: Zed Books.

Tuck, E., & Yang, K. W. (2012). Decolonization is not a metaphor. *Decolonization: Indigene-ity, Education, and Society, 1*(1), 1–40.

Wilson, D. D., & Restoule, J.-P. (2010). Tobacco ties: The relationship of the sacred to re-search. *Canadian Journal of Native Education, 33*(1), 29.

Wilson, S. (2007). Guest editorial: What is an Indigenist research paradigm? *Canadian Journal of Native Education, 30*(2), 193.

Wilson, S. (2008). *Research is ceremony: Indigenous research methods.* Halifax: Fernwood.

# CHAPTER 14

# Tentsitewatenronhste: We Will Become Friends Again

*by Kawennakon Bonnie Whitlow and Vanessa Oliver*

———

Kawennakon Ni: yonkya'ts (My name is Kawennakon). My English name is Bonnie Whitlow. Wakskarewake (I am Bear Clan). Kanyen'kehaka niwakonhwentsyo:ten (I am Mohawk woman). Ohsweken nitewake:non (I come from Six Nations). Rawennahatyes ronwa:ya'ts ne ri:yen (My son's name is Rawennahatyes). He doesn't have an English name, because he isn't English.

My name is Vanessa Oliver. I'm a settler woman who grew up in Bobcaygeon on the territories of the Anishnaabeg people. I am thankful for their care and respect for the land, the people, and all of our relations. I was raised on those territories by my dad and my grandma with a lot of love from family and friends. I am trained as an academic through colonial institutions, but I have also had the good fortune to develop relationships with Indigenous people who have generously told me their stories and shared their knowledge. And one of those stories comes from, or maybe becomes, the TAG project that we built and worked on and talk about here.

———

The TAG project is an Indigenous-led research project that is infused with the spiritual power of dreamtime, includes elements of prophecy (the Eagle and the Condor), and follows a path of practice that was governed by the Spirit World or Ancestors. For our team, TAG was an experiment in both faith and consent, learning to navigate the world according to Indigenous ways of knowing. TAG is a project that involves Indigenous youth from communities within Six Nations, and Indigenous and non-Indigenous youth from the surrounding communities and Wilfrid Laurier University. Together, we participated in cultural healing and arts practice workshops to create community graffiti murals, one in Brantford (at the university) and one on Six Nations, exploring the interwoven themes of identity, healing, friendship, and cultural pride. This chapter is a conversation between the co-investigators on our team that uses storytelling as a vehicle to traverse the unique journey that led to the creation of these two beautiful murals. This conversation demonstrates the ways in which the murals and, indeed, the project itself, reflect Haudenosaunee teachings shared in ceremony and in dreamwork. By focusing in on various pieces of our research process, we talk through what reconciliation through research might look like.

**Kawennakon:** Okay. So where do we start?

**Vanessa:** I think we start where we always start.

**Both:** With the dream.

**Kawennakon:** Okay. I think it's important to come back to the importance of dreaming in Haudenosaunee culture later. There's no corollary in the settler academy, so how do we create a bridge between our culture and theirs? For us, a dream or vision takes complete precedence and completely changes your future path and the paths of those with whom you share it. In settler culture, dreams are dismissed as irrelevant and unimportant. The only way to bridge this is for us to show you. Back to you and I sharing and manifesting the dream.

The dream came to me after having visited with the Mapuche muralists, who were in Canada to paint a mural in Kitchener. They asked to meet the Onkwehonwe (The Original People, or Indigenous People) of Canada, who were reconnecting with their ancestral teachings despite colonial disruption, as this was to be the theme of their mural. I was asked to arrange a meeting with the people of Six Nations.

We invited them to Six Nations for supper and then stayed up late telling stories, singing songs, and sharing dances. Then they returned to Kitchener, leaving us with an invitation to visit them at "the wall" to see the mural and learn to spray-paint. When we arrived, it was lunch and they were finishing a presentation in the back room of a nearby café.

At the end of their talk, a woman stood up and asked, "If you are all artists in your own right, how do you collaborate on large mural projects like this?" Gabriel, one of the artists, explained that after they listened to the stories, all of the members of the collective go back and get out their notepads and begin to sketch. They generally find that the same imagery is occurring to all of them at the same time. They simply put the pieces together. However, sometimes they find one guy is limping way off to the left and drawing something completely different from everybody else. When that happens, they all join him and limp along so that he may complete his vision.

His simple story pierced my heart. *That* is Indigenous practice. That is Indigeneity. As I was coming home, I was thinking about all the gifted and created youth in our community who long to express themselves through the arts but don't know how to get started, or think that art is a waste of their time. I wanted them to meet these young men who were travelling the world sharing their gift with so many different nations of people. I wanted them to see how they could do the same thing and live their lives through their art. I wanted them to see what's possible. I wished they could see a path that would allow their gifts to manifest.

That night in dreamtime, I was flying across the land. I could hear the whipping of the wind in my ears and feel the cool breeze blowing and pushing my whole body. A feeling of separation, lightness, flight, and travel. Sometimes I fight this separation in my dreams and sometimes I just allow it to happen. I have come to recognize dream signs like this as a call to pay close attention. I know that our Ancestors are about to show me something important.

That night I found myself flying over the landscape down in the desert by the Navajo territories as I flew over the canyon. I saw hundreds of people who were climbing up on the canyon wall. I could see they were on ladders. I flew down into the canyon behind them and I noticed that they were Shakotinenyo:yaks, the little people wearing the traditional dress from all over the world. You could see very old-school Asian clothing, Viking clothing, Kanyen'kehaka and Navajo clothing; hundreds of nations were represented. I flew up closer to the wall and noticed they were chipping and spray-painting. In my dream I was offended. I thought, why do that to a sacred space?

I flew closer to investigate. I noticed that their ladders were made of old wood and tied together with sinew and, in anger, I flew back to the other side of the canyon and stopped in mid-air. I turned around. When I looked back there was this incredible, sparkling, crystallized image on the wall of Mother Earth. In the dream, she was lying down. At that point, I was sitting up in bed saying, "I want to do that."

My dream had a sparkling quality, incandescent. This is another dream sign that tells me I've been given a message. If I've been given a message, then I don't have a choice. I have to act on it. I had the dream on a Friday and on Monday or Tuesday we met. I was asked to speak at Laurier's workshop about doing research in Native communities. You introduced yourself and said you did arts-based healing research with youth. It was a sign.

I don't always immediately know what my dreams mean. Sometimes I get it wrong at first and then the message reveals itself over time. Sometimes it's not for me, or not just me, but is meant to be shared with someone else. Then, I am the vessel that carries the story and each person can hear a message that is just for them. I have been very fortunate to have many great teachers who share their dream knowledge with me.

**Vanessa:** Yes. You and I met at that forum about doing research in and with Indigenous communities. I'd been doing work in the years previous with the Taking Action project, which was partnered with the Native Youth Sexual Health Network. I had some incredible Haudenosaunee teachers who taught me so much about working in an Indigenous context. But when you and I met, I was new to Laurier and on Six Nations territory and wanted to learn more about Six Nations specifically. So, as we've talked about many times, it wasn't by coincidence that we happened to be in the same room at the same time. You asked me to come and meet you in your office because you had an idea you wanted to talk about.

**Kawennakon:** I always like to reflect on my feelings that day (*laughter*). I had never been given a message that was to be shared with (*both laughing*) this blonde-haired, blue-eyed representative of a settler nation. So, I second-guessed, even though I know to just go with the flow of the universe. I couldn't help but question that. I mean I was…

**Vanessa:** …understandably concerned.

(*laughter*)

**Kawennakon:** An odd experience for me, but I thought, "If this is who the universe gives me then okay, I'll do it. So, I extended the invitation to come and talk.

**Vanessa:** Yes. Which felt like a tremendous amount of responsibility for me (*laughing*). Because I recognized that it was a privilege and having known you only a little bit before that time, I was also surprised that you put your trust in me. We met at your office and you told me that dream, which anybody hearing it, or reading it in this case, couldn't help but be completely affected by. It's visceral and emotional and the weight of it and the importance of it were clear to me from the outset. But the question was, of course, okay, so we need to make this happen, how do we make it into research so that we can get the funding to manifest the dream? And this is one of the places where the research as a reconciliation piece becomes very frustrating.

(*laughter*)

**Kawennakon:** Yes. Is that government grant process really reconciliation? Come on.

(*laughter*)

**Vanessa:** Exactly. Money and templates and top-down structures. Doesn't sound anything like it.

**Kawennakon:** The experience of it wasn't really reconciliatory.

**Vanessa:** We had the option of applying for Tri-Council grants because that was the kind of money we were going to need. We wanted to bring the mural team from Chile, which was going to be a significant cost. We needed to bring them and host them here for a month or so to do the work—not to mention the cost of paint and machinery and equipment for massive works of art! And we wanted the art to be astounding, like it was in Kawennakon's dream. The murals had to be big and bright and bold and they needed to involve youth from Indigenous and non-Indigenous communities. We sat down and thought about what we would actually do as a research project that would make all these things possible: involve the youth, involve the artists, be led by Six Nations, be driven by Haudenosaunee ways of knowing. Trying to fit Haudenosaunee ways of knowing into this academic box that, you know, is built in the image of settler colonialism was probably the most difficult part. In order to write what we needed to write to impress upon people that this was academic research, we, as we've come to say, kind of had to suck the life out of the dream. The dream was absolutely critical, but it all but disappeared from the 10,000 characters allotted in the online application or the limited drop-down menu choices in the online CV.

(*laughter*)

**Kawennakon:** It did not feel reconciliatory at all. In order for us to fit into the settler colonial spaces—the institutions and even the Tri-Council grants process—we essentially have to suck the life out of our work and create a dead, clinical description for our research. When I read the final version of the grant application approved for funding, it was lifeless and academic. If you had come to me with that and asked me to participate, I would have refused to be involved with it.

**Vanessa:** Right? It was a completely assimilated rendering of the dream.

**Kawennakon:** We had to cut off all of our own beautiful edges and curves to create this square peg to fit into that square hole. It was soul crushing at times. But it was also useful to see how the whole process works.

**Vanessa:** Yes. I think we tried to do a few things that mattered. For example, the letters of support that came not just from the elected council, but also from traditional council. I think really importantly for this project, making it clear that although I was the academic lead or "principal investigator," which is a term that we could critique all day, I was not leading the process—the dream was and then the community was. I was there to make the logistical pieces happen. My name and my credentials were important to getting the funding to make the dream a reality, but your name, your experience, your life, and your teachings were the most important part. Both of our names needed to be at the top of that grant, not just mine. That was a symbol of the type of partnership that we had and needed to have and wanted to have, but even that was not without its problems.

(*both laughing*)

**Kawennakon:** It's important to note all of the bureaucratic and institutional barriers that were placed before us and how access to the halls of power and funding were completely closed off to Onkwehon:we who don't have PhDs, and how Indigenous communities are in many ways closed to non-Onkwehon:we researchers. I didn't have the academic credentials and you didn't have community credentials. Neither community recognized each other's definition of expertise.

I really want to include (*laughter*) my naïveté at what I was asking you to do. You know? Just innocently asking, "Let's do this project, what do you say?" I had no idea how much work went into writing these grants, doing the finances, administration, meetings, hiring research assistants, and so much more.

Despite the fact that the grant application was rejected the first time we submitted it and it scored almost last, 28th of 30, I never doubted. It would be approved, the ancestral dimension was saying, "We want this thing to happen and we're going to open up the doors if you, Kawennakon, would just trust us, and just read the signs that we put in front of you."

I also want to share a story that reveals the nature of the grants process. At a language colloquium in Toronto, an Onkwehon:we lady stood up and proclaimed that she couldn't get SSHRC or Tri-Council funding because she did not have the requisite academic credentials. I was genuinely surprised, because we had just been approved. I didn't know that we were doing something new or different. Several people mentioned they were denied access. I had to come back and ask you some questions about how I had been approved as a co-investigator. You explained the struggle you experienced trying to put the project through with my name on it. I was surprised to learn how you had protected me from the pushback you faced. Yet you emphasized co-leadership and refused to remove me from the ownership of the project, which finally received approval.

**Vanessa:** My learning from the Native Youth Sexual Health Network told me that this is what it means to be a continuing ally working with Onkwehon:we people: if you're doing work with Indigenous people, it's Indigenous-led, end of story. To me, a White person in neocolonial Canada, reconciliation means taking a huge step back and humbling yourself. It's doing a lot of unglamorous work and building trust. A lesson I learned early on, also from Haudenosaunee people, is that you have one mouth and two ears, so you should listen twice as much as you speak. I think in the case of White folks in this particular historical moment, as it should have been originally, the lesson is to listen and to realize you're not the expert—you're a learner and will always be a learner. Respect sovereignty and show up when you're invited. Much more listening, a lot of visiting, and very little talking. What that meant for me, here, in this case, was that your voice was the loudest, your community was the loudest, and I played more of a support and administration role. Having your name and my name written together on equal terms was important. We had other checks and balances for this, too. I think this is happening more often now, but Six Nations was one of the first communities to have an independent research ethics board. The same thing happened with ethics approval, where we had Haudenosaunee approval before we could get the university approvals, and that's how it should work. And, again, I don't think that process is the same at all universities. In terms of the question, are we really in a space of reconciliation yet, the answer is no, we still have a very long way to go if there's a rule, for example, that an Indigenous person without a PhD shouldn't be allowed to be a co-principal investigator on a project that's happening in their community. The project was born of your dream, your vision, your ancestors. Why would I be the one to claim it?

**Kawennakon:** Right. It wasn't even really mine. I was simply the human vehicle for ancestral desire, right? It was shown to me and, if I didn't do my human work to manifest it, then that idea would have moved on to somebody else. I was so lucky to have been able to follow the signs on a well-lit path.

**Vanessa:** Right. In terms of thinking about ways of knowing, that individualism comes up over and over again in the academy. It's also rooted in the academic culture. That individualistic drive is nowhere to be found in Haudenosaunee ways of knowing. That's what we wanted to avoid in the project and that's what it really meant to have the leadership coming from Six Nations. Because from the very outset the Haudenosaunee way of seeing has to be structured into the project. You have to build it in from the ground up; it's not something you can add on later or do some consultation on. It has to be built that way in its foundation.

**Kawennakon:** Yeah, you just can't slap brown on some existing program in the university and call it Onkwehon:we. It has to be Onkwehon:we at its core, the very essence. The ground and the foundations all have to be Indigenous.

**Vanessa:** The Eagle and the Condor prophecy is another perfect example of how difficult it was to put the essence of this work into grant-speak. That was a story that we wanted to highlight in the grant and there was just no way to put it in, although it was a crucial piece in many ways. After the dream, the Eagle and the Condor prophecy was the next most important story.

**Kawennakon:** In the Southern territories, the Eagle and the Condor prophecy says that long ago human societies divided and followed separate paths to different places, some North and some South. The North is represented by the Eagle and the South by the Condor. Eventually, when the time or moment called for the people to come back together, the people of the North and the South would reconnect to bring forward an era of peace and prosperity for the entire human family. What I found amazing about the whole process is that the Eagle and the Condor was a part of our own discussions that were just you and I in the beginning and I don't remember ever talking about it outside of that.

**Vanessa:** No, I don't either.

**Kawennakon:** I found it so comforting that it appeared in this final mural without any conversation about it. The way that the artists captured the cultural mingling and the reconnection in one piece; the Eagle and the Condor flying in the background, the two medallions in Sky Woman's hair—one represents their sacred plants in the South, the other represents our sacred plants in the North. The piece is just so culturally dense.

At the grand opening of the Youth and Elders building in Six Nations, I learned Dave General had also created a stone monument in honour of Tom Longboat at the front entrance. Unbeknownst to the entire community, on the back side of his piece was the Eagle and the Condor prophecy. I found it serendipitous that the prophecy manifested twice, at the front and the back of the building. That's much more than coincidence. It's confirmation that we fulfilled our human duty to the original vision.

**Vanessa:** It's amazing! And so those are all thoughts on creating the project, trying to get it funded, and the barriers to reconciliation that are placed in our way by institutional and systemic barriers. Now we should talk about the process and the project itself so that folks have a sense of what it actually was and why that prophecy is so crucial. We invited the Alapinta muralists from Chile to work with Onkwehon:we and non-Onkwehon:we youth on creating graffiti art murals that would be visual representations of what the young people would learn from experiential workshops hosted in Six Nations. Several of the Alapinta muralists are Mapuche people (Indigenous people from what is now called Chile). They brought Silvia Ancan Painemilla with them. Silvia is a Mapuche community leader working on sovereignty, reclamation, language, and education for her people. The South American delegation was the three artists, their cultural producer, Rodrigo, and Silvia, who came from the Mapuche community of Kompu Lof. Silvia has done so much work in her community around reclamation of language and culture and has fought politically in a number of ways both on micro and macro levels for the sovereignty of the Mapuche people. When they came here, they were working very closely with people in Six Nations doing similar work. That was an additional layer to the project—while it was a research project that was working with youth, there was also this separate piece where two communities that had experienced colonization in similar ways, thousands and thousands of miles apart, came together to talk about the original ways of knowing. While the project was at one time about the youth and the art and the workshops that taught young people about the beauty and importance of Haudenosaunee culture, it was also about international partnerships between Indigenous people.

**Kawennakon:** Yes, different levels of reconciliation, not just between a settler nation and the Onkwehonwe, but also a reconnection of ancient trade roots from the North to the South, a different form of reconciliation.

**Vanessa:** We sucked the life out of the beautiful idea to get the money that allowed us to do all of this work. Then we set to work revitalizing the idea and the excitement that came with the idea. We hired Stephanie, who was the leader of the youth advisory council, and she was so excited about the idea that her enthusiasm became contagious. Thanks to her, there were other young Indigenous people who became excited about the project. Kaienkwinehtha, another fabulous Haudenosaunee young woman, started working with us around how to make the project youth-positive and engaging. Now that we had the means to do what we wanted to do to, we made sure the Onkwehon:we community was leading and centred in all that we did. What that meant for the whole project was that every single thing we did, from where we spent money, to who the service providers were, to where the leadership came from, to who provided food—all of it—was about the community, the Six Nations community, Haudenosaunee people, and to some extent the Mapuche people as well. We wanted all the resources going back into the communities and we wanted to showcase all the talent that lives in those communities.

**Kawennakon:** Yes. It was always the guiding principle that as much as possible, the funding, the benefit, and everything belongs in the community

**Vanessa:** From that point, what we ended up doing was three days of workshops. The first night we hosted a social that introduced the 25 young people participating in the research to one another, to our team, and to the many community members that came out to eat, sing, dance, and visit. Half the youth were Onkwehon:we, half were non-Onkwehon:we. They were invited to Haudenosaunee territory to participate in Haudenosaunee teachings, ceremony, and hospitality. At the workshops the youth learned about a lot of the positive sides of Haudenosaunee culture—the beauty of the culture and the importance of the cultural teachings to all of our survival. I think we can't overstate the importance of having hosted the workshops on Haudenosaunee territory. All of the youth live on unceded Haudenosaunee territory, but to host the workshops in Six Nations was really special. Especially for the non-Indigenous kids be invited into the community—most of them had never even been there before, and that was so important to their experience and to their learning. The Onkwehon:we young people were really proud of who they are and where they come from. All of these outcomes were about being on the territory.

**Kawennakon:** In the university, I often find myself being that cultural bridge. And I have people in front of me who have never been to the reserve, never seen a powwow, haven't gone to a lacrosse game. I think one of the most powerful ways for those people to learn is to get out of their cute, cozy, little settler spaces and get down to the reserve. I would even go further and suggest settler people should do it with a friend. See and experience what it's like to be the marginalized minority in a space. Most settler nation people have no idea. Do not be surprised if you have a great experience. Do not be surprised if you have a bad experience, if you get vibed or put in your place in Indigenous spaces. Take your moment to regroup, but also do what you need to do to find the courage to try again. Complain to somebody you know, counsel yourself, meditate, whatever you need. Reconciliation is not going to be all loving and singing "Kumbaya" around the campfire. It is going to be messy. You must have the personal wherewithal to take the good and the bad.

**Vanessa:** Right. Just to understand that being the outsider is a lot of people's daily experience. I think more White folks need to experience that othering that rarely occurs in White-dominated spaces—so, you know, basically everywhere else. And that being said, when the settler youth did come down to Six Nations and everything was open to them and there was ceremony and the social and feasting and dancing, I mean, they all loved it—no one was anything but totally welcoming to them. They had access to all these experiences that they never dreamed they would have access to and it made a huge difference, but that was the generosity of the community opening itself up to guests and that's how they were treated. The hospitality, the Haudenosaunee hospitality, was one of those pieces that you really wanted everybody to see and did they ever see it.

**Kawennakon:** That was really important. Enough of the negativity. Let's show you the hidden side of the coin. I will never understand why the powers that be hide the beautiful and positive Haudenosaunee experience. Or maybe I do: the powers that be cannot manufacture hate if you see the beauty and the depths of the people and the culture. It is deliberate.

I remember when I asked you to be the colonizer for the wampum circle exercise and the emotional impact it had for you. Can you talk about your experience in the circle where we're trying to make colonization visible to the non-Native students and make decolonization visible and practical to the Indigenous students?

**Vanessa:** It's an exercise that you lead where people put the things that are the most special to them in the centre of a circle and then two people are selected to represent the colonizers—in this case, those people were me and the other blonde-haired, blue-eyed academic on the project. I got to have an experience that's very familiar to Indigenous folks, especially on university campuses, where you asked me to speak for all White people for all time (*both laugh*). You asked that I represent all of colonization and be the embodiment of the colonizer. In other words, be the person who's going to steal everything that matters to people right from underneath them. Obviously, that's not going to feel good, but that's what you asked of me, so that was the job. Feeling the shame and pain of stealing from people and taking the things that are most precious to them, of course, that is what colonization is, but to be the stand-in, the token person who causes all that pain and suffering, is emotional and painful. To be in that role and feeling all those feelings while at the same time recognizing that this is exactly why White privilege exists and White supremacy exists and all the privileges that I have exist. The intellectual understanding is one thing but experiencing the emotional side of that is another thing altogether. The exercise was a very micro, very personal, very emotional version of the larger issues that we were talking about with the youth. When we went back to the interviews with the young people and asked them about the most powerful parts of the workshops, they all said that exercise had the most important impact on them, too.

**Kawennakon:** I shouldn't be surprised by the impact of the circle wampum exercise because it is based on understanding the Haudenosaunee elements of condoling the people and making them human again. I was shown that exercise by my ancestral guides and am lucky to be in a place where I get to participate in meaningful change in such a powerful way.

There are ways to think about reconciliation from within a strictly Haudenosaunee framework, like using elements in the Kayanere'kowa (The Great Law) and the principles of Peace, Power, and the Good-Mind. I always try to ground my thinking in ancestral thought, and more specifically, in our ancestral tongue.

We need to use one of our words for reconciliation, like Tentsitewaten-ronhste, which could be translated as "we will become friends again." The challenge here becomes the ability of the person explaining both cultural teachings and cultural translations. We are still boxed in by colonial thought by using the English language and expressions. How different would this conversation be if we were both speaking Kanyen'keha? What kinds of actions are required for us to reach that place? This is why I insisted we include Kanyen'keha translations in the final research report. As an act of reconciliation. We must recognize that cross-cultural understanding really depends on the efficacy of the cultural translator doing the interpretations. It is very difficult to be the cultural bridge.

**Vanessa:** It's a very powerful experience. These kinds of experiences, in all of their discomfort and emotion and humanity, really were central to our learning. Not just as researchers or participants, but as a team.

**Kawennakon:** I think it pinpoints the human foibles that come along with the project and what we all had to deal with in order to do it well. Even our irritation with each other. Everything wasn't always smooth and simple, it got messy—that's all part of reconciliation. The concept of reconciliation is captivating, but, in practice, it is frustrating.

**Vanessa:** It is frustrating. There were a lot of successes and so many amazing relationships built, but there was a lot of tension and challenge that accompanied those. None of it is easy or painless, but reconciliation is absolutely about creating and honouring relationships—even when they're difficult and accompanied by guilt or anger or sadness.

**Kawennakon:** We confronted our own human foibles and learned more about our personal challenges; we still had to remember, "I am in this with this person." We had to nail it down. We had to set our baggage aside to remember to recognize the value of the other people and what they bring to the table. It was like a busy, intense marriage.

I think we can look at reconciliation between individuals and apply the same principles at community and nation levels. Realize it's going to be emotional humanity. As that stuff boils up, we have to look at it and learn how to deal with our baggage in the moment, or shortly after. We have to learn how to say, "Okay. Here is my chance to work on this problem and resolve it." Those are what I think are the keys to reconciliation.

I have recently been thinking about a reconciliation analogy in terms of a deeply dysfunctional relationship. The patriarchy (Canada) is the violent abusive husband, and the Onkwehon:we is the violated wife. The husband has tortured and killed her entire family, gram and gramps, mom and dad, brothers, sisters, and cousins whenever he can find them. He has taken over her house and locked her in the basement. For centuries, he has violently raped her with a knife to her throat and violated her in every way possible. She has an inner strength—culture and ceremony—that has helped her survive and maintain hope.

Recently, some of his nieces and nephews met her distant cousins at school and heard the rumours of his molestations. The husband has tried to pretend innocence and deny his abuse, but the truth found a way. She found her voice and now his family are asking him uncomfortable questions. He has had to be more devious; the physical violence is muted and hidden but it remains. He doesn't want to leave marks people can see. Now that his violent past is public, his abuse has become subtler, more indirect, more mental and emotional—an example would be through legislation or institutional bureaucracy. She is still locked in the basement, but she used her ancestral knowledge to heal herself and now she is raising her voice. More of his family are listening for her. They have asked about her and want to meet her.

I think this is where we find ourselves now. I think we have a lot of work to do. We need to think of reconciliation in terms of the healing work we still need to undertake. How does he deal with his violent nature? How does she reclaim her dignity and safety? How does she forgive him? How do they both reclaim their humanity? How do they learn to love themselves again? How do they learn to know the other's love? We currently find ourselves looking for the answers to these questions and many more.

For me, the answer is we conduct our own research. Research that answers questions we have about ourselves and others. We operate within Onkwehon:we frameworks, according to Onkwehon:we theory and using Onkwehon:we methodologies. Contrary to what Canada might think, we are not creating new Indigenous frameworks, we are simply introducing you to them. They might be new to the academy, but they have been in operation on our lands for tens of thousands of years. They are ancient. That we still carry this knowledge amidst such colonial violence and oppression is testament to its power. Our models have been tested and vetted across the millennia. We are fortunate that we still speak our languages and practice our ceremonies because that's where we find the answers. We know the answer. The answer is research. Research is ceremony. Research is healing. *Research is reconciliation.*

And I think that's actually my message for this era of reconciliation: you better be prepared to face yourself. You have to learn how to deal with you and all your baggage. That's what our ancestors mean by becoming human. Becoming more kind, more loving, more compassionate. You better be prepared to cry. You better be prepared for the feels. That's what the ancestors are trying to show us. It's like amidst all of the human foibles, there are these moments of exquisite beauty and joy.

Here's what it looks like in a piece of community art. Look at the love and the power that we were able to help or allow to manifest in our communities. Where did that come from? That's not a human hand. That is a whole bunch of people with diverse gifts from diverse places, all coming together in unity. That's what unity looks like. It's freaking beautiful.

For more information on this project, please visit www.tagsix.net.

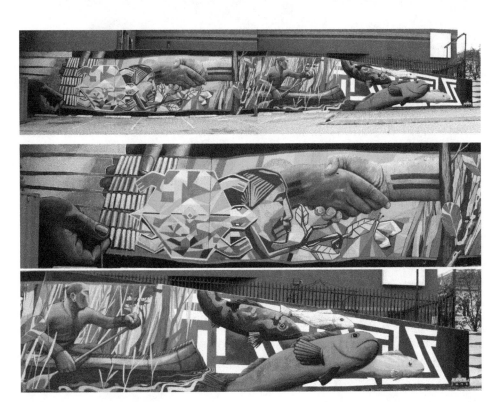

*Source:* TAG: Transformation Action Graffiti, project website, www.tagsix.net.

## Landmark Study Reveals What First Nations Have Already Been Saying for Decades

Whatever First Nations have already been saying loudly and clearly for decades is pretty much true, I guess, according to a landmark, government-funded study.

"Although First Nations communities and people and media and even some white people have been saying this is true, our extensive research and this remarkable report now lay bare that yes, I guess what they were saying is true," says Jerry Markel, the report's lead author.

"And it's all thanks to our tireless work."

A spokesperson for the federal government said that while it is reviewing the findings of the report, more study is likely needed before action can be taken.

## CHAPTER 15

# Considering a Truth Commission in Norway with Respect to the Past Forcible Assimilation of the Sámi People

*by Stephen James Minton and Hadi Strømmen Lile*

———

My name is Stephen James Minton. I am the father of a daughter and a son, and a psychologist of education. My paternal grandparents were workhouse children, so little to nothing is known about their origins. My maternal grandmother and my mother were born in Lancashire, England, where I grew up, and my maternal grandfather, who, whilst having passed over 40 years ago, remains a huge influence on my life, was a Scot. Since 1995, I have made my home in Ireland, where I have spent the bulk of my career working as a researcher and practitioner in addressing bullying, cyberbullying, prejudice, discrimination, and violence in school communities. Since 2012, I have had the privilege of collaborating with Sámi scholars, including the co-author of this chapter.

My name is Hadi Strømmen Lile. I am a Sámi Iranian scholar of sociology of law. My mother is from Iran, although she grew up in Kuwait. My father was a Sámi. His father (my grandfather) was the school principal at a boarding school in a small village called Snefjord, in the north of Norway. He was one of the very few Sámi teachers in the Norwegianization period. He was part of the system, but he had great affection for the Sámi culture and language. I guess he was not very loyal to the aims of the Norwegianization policy. However, none of his eight children, including my father, learned to speak Sámi. I could say a lot about my grandfather. I think he was a great man and he did great service. Thus, although I am pretty critical toward the Norwegianization policy, I do not blame the teachers, and I guess I see the history from more sides than expressed in this chapter.

———

In June 2017, it was announced in the Norwegian national Parliament that a commission would be established to examine the past "Norwegianization" policy[1] (the forcible assimilation of the Sámi and Kven people[2]). In an experience shared by many Indigenous Peoples around the globe, Sámi and Kven children were deliberately enrolled in residential schools, in which their native tongues and other artifacts of culture were forbidden, and the learning of the dominant language and culture was enforced. This chapter takes the form of a dialogue between the two authors; we discuss Norwegianization, and what might be learnt from both the implementation and the critique of the underlying philosophies, legal frameworks, and practical operations of truth and reconciliation processes conducted with Indigenous Peoples elsewhere in informing the work of the nascent Norwegian commission. When this conversation took place (December 2017), the mandate and the name of the commission had not yet been decided. The mandate was announced in June 2018, shortly before this chapter was submitted.[3] We feel that many, if not all, of the concerns that we discuss in this chapter still stand, and are relevant to the work of the commission.

**Stephen:** I'd like to talk with you about this proposal for a truth and reconciliation process, or similar, for the Sámi and Kven peoples in Norway. I know that this is something you have been talking about for a long time, so can you tell me a bit more about it?

**Hadi:** When I wrote my PhD—I submitted it at the end of 2011 (Lile, 2011a)—I wrote about what Norwegian children should learn about the Sámi people, according to Article 29 of the United Nations Convention on the Rights of the Child (CRC). This provision is supposed to be a standard for education according to the law. I tried, like any good researcher, to get attention for my research. I wanted to make it a national issue, so I focused on history education, and the word *Norwegianization*. What makes this history in Norway unique is that it lasted so long; it was more than a hundred years. It was not just about teaching Sámi and Kven people the Norwegian language—it quickly became about how to fight the Sámi culture: how to make Sámi people forget about their own culture and adopt the Norwegian culture.

**Stephen:** I think just there, in the comparisons with other Indigenous Peoples, the whole story's quite interesting. Because we're talking about the same historical period—you know, the late 19th century to sometime after the Second World War. You see the same type of experiences in North America with the residential schools for Indians; when the European settlers stopped physically slaughtering them, there was the idea of putting the Indian children in schools and remaking them as White children. The same way in which Sámi people were taught not only "Well, don't speak Sámi," but also "Don't *be* Sámi," and we will make you into proper Norwegian citizens, and then you won't be stuck in the past.

## THE ISSUE OF NATION-STATES

**Hadi:** Exactly, and the thing is also, I think in Norway, there was this international movement, and this thing about nation-states—the ideal of how a state should be. One people, one state, one language—the unity of a state was very important. Some people would argue that that's not the only reason for the Norwegianization policy; Einar Niemi and Knut Einar Eriksen argued that it was also an issue of self-defence policies against Finland. In Finnmark—it's on the border with Finland—there were "too many" Finnish people: the Kvens. And at least some elements of the government were afraid that Finland was going to make claims on the northern part of the country. So, they had to Norwegianize, and consolidate the Norwegian claim.

**Stephen:** It's a funny thought, really, you know—today, you think about the cooperation between Norwegians and Finns. So, the idea that there could have been different territorial claims and real disturbances up there is hard to imagine.

**Hadi:** Yeah, I mean, it's a long time ago. But it was, at that time at least, a real issue. In the book *Den finske fare*, Einar Niemi makes this claim that it was an important issue.[4] But anyway, this whole history of the Norwegianization was not included in the school curriculum plan in 2011. And that was my angle on the whole issue. One of the important aims of Article 29 of the CRC is that children should learn respect for human rights. If you're going to talk about human rights education in Norway, you have to talk about promoting respect for the Sámi. It is impossible to learn respect for the Sámi people if you don't know anything about their history—and the oppression.

**Stephen:** But I think that there's almost a challenge there, because, I mean, if a Norwegian child is really going to learn about the history of the Norwegianization of Sámi and Kven people, then there has to be that engagement with their predecessors as oppressors, which I think people really don't want to do. I mean, growing up in Britain as I did, when we learnt about human rights abuses, it was always those in Nazi Germany. We didn't learn about human rights abuses in the British Empire, for example. Which, as a British person who's lived in Ireland for 22 years, I know that there are certain pubs in which I could be reminded about that fairly quickly!

# PROGRESSION TOWARD A TRUTH COMMISSION IN NORWAY

**Hadi:** Exactly. That's why it became my angle to it, and I wrote an article in *Dagbladet* called "Whitewashed History Education" (Lile, 2011b). And so, at the end of that article, I contemplated: Is it enough just to include the word *Norwegianization* in the curriculum plan? I pointed to what had happened in Canada and in Australia. At that point, a truth and reconciliation committee had just been established in Canada, but they had not submitted their report—this was in 2011, in December.

**Stephen:** Yeah, I think that things were just getting going then in Canada.

**Hadi:** I was inspired by that. And I said, "Well, why shouldn't we do something here about that, too?" I think that would be a way for the state, and especially for the (Norwegian) Parliament, to deal with the past in a fair way. That could bring the issue into the national agenda. Because when I wrote my PhD about Norwegian children and education about the Sámi people, the Sámi Parliament had been working mostly on rights of Sámi children, and Sámi rights. They had not really been that engaged with, "What about the Norwegian community, and how do we change them?" They hadn't come to that stage. So I was one of the first to start to addressing that—and I repeated this call for a truth commission, in lectures and at conferences, and whenever I was invited somewhere, I would repeat this proposal—that we should do something similar to what they had done in Canada and Australia. So, in the spring of 2017, the Parliament organized this open hearing about the issue. The Sámi Parliament and a range of Sámi organizations and the Kven Organization were present there. I also attended that. Actually, it was streamed online, and you can see the whole thing on the (Norwegian) Parliament's website.[5] There was almost unanimous support for the establishment of the commission. All except one organization supported it. The only organization that opposed it was the Norsk-finsk forbund (Norwegian Finnish Association) in Norway. At that point, Inger Elin Eriksen was vice-president of the Sámi Parliament. She was the main representative for the Sámi Parliament. She is a very competent woman. She is a lawyer by training and a former judge. She had a very good and strong presentation. I would say the whole thing was a very strong experience. It was really sad that it was not broadcast nationally, because it was such a profound, historical, and powerful meeting. There were the Sámi youth organizations giving strong statements, and the elderly Sámi organizations, these old ladies talking about their own experiences and saying this is really important, not just for us, but for the future generations.

**Stephen:** So, now you have this in-principle decision from the Parliament concerning the establishment of some sort of truth process, but the mandate had yet to be worked out?

**Hadi:** Yes. On June 20, 2017, the national Parliament, with the support of all the political parties except the Conservative party and the Progress party—the government parties—voted for this. The Conservative party was not that negative, actually. Their thought was more along the lines of, "We do not really see the need for this now," but the Progress party was really against it. They said, "This is going to create conflict, and we are very much against this." They were the only ones that expressed a real opposition to the establishment of the commission.

**Stephen:** Yes, but the Progress party would not generally be known for their support for Sámi issues.

**Hadi:** So, this is where we stand today. The Parliament has voted for this commission and now the name and the mandate will be decided by the new Norwegian Parliament and the new Sámi Parliament. We just had an election in Norway and traditionally the election for the Sámi Parliament is at the same time as the election for the Norwegian Parliament. So, they will get together soon to agree on the remaining issues.

**Stephen:** That is an interesting one, because we've mentioned the Canadian truth and reconciliation process and, to an extent, Australia's *Bringing Them Home*.[6] And there is the possibility to learn from outcomes, positive and perhaps negative, from those processes.

## CONCERNS ABOUT A MANDATE FOR THE TRUTH COMMISSION IN NORWAY

**Hadi:** I have not contemplated all the consequences of a commission. I mean, the whole issue of reconciliation and digging up the past—will it be positive or negative? I do not really know. From my point of view, Norwegianization has been an issue of the Sámi people, not just in terms of the history, but also the existence and presence of the Sámi people, is invisible in Norway. The truth commission in Norway is about combatting the power of making the Sámi people and everything associated with Sámi insignificant. The commission is about making the Sámi people visible. There are strong political interests and attitudes among Norwegian people to sort of make Sámi people invisible. It is a form of power needed to make something invisible. And that the commission is about taking on those attitudes and interests, that sort of power. Maybe my biggest fear is that when this commission submits its report nobody is going to care. But if a truth process becomes an issue that the whole of Norway is involved in, it will lift the Sámi issue and make us visible. But then again maybe the debate will turn ugly and it will have very negative effects? I don't know.

**Stephen:** Part of the Canadian mandate was that all Canadian citizens should be educated on the history of residential schooling. And I don't really know how far they have gotten with that, or it may be that this process of education will take a few years to be realized.

**Hadi:** I am hoping that there will be a movie—a good blockbuster movie—about the Norwegianization history. I mean, we have this recent movie called *Sámi Blood*, but that is about what happened in Sweden, and the history in Norway and Sweden was not the same. Some years ago, we had this film about the Kautokeino Rebellion,[7] which almost every school class in Norway watched. Whenever the teacher had something to cover on the Sámi, this film became a good angle for them to talk about it with the students. But the Kautokeino Rebellion is not really a central part of the history; it has very little to do with the Norwegianization and assimilation policies.

**Stephen:** I think that a film is always interesting to an extent, but a film is sort of self-selecting, in that people who are already interested in the issue will go and watch the movie, and probably have their pre-existing beliefs confirmed. If you look at the United States, where the film industry is so prominent, and the whole issue of the depiction of Indians, you have some good and significant movies, but so many terrible depictions of Indians. And some popular films like *Soldier Blue* and *Dances with Wolves* have had rather mixed receptions. On the one hand, many Indian activists thought that *Dances with Wolves* was a terrible "White saviour" movie, but on the other hand, it did sort of raise awareness of the treatment of Indians amongst White people. It is difficult even now to say what its real value was. I think your earlier idea of looking more at what children learn in schools might be more beneficial, because schools educate all citizens. Could we, say, make it compulsory that every student in Norway learns about Norwegianization, and its effects?

**Hadi:** Yes, actually that is there. Two years after I pointed out that this history was missing from the curriculum plan in 2011, the Sámi Parliament was able to include the Norwegianization history in one of the learning outcomes of the school curriculum for grade 10 students.

**Stephen:** Yes, but this was what I was getting at: if Norwegianization is just taught as historical fact, a term to be learnt, then there is no proper engagement with the shadow *effects* of having that period in one's history.

**Hadi:** Yes, but what if I ask you about *Rabbit-Proof Fence*?

**Stephen:** Yeah, it's a good movie.

**Hadi:** I was hoping maybe we could get a movie similar to that in Norway. Don't you think it changed anything in Australia?

## A PACKAGE OF MEASURES?

**Stephen:** I am not devaluing the power of movies as a communicative medium. I think there are movies that have genuinely changed the way people look at the world. We could talk about a list of those until the kids go out for pints! But I see a good film being useful as *part* of something bigger. I really think that your idea of looking at what children learn in school would be very valuable indeed.

**Hadi:** The thing is, I just know that the schools can't do this alone, and I always have this perspective in the back of my head. When I talk about this history of oppression, I always see it in the light of the overall and most important aim, which is to promote respect for the Sámi people's rights, and to promote understanding and tolerance toward this people, which is a legal obligation of the government. And it is not just a legal obligation for the Ministry of Education and schools, it is an obligation on the part of the whole government to realize these aims, to just make it a reality. Now, how do you do that? And what I have been contemplating is that you have to look at what happened. The Committee on the Rights of the Child also points out this fact in General Comment 1, which outlines their interpretation of Article 29 of the Convention on the Rights of the Child. It states that "emphasis must also be placed upon the importance of teaching about racism as it has been practised historically, and particularly as it manifests or has manifested itself within particular communities." Thus they say that one has to look at "what happened." Why are the Sámi so few today? What sort of racism and oppression were directed against the Sámi? But then again one cannot just talk about what oppression there was. You cannot just do that. It will not work if the teaching focuses only on the oppression: "Oh, look at these poor people, how they were oppressed and it is terrible." You have to also, subsequently maybe, talk about the fight for human rights. Who has been standing up against this oppression? Why do we have rights today? Why did anything change? If you can lift up these protagonists against the oppression, at least for some people, it would be inspiring.

**Stephen:** Yes, I think you are right, and I think we are coming at this from different angles. I think there has to be a package of measures. You cannot just leave it up to the administration of education, no. But I think changes in the education curriculum are going to be helpful, and I agree that making a good film would be helpful. Also—and I think you as a legal scholar would know more about this—should there potentially be legal reforms as well? I mean, this was a fucked up situation that stayed fucked up for generations, so there is not just one pin you can take to the bubble and have everything fall down in a beautiful way. You know, I've worked on these bullying intervention programs. I look at bullying from a community approach; it's no good in just talking to the kids or training up the teachers—you've got to actively engage entire school communities, otherwise it is really largely a waste of time.

## RESPECTING THE IMPORTANCE OF CULTURE

**Hadi:** Yes, I agree with you. And I think there are going to be bumps along the road. Maybe I fear that at a certain point the debate is going to turn ugly. And it might affect Sámi children, and increase bullying against them. Because when you start to confront people with this issue of the past, it is a very sensitive issue in Norway. I mean, there are slumbering emotions, prejudice, and negative attitudes still there. And some people are going to say things along the lines of, "Oh these Sámi people, they are always thinking they are so special, and now they come again starting to complain and complain. Are they never going to be satisfied?" I picture a bully in school approaching a Sámi kid, going, "Oh, so you're oppressed? You little shit-bag, I'm going to show you oppression!" It is also the thing about being in a majority. Norway is a country with a huge ethnic Norwegian majority. They do not understand the importance of culture. They take it for granted, and they ask, "Why can't you just be Norwegian, why do you have to be Sámi? Why make such a fuss about it—is it not good to be Norwegian?" Ole Henrik Magga used to say that culture is like air—you do not notice it until it starts to disappear, because then you suffocate.[8]

**Stephen:** I think that is a really interesting, and I think that if I had a wish for the educative component of a truth process in Norway, it would be that it would remind ethnic Norwegians of the privilege that they enjoy as a majority. Because the problem is one of ethnocentrism—generally, people find their *own* culture as natural, as abundant, and as *universal* as the air that they breathe. And if someone says that they breathe a different sort of air, and that this is equally important, then they must be some sort of odd person.

**Hadi:** Actually, you are not far from the truth. One of my questions when I did my PhD was about a statement: "Sámi people are a part of the Norwegian people. To what extent do you agree with this statement?" None of the teacher participants said that they fully disagreed with this statement. And in the interviews

I confronted them with this, and asked them about the Basque people: "Are the Basque people part of the Spanish people?" And they said things like "Oh no, you can't say that." But what is the difference? In Norway, there is this perception that it is a Norwegian country, and they do not distinguish between Norwegian ethnicity and Norwegian citizenship.

## NORWAY AND ITS PEOPLES

**Stephen:** But you have this statement made by the King of Norway in 1997, that Norway is founded on the territory of two peoples. I can imagine that being quite an emotive thing to hear for Sámi people. Because then he was indicating two peoples that are equal.

**Hadi:** Yes, it was a huge thing!

**Stephen:** I don't know, but maybe that statement is not as significant for a Norwegian person as it is for Sámi person?

**Hadi:** No! Most Norwegians do not know about it.

**Stephen:** As you said, this is all indicative that the equality between the two peoples is not there. They *are* two peoples, but not two *equal* peoples. And this I think is a problem with the concept of reconciliation.

**Hadi:** Hmm…?

**Stephen:** Roland Chrisjohn has been critical of the Canadian process.[9] He points out that if you look logically at *re*-conciliation between peoples, this presupposes that at some point in history, these people have been *conciled*. That they were equal at some point, then fell out, and now the reconciliation process brings them together again, almost like marriage counselling. But that it is not the situation with colonization at all.[10] And as with the colonization Chrisjohn was talking about, with Norwegianization, it's not like you're arguing about the backyard fence—you're talking about forcible assimilation. And I think that this is something that informs things on all sorts of levels, including many Norwegian people actually not seeing the Sámi people as equal.

**Hadi:** Yeah, maybe. So, what do you mean? Shall we have this commission or not?

**Stephen:** Getting to the truth is an interesting journey. But I wonder whether *reconciliation* is actually the word that people should think about.

## "THE GREAT NORWEGIAN IGNORANCE"[11]

**Hadi:** I mean, from my perspective, I just see this enormous ignorance toward the Sámi people. It is just mind-blowingly stupid. Norwegian people in general do not know the most basic things about their own history and their own country. How do you address that? I have tried to look at it from different angles. You can start with the schools and include a sentence or two in the learning outputs of the school curriculum plan, but we really need something more, something spectacular, to awaken people from their indifference. Some years ago, the Directory of Education in Norway organized these courses for teachers on Sámi issues. They were going to pay for teachers to come to these courses, to come to a conference and learn about the Sámi issues in the curriculum. They had to cancel it because nobody came. So how do you deal with that? You can try to educate people, but if they are not interested it's not going to happen, so you have to somehow lift this issue up to a level that it becomes interesting. That is why I say that my biggest fear is that this commission and its report is going to be ignored, that nobody is going to care. Because then we haven't achieved anything.

**Stephen:** Yes, it is a realistic fear, and that is why the *truth* aspect of a commission might be the most important part of it.

**Hadi:** Maybe we should call it a "knowledge" commission, or an "enlightenment" commission, or something.

**Stephen:** I agree that the level of ignorance seems astonishing, even in my far, far more limited experience. I remember I was teaching a class in a Norwegian university and we got talking about Sámi issues. Later, I gave the students a discussion exercise, and I heard some students discussing things in Norwegian, a language I don't know very much of, and one said the word *Færøyene*. So, I thought that meant the Faroe Islands (I was right!), and I was thinking, "This is crazy, does she think that Sámi people live in the Faroe Islands?" But no—I later found out that she had been suggesting that the Sámi people should be *deported* to the Faroe Islands! And this was a master's student!

**Hadi:** Oh? Was she joking, or....?

**Stephen:** No! She was deadly serious! This was the one of most stupid things that I have heard in my life. I mean, I know these are sort of strange footnotes, but I think they are indicative of the monumental scale of the ignorance. I think maybe that is why I keep coming back to compulsory education as a good avenue. But then what do you do with the existing adult population? Because if you say every kid in Norway is going to do a mandatory subject on Sámi history, yeah, great, but we'll have to wait to see the effects in 10 to 20 years' time. What do you do at the moment?

**Hadi:** Yes, well, I am a sociology of law scholar, and within sociology of law there is this issue of how do you study the effects of laws. Thomas Mathiesen is one of the grand old professors of the sociology of law, and he says that in order for a law to function it has to fall into a social and normative landscape consisting of values and attitudes that somehow fit or harmonize with the norms of the law. If there is a huge discrepancy between how the landscape looks and intentions of the law, it is not going to work.[12] We have been working for Sámi rights for so many years, but we haven't been able to address this issue. We have these rights on paper, but how do we actually benefit from them? So, education is about changing the culture, changing that landscape. You have to change norms, culture, and attitudes. It is not just about knowledge; you have to do something about feelings, identity, and how people look at themselves. It is a very difficult pedagogical challenge. In the north, there are outright negative attitudes towards the Sámi. I mean, hostile attitudes. In the south, they are not hostile, not negative. They are just ignorant, and they view the Sámi people as funny people. You may just mention the word *Sámi* and people start laughing: "Oh, ha, ha! The Sámi are so funny!" But it is also derogatory, because they actually think the Sámi are quite stupid, but they do not feel threatened by them. And I don't know what is going to happen. I mean, you have these liberals in the south and if they are educated they will change their attitudes in a positive way. Thus, I am hoping at least we can do something about them. What to do with those in the north with these hostile attitudes and how they will react to this, oh, I don't know. I don't know how it is going to play out.

**Stephen:** Maybe if you look at civil rights in the United States … you could almost reverse the compass direction, couldn't you? Didn't Dr. Martin Luther King get some support from the northern liberals?

**Hadi:** Yes, but if you read Dr. King's (1964/2001) book *Why We Can't Wait*, he criticized the liberals in the north. He said, maybe they are the biggest problem, because we can deal with those outright racists in the south, they are at least honest about their position, but some of these people in the north who say they are tolerant are not really honest.

**Stephen:** I can understand that psychologically. I mean, if somebody has their cards on the table, so to speak, you can at least engage with an honest debate, whereas if somebody has a pseudo-liberal attitude, that might just be a sort of latent prejudice layered over with privilege, you know?

**Hadi:** Yes, and in Norway you have this issue of the Norwegian culture being seen as the best culture in the world. Norwegians: "We are good people, we are rational people, we are the most advanced people."[13] The more similar you are to a Norwegian, having similar attitudes, the more you are accepted, and the more people like you. But if you start to say, "I want to be different, I am not like you," they see it as a threat.

# THE RESIDENTIAL SCHOOLS AND THE POTENTIAL OPERATION OF A TRUTH COMMISSION IN NORWAY

**Stephen:** I was just wondering—are the Sámi and Kven people who went to the boarding schools old, or...?

**Hadi:** No, not really! Ánde Somby was at a boarding school. And Ole Henrik Magga was at a boarding school.[14] Magga did not understand anything about what the teacher said during his first four years of school, he told me.

**Stephen:** So, let's say how these truth commissions generally work: they talk with people who can give a first-person account. Are there enough of those people?

**Hadi:** Yes and no; there are some. I mean, this Wexelsplakaten, which was this instruction to the teachers that they should not speak Sámi, was officially disbanded in 1963. But although the law was formally changed, it was practiced for much longer in many places.

**Stephen:** It is something that I came across in Ireland, when there was a commission on child abuse after the industrial schools.[15] The last industrial school finished, I think, in the late 1960s. One problem was that a lot of people said, "Well, many of those who were interred as children in the industrial school system might now be dead, because that was 30 years ago." I think that there are factors of age and willingness to engage in getting those first-person accounts.

**Hadi:** Absolutely—you are only going to get first-person accounts from a small part of that history. I do not know, but I think that is important, too. But Ole Henrik Magga, who I mentioned, was not very supportive of the whole truth commission project. He said something like, "This was a long time ago, and now we should just move on and not dwell on the past."

**Stephen:** I think there are problems. Again, thinking about Roland Chrisjohn, he said that there is a real problem when people assume that engaging with a so-called truth process is *in itself* an act of reconciliation. And what he wrote really struck a chord in me, in terms of what happened in Ireland: that people would go and tell their painful stories to representatives of the religious order that provided the so-called schools in which they were interred, and that this was seen as an act of apology and, at worst, as Chrisjohn says, catharsis in itself—as an act of "healing." And he says that it is absolutely nonsense, because if you look at the abuse that was perpetrated, if people had been sexually and physically abused outside of the school system, would telling the representatives of those that abused you 30 years later on about the abuse be seen as enough, in terms of a sense of justice?[16] I think that in a way, this could be off-putting: people might ask what really is the point of collecting these horrible stories that are so painful to tell. Will this really lead to anything, or is this just going to end up in some sort of academic vault?

## SOME ISSUES OF THE LEGACY OF NORWEGIANIZATION

**Hadi:** Okay, but let me take an example. If I come to a new workplace in which horrible things have happened, or there has been a bad conflict, I cannot pretend as if nothing has happened. I can try to say, "That was in the past, let us just move on." But it is not that simple—you have to deal with the issue that some people are traumatized by the past. People that are scarred in some way have a tendency to react in certain ways in certain situations because things have happened to them, in certain situations, debates, and topics. If you have been abused, you will react to certain situations based on that experience. And the same thing is happening here. Because it kind of goes into generations, too. In relation to certain issues that we talk about and some debates there is this tension beneath the surface. And it affects policies, it affects rights, decisions, services, and so many things. And just to ignore that and say, "Let's just move on, let the past be past," I do not think that is a wise and constructive way of dealing with the future.

**Stephen:** I think sometimes when things get lost it is actually down to the way in which many psychologists approach things. I mean, I hold many members of my own profession to account here. People will talk about different individual responses to traumatic experiences and talk about post-traumatic stress—and to a certain extent, that there can be significant variations in individuals' responses *is* true. But I think that one really has to look more systemically at this: the events of the past have substantially limited the life opportunities of certain groups of people today. If you look at it entirely individually, these people can then be seen as "pathological," and some will say, "Well, they should just get over it." The *real* broader historical problem is treated as if it is located within the so-called sick individual. So, if you are still moaning on about the past, then that is your fault; you are the broken person, and you either need to "fix" yourself or, perhaps if you're lucky, we can grudgingly set aside some money to get you "fixed." And that is just fucking disgusting! But I think it is far more important to look at how these policies have led to lower levels of resources. Look at the situation in the United States: generations of people have ended up living on reservations or in urban poverty with a low life expectancy, and a 20 times higher risk of type 2 diabetes, suicide, and all manner of things.

**Hadi:** But I am trying to get at something more subtle than just the brute material consequences. You would meet these people who would say, "My father (or my grandmother) spoke Sámi," but not say they were themselves Sámi. Why? I mean, it is a way of distancing yourself from the culture. So, there are all these sorts of strange patterns in relation to how people speak about Sámi matters.

**Stephen:** That is what I am trying to get at really in terms of legacy issues and issues of identity. I think we can say, sort of first of all as I understand it: Who is Sámi? It has often been associated with the language or self-identification as Sámi, rather than, shall we say, the racial or religious differences that might be markers of some other peoples. But the idea of not wishing to identify as Sámi, that is important. Norwegianization in the past affects Sámi identity today; not only does that link have to be made, but it also has to be communicated. And I think it will be important to find the most expedient way of doing that.

**Hadi:** At the open hearing about the truth commission at the Norwegian Parliament, this issue came up a lot. And I strongly agree with this—that the mandate of the truth commission cannot only be to look at what happened in the past, but it also has to look into the situation today and how that history affects the situation today. Maybe the mandate should also point forward, but that might be more difficult.

## STILL HERE!

**Stephen:** It might be more difficult, but I think it's very important, so that Norwegianization does not just become relegated as just some past event. Because both you and our friend Ketil Lenert Hansen have shown in your doctoral research what some of the contemporary consequences of Norwegianization are. Your PhD (Lile, 2011a) showed that most Norwegian people learn nothing, and know nothing, about this. Ketil's PhD (Hansen, 2011) and a lot of what he's published since (see, for example, Hansen, Minton, Friborg, & Sørlie, 2016; Hansen & Sørlie, 2012) show that Sámi people, especially in mixed ethnicity areas, are experiencing unacceptably high levels of discrimination and poorer health outcomes. Unless one sees these findings as at least strongly influenced by, if not direct outcomes of, Norwegianization, any other explanation is ridiculous. What else is possible? "Oh, there are some people living up there, and they have a hard time, but we don't know why?" Bollocks! But you spoke earlier about your difficulties in trying to interest people in your PhD research results...

**Hadi:** Yes, the argument is always that "the Sámi are so few, so nobody cares about them." So, there is no market for it.

**Stephen:** Yes, but shouldn't one ask *why* are they so few?

**Hadi:** Yes, but if you talk to a publisher ... I mean, I wanted to publish my PhD as a book. But I found it very difficult, because publishers said there is no market for it. Nobody is going to buy it. They would say that it is a good PhD, the quality is good, but it is about Sámi people, thus nobody cares about that. I tried to say that it was not just about the Sámi, that it was about international laws on education, about new methods of sociology of law, and these sort of things. I can adjust it to that, I said. But no, no, it was too much about the Sámi, they argued.

**Stephen:** I think that it might be difficult for people who want to publish work on Indigenous Peoples in a majority society. Partly one can argue that there are so few Sámi—but part of it is surely also about power.

**Hadi:** Of course. It is also partly about how you frame it. If you say this is the history of Norway and the Norwegians, because it really is that too, that might at least be seen as relevant. But if you say this is the history of the Sámi, nobody is going to care. So, you have to get across this message that this is your own history, it is not "their" history, this tiny little group that nobody cares about, which has not yet entirely disappeared. It is almost this paradox, that because the Norwegianization process was not oppressive enough, because it did not completely succeed in its mission to extinguish the Sámi, today we have the call for a truth commission, and there are at least some forces working for that. What if there were no Sámi left? What if it had been a complete genocide? Would that not have been a more serious and an even worse history, which would have been more important? However, in practice, it would have had the effect that, then we can for sure forget about it, because then nobody would care. Because the policy, to some extent, failed, despite lasting for more than 112 years, today it can be called out by some of the remaining Sámi and remembered as a black stain on Norway's history.

**Stephen:** Well, the Sámi people might be few, but you are still there!

**Hadi:** Certainly, we are still here, and we are not going to disappear!

## NOTES

1. An excellent introduction to this policy in English can be found in Minde (2005).
2. The Kven people are the descendants of immigrants to Norway from neighbouring northern parts of Sweden and Finland in the 18th and 19th centuries, who were escaping poverty and famine. The present-day Kven population in Norway is estimated to be between 10,000 and 15,000; traditionally, they speak an old dialect of Finnish, also called Kven, and they share the Sámi people's history of forcible assimilation in Norway. For the purposes of this chapter, we shall be examining the situation of the Sámi people in Norway, but for the interested reader who wishes to learn more about the Kven people, there is a Norwegian Kven Organization (Norske Kveners forbund/Ruijan Kveenilitto), whose website can be found at www.kvener.no (in Norwegian and Kven

only). In English, Marjut Aikio (1989) has written an interesting article on the history and language of the Kven.

3. The short name of the commission is the Truth and Reconciliation Commission. The mandate of the commission is threefold: (1) mapping the history, including personal accounts and stories; (2) contemplating the consequences of the Norwegianization policy; and (3) giving advice for the future (see Stortinget, 2018).

4. This translates as "the Finnish danger" in English (see Eriksen & Niemi, 1981). Knut Einar Eriksen later became a professor at the University of Tromsø, and from 1988 to 1990, he was the chairman of the Norwegian History Association.

5. See Stortinget (2017).

6. See Human Rights and Equal Opportunity Commission (1997).

7. The Kautokeino Rebellion (also known as the Sámi revolt in Guovdageaidnu) was an 1852 revolt in which a group of Sámi people attacked representatives of the Norwegian authorities. The rebels burnt the house of and killed the local merchant and the local fief holder, and whipped their servants and the village priest. Two of the leaders were subsequently executed by the Norwegian government. The film to which Hadi refers is 2008's *Kautokeino-opprøret* (in Northern Sámi, *Guovdageainnu Stuimmit*; in English, *The Kautokeino Rebellion*). For an account of the event in English, see Kristiansen (2018).

8. Ole Henrik Magga is a Sámi linguist and politician who led the Norwegian Sámi Association from 1980 to 1985, and was the first president of the Sámi Parliament of Norway (1989 to 1997).

9. Roland Chrisjohn is a member of the Oneida Nation of the Confederacy of the Haudenosaunee (Iroquois), and is a world-renowned author and academic who has written extensively on the residential schools in Canada for over a quarter of a century, and more recently on the truth and reconciliation process in Canada.

10. See Chrisjohn and Wasacase (2009).

11. A phrase coined by Ánde Somby, who is a traditional Sámi joik artist, an associate professor in the Faculty of Law at the University of Tromsø, and a friend of Hadi.

12. See Mathiesen (2011).

13. In a recent survey by the Pew Research Centre, 58 percent of Norwegians expressed that they thought that their culture was "superior to others"; Norway was the only country in Europe where such a majority was found. See Sahgal and colleagues (2018).

14. The point being made here is that neither of these two individuals, whom we have mentioned previously in this chapter, are particularly old: Ánde Somby was born on May 12, 1958, and Ole Henrik Magga was born on August 12, 1947.

15. See Commission to Inquire into Child Abuse (2009).

16. See Chrisjohn and Wasacase (2009).

# REFERENCES

Aikio, M. (1989). The Kven and cultural linguistic pluralism. *Acta Borealia: A Nordic Journal of Circumpolar Societies, 6*(1), 86–97.

Being Christian in Western Europe. (2018, May 29). Pew Research Center, Religion and Public Life. Retrieved from http://www.pewforum.org/2018/05/29/nationalism-immigration-and-minorities/

Chrisjohn, R. D., & Wasacase, T. (2009). Half-truths and whole lies: Rhetoric in the "apology" and the Truth and Reconciliation Commission. In G. Younging, J. Dewar, & M. DeGagné (Eds.), *Response, responsibility, and renewal: Canada's truth and reconciliation journey* (pp. 217–229). Ottawa: Aboriginal Healing Foundation.

Commission to Inquire into Child Abuse. (2009). *Report of the Commission to Inquire into Child Abuse.* Dublin: Stationery Office.

Eriksen, K. E., & Niemi, E. (1981). *Den finske fare. Sikkerhetsproblemer og minoritetspolitikk I nord 1860–1940* [The Finnish danger: Security problems and minority politics in the north 1860–1940]. Oslo: Universitetsforlaget.

Hansen, K. L. (2011). *Ethnic discrimination and bullying in relation to self-reported physical and mental health in Sámi settlement areas in Norway: The SAMINOR study.* Doctoral dissertation, University of Tromsø, Norway. Retrieved from http://munin.uit.no/handle/10037/3259

Hansen, K. L., Minton, S. J., Friborg, O., & Sørlie, T. (2016). Discrimination amongst Arctic Indigenous Sámi and non-Sámi populations in Norway: The SAMINOR 2 questionnaire study. *Journal of Northern Studies, 10*(2), 45–84.

Hansen, K. L., & Sørlie, T. (2012). Ethnic discrimination and psychological distress: A study of Sámi and non-Sámi populations in Norway. *Transcultural Psychiatry, 49*(1), 26–50.

Human Rights and Equal Opportunity Commission. (1997). *Bringing them home: National overview.* Indigenous Law Resources, Reconciliation and Social Justice Library. Retrieved from http://www.austlii.edu.au/au/other/IndigLRes/stolen/stolen08.html

King, M. L. (2001). *Why we can't wait.* London: Longman. (Original work published 1964).

Kristiansen, R. E. (2018). The Kautokeino Rebellion 1852. Sámi Culture. Retrieved from http://www.laits.utexas.edu/sami/dieda/hist/kautokeino.htm

Lile, H. K. (2011a). *FNs barnekonvensjon artikkel 29 (1) om formålet med opplæring: En rettssosiologisk studie om hva barn lærer om det Sámiske folk* [The UN's Convention on Children Article 29(1) on the purpose of education: A sociology of law study on what children learn about the Sámi people]. ISSN 1890-2375. Doctoral dissertation, Faculty of Law, University of Oslo, Norway.

Lile, H. K. (2011b, November 16). *Hvitvasket historieundervisning* [Whitewashed history education]. *Dagbladet*.

Mathiesen, T. (2011). *Retten I Samfunnet: En innføring I rettssosiologi* [Law in Society: An introduction to sociology of law]. Oslo: Pax forlag.

Minde, H. (2005). Assimilation of the Sámi: Implementation and consequences. *Journal of Indigenous Peoples' Rights*, *3*, 1–33.

Stortinget. (2017, May 15). Open hearing in the Standing Committee on Scrutiny and Constitutional Affairs [Video file]. Retrieved from https://www.stortinget.no/no/Hva-skjer-pa-Stortinget/Videoarkiv/Arkiv-TV-sendinger/?mbid=/2017/H264-full/Hoeringssal1/05/15/Hoeringssal1-20170515-091119.mp4&msid=0&dateid=10004071

Stortinget. (2018). Innst. 408 S (2017–2018). Retrieved from https://www.stortinget.no/no/Saker-og-publikasjoner/Publikasjoner/Innstillinger/Stortinget/2017-2018/inns-201718-408s/#m3

CHAPTER 16

# Nipivut (Our Voices): A Discussion about an Inuit Values-Based Research Framework and Its Application in Nunavut

*by Gwen Healey Akearok and Moriah Sallaffie*

---

ᒍᐊᓐ ᕼᐄᓕ ᐊᖅᑭᐊᕈᔪᖓ. ᐃᖃᓗᓐᒥᐅᑕᐅᔪᖓ. ᐃᓱᒻᒥᖅᑐᐃᔨᐅᔪᖓ. My name is Gwen Healey Akearok. I was born and raised in Iqaluit, Nunavut. My parents are Greg and Sylvia Healey. I am married to Jason Akearok, from Sanirajaq, and our children are named Qatturainnuk and Qammaniq. I am the executive and scientific director of the Qaujigiartiit Health Research Centre.

My name is Moriah Sallaffie. I am Uliggaq, Moriah Sallaffie, from Mamterilleq and Siqnasuaq (Bethel and Nome, Alaska). My parents are Sine' Holly and David Holly from Nome, and Elia Sallaffie Jr. from Bethel. My partner is Jesse Mike from Iqaluit, Nunavut, and our daughter is Niviaq. Wiinga Yup'iuga, I'm Yup'ik. The Yup'iit are politically, culturally, and linguistically Inuit. I am grateful and humbled to be living and working here in Iqaluit with my family and in my wife's community. I am the youth research coordinator at Qaujigiartiit.

---

ᖃᐅᔨᒋᐊᖅᑏᑦ Qaujigiartiit Health Research Centre is an independent, non-profit, community-based research centre located in Iqaluit, Nunavut. Qaujigiartiit is a small organization that has been steadily growing since 2006. We are grateful to be able to contribute to the conversation around reconciliation in Canada and discuss how Qaujigiartiit is situated in this landscape. The best way to express our history and role in research is by sharing a conversation between two of our staff members: Gwen Healey, executive and scientific director, and Moriah Sallaffie, youth research coordinator. Gwen and Moriah travelled to Gwen's family campsite by the Sylvia Grinnell River in Iqaluit in early July 2018.

**Gwen:** We should begin by describing where we are so the readers will understand. We're in my tent at the river, the kuuk. This was one of the traditional summer camp areas for this region, known for Arctic char. It still is used widely today by the community. I have been camping and fishing here all my life. We can hear the river burbling beside us. The sky is a little grey and rainy. We are sharing tea while we talk.

**Moriah:** I was hoping that we could talk about Qaujigiartiit—the origins of the centre and what you do there?

**Gwen:** I was born and raised here in Iqaluit. As a young person, I was involved in initiatives for youth. I helped start our high school daycare—I was part of a group involved in different activities to change things we thought weren't right. And we tried to find solutions. As I got older, I left and went to university. Then I had an opportunity to work as an intern for the University of the Arctic and I saw Arctic communities with incredible infrastructure. It was different from our community, where we don't have that infrastructure, where we're at the mercy of a narrative that tells us our communities are terrible places, not worthy of investment. Yet much was happening in other countries where their Arctic seemed to be worth more to them than ours did to Canada. I spent a year on an internship in the Nordic countries and I visited all the Arctic countries. I was so inspired. I came back to Canada to go to grad school and I studied community health and epidemiology. I talked to people about what my research topic should be and a number of community members said it should focus on women's health. As I was doing that, I was working with the late Andrew Tagak Sr., who was the Inuit Qaujimajatuqangit coordinator for the Department of Health at the time. I knew Andrew quite well from my childhood. He and I had conversations about terminology in Inuktitut and about health and wellness. I really enjoyed learning from Andrew. As I was finishing grad school, we were talking about how research in the North focused more on what was of interest to other researchers, and not necessarily what was of benefit to us. I happened to meet two other women from White-horse and Yellowknife who felt the same way. We decided to work together across the territories to cultivate a space where research was community led. The centre grew out of that—a climate where we weren't getting the information that we needed to address the challenges in our communities and the existing information wasn't building on the strengths of our communities. The right kind of research funding came along that allowed us to form our three sites across the territories. Originally, we were all working together and over the years we drifted apart as we responded to specific requests from our communities, but we still collaborate. Andrew was the founding chairperson of our board until his passing.

**Moriah:** I appreciate hearing that origin story. I'm very fascinated by the research model that's used at Qaujigiartiit. How was it developed, and what does it look like?

**Gwen:** How about you describe what you do at the centre first? (*laughter*)

**Moriah:** I'm the youth research coordinator. I focus on youth mental health and well-ness in the territory. My primary focus area is training community members to become facilitators of the Makimautiksat Youth Wellness and Empowerment Camps. Other areas I get to focus on are research projects that help us get a bet-ter understanding of what our youth need to be well.

**Gwen:** When you were moving here, what drew you to work for us, where you have little to no job security and a little old building to work out of? (*laughter*)

**Moriah:** I'm extremely grateful that I'm able to work at the centre. I'm going to build my answer a little bit off of the research model that's used and the communities that we focus on. The majority of people who reside in Nunavut are Inuit, and I'm Yup'ik from Bethel and Nome, Alaska. Before moving to Iqaluit, all of the work that I had done was focused on self-determination and wellness of Alaska Native people. I've worked for tribal organizations, I've worked for non-profits, and that's always been at the heart of the work that I get to do. It's important to my well-ness that I'm able to focus on helping our communities become whole again, to become well. The fact that I get to work for an organization that is really based in the community and what communities are asking for is incredible. The work that we do gives us the space to be creative. You give us the space to bring our whole selves to the work that we're doing. I'm hopefully making a difference in Nunavut, but it gives me the opportunity to nurture in that sense my own spiritual, mental, and emotional well-being because I'm allowed to bring my whole self to work. I don't know if I'm describing that well enough.

**Gwen:** It makes sense to me. That's a good segue into the research model. When Andrew and I were forming the centre, we were talking about the ways in which people do research. Even though I studied epidemiology, my research focused on storytelling and narrative collection methods because they were more useful for deriving meaning and understanding about women's health issues in our communities. Andrew and I were talking about why people do research, why do they come here, why do we study what we study, why do we want to understand the things that we want to understand? And then how do we come to that place of understanding? From these conversations, the Piliriqatigiinniq model came to be (Healey & Tagak, 2014). Piliriqatigiinniq is that we're all working for a common cause or we're all working toward a common good. That was why we wanted the centre—because we ultimately want to work for the betterment of our communities. We need knowledge and evidence to help support us to get there and make arguments for the resources we need or whatever it is we're working towards. That was the first concept; then we had some conversations about ethics. One of the key focus areas for the centre was to articulate what it meant to be ethical because researchers had come here and done terrible things in the past. There was a skin graft study in Igloolik where squares of skin were grafted on to siblings from each other and other relatives to see what would happen—if they would have the same rejection reaction to other sort of transplants as other groups of people.

**Moriah:** That's horrific.

**Gwen:** It is absolutely horrific. It had been done without informed consent, of course; it had been done without the subjects having any knowledge of what was happening. People abused their power and authority in order to conduct this experiment. There was another example in Pannniqtuq, where anthropologists called people to the health centre and pulled their teeth out. This is not hundreds of years ago—this was in the 1960s and 1970s. It's still in the recent memory of many of our community members. To be ethical means to be respectful and to be good and kind. We'd had a conversation as well with Janet Tamalik McGrath, who grew up in Taloyoak and Rankin Inlet. She had done an investigation into how people talk about ethics in our communities and she had talked about Pittiarniq, to be good or kind, and so that was what we focused on in our model (McGrath, 2004). It's like when my little one, my daughter, is picking on her big sister, we say, "Pittiarniaqputit—just be nice. Be good." That's how we conduct ourselves in our research. The first principle is to be kind.

The next part of the model was about the stories, Unikkaaqatiginniq. We were talking about my master's research—women and stories—and how I was supposed to be doing a thesis that was based on epidemiological methods. I knew that wasn't going to get at the root of women's health challenges and strengths here, so I collected stories and talked to women. I found that when I went back down south and told this to my supervisor and committee, they couldn't understand it. They would say, "Well, that's just artifact or anecdotal." If I interviewed a woman and she told me about what happened to her sister, their perception was that it was artifact, not a genuine piece of data because it didn't happen to her. And I'm saying, "It did happen to her—via her sister." That's why the story is important, because she's trying to explain a circumstance that impacts her health and the health of women around her. My supervisor and committee began to understand this way of communicating and sharing information. We recognized the need for Unikkaaqatiginniq to be a core element of our research model. In our research process we include all aspects of story: the power of story, the meaning of story, how knowledge is shared or conveyed through story, what it means to the storyteller and the listener. The information and the knowledge that are transmitted in different ways through stories: metaphorically and literally.

The next part of the model is this concept from Andrew that I absolutely love. It's one of my favourite philosophical ideas, Iqqaumaqatigiinniq, which is described as all-knowing—everything you've ever known since kindergarten and before—all coming to a point of understanding. Coming to a point of crystallization. You just reach a moment—"Oh, I finally understand." And that changes over time—the point at which we come to develop understanding—it depends on our own experience, our age, our life, and what we understand at that point in time. Ten years later we may see things with even more meaning and more deeply as we develop more understanding about life and the world around us. I love that concept. That was how he had articulated analysis.

The fifth part, Inuuqatigiittiarniq, is to work in a way in which we show respect for all human beings. For us that was about motivations: Why are you here? Why are you asking me these questions? Why are we doing this? Is part of the end goal of your project to articulate a respectful worldview to our communities? To respect the need for knowledge to be shared in a way that's useable or actionable? All of those questions.

Those are the five components of the model. Every project that goes through our centre follows this model. We work in an environment of respect for others and their beliefs and values. We work with goodness and kindness, we are heart-centred in that way. We value and cherish the power of story in our work and how we come to a place of understanding. Those are the five philosophical ideas behind our model. What do you think about the Piliriqatigiinniq model?

**Moriah:** I think the model is beautiful. I'm trying to learn Inuktitut and speak it without stumbling over my words—it is not just the model, but in all of our programs we incorporate Inuit values and traditions and ways of knowing and understanding and culture, and I get to practice using these words and having a deeper understanding of what they mean. This goes back to what I was saying earlier about the work we get to do—it allows me to bring my whole self to the work. Being Yup'ik, we generally don't call ourselves Inuk or consider ourselves Inuit, but culturally and politically and linguistically we are, we're all related. The values that are inherent in the model are values that I've always practiced in my work, in my life. Those are the values that I was taught from a young age and I'm now able to apply my unique worldview in the work, supported by the model. That's another way that I'm allowed to bring my whole self to the work that we do and that's really special.

Does Qaujigiartiit have a role in the reconciliation process?

**Gwen:** I checked the definition of *reconciliation* in preparation for our discussion, to really make sure we were starting from a common definition. *Reconciliation* means "to make amends; the restoration of friendly relations; and/or the action of making one point of view or belief to be compatible with another" (Merriam-Webster, 2018). The third definition piqued my interest because in some ways that's what we're trying to do with our model: reconcile different ways of coming to an understanding when it comes to knowledge production or research. Our model, our centre, exists to bring all kinds of ways of knowing together. Not just Inuit or Western or Eastern, Northern, Southern ways of knowing. If it helps us to achieve understanding and ultimately improve the health of our communities, we're not limiting. We're welcoming and inclusive. We are reconciling different ways of knowing as the core of our research framework. I see our centre more in the self-determination realm. Our centre exists because our communities are capable of doing their own research. What do you think? What you think about reconciliation in our centre?

**Moriah:** Definitely what you said—reconciling different ways of knowing and doing and bringing that to the forefront of all the work that we do. Challenging the narrative that we can't do things for ourselves. When it comes to Canada, how can there be reconciliation without conciliation? Colonization is ongoing and continues to have detrimental effects on all communities, especially Indigenous communities. The work that I've been lucky enough to do has always been around self-determination for Indigenous people and that's the work that we continue to do with or without reconciliation happening in the rest of the country.

**Gwen:** We're still working through it. There are many definitions of and different ways people use the word *reconciliation*. In Inuktitut—what's the terminology people would use for explaining that? It's an English word with multiple definitions. I don't think our centre is here to make amends—we're not part of that definition of reconciliation. We're reconciling ways of going forward and understanding what's happening in our communities and finding the solutions and actions that help people feel better. That's the space we're in. There were colonial policies and processes at the time of settlement. The experiences of communities and the outcomes of those interactions are different based on the epistemology of every community. There are degrees of differences and outcomes related to how colonial processes unfolded across Canada—and the length of time in which people have been exposed to those colonial presences—there's diversity there. I find I reflect on my own experience—my parents are not Inuit. They were welcomed into Inuit families and much of my upbringing was to be Inuk. Families who are from here, originally from this area, refer to me as "original Iqalungmiut." I'll be at gatherings with someone from here and they'll say, "Original Iqalungmiut like myself and Gwen, this is how we feel about these things." I never grew up differentiating myself or feeling differentiated from anyone around me. My husband is Inuk and my children are Inuit and there's a beauty in belonging to more than one family—the web of connections that weave our communities together like fabric. My parents were taught how to hunt and sew; we grew up with these activities. We camped here at the river, like everyone else, and it was never really pointed out to me that maybe I was different until I was a teenager, and it was by a teacher from the south who didn't understand. Inuit are very welcoming in our community. That's why there are so many non-Inuit with Inuit names, myself included. It's about participation in the Inuit community, not just whether or not you're a beneficiary of the land claim. It's based on the qualities you bring to the camp or community, which make you Inuk or not, historically. That's one of the things Andrew would say, too. It can be difficult for our communities and our young people to reconcile different definitions of identity.

**Moriah:** In Inuit communities, both here in Nunavut and in Alaska, the definitions of what qualifies a person as Inuk have, in part, been shaped and structured by colonization. Different structures of governance have developed a somewhat colonial understanding of who is Inuk and who is not. Precolonization we did not exclude community members or keep people out who contributed to the community and were not harmful. Our survival was dependent on one another and nobody was expendable; all community members were valued. Developing arbitrary definitions of identity as a means of exclusion is a tool of oppression and colonization. As Inuit, part of it is us actively working to reclaim our cultures and identity and part of it is having those difficult conversations among ourselves. We have to have these conversations in our communities among ourselves and answer these difficult questions. Like, how do we maintain our unique identities without pushing others away? How do we do that without isolating ourselves, as well? Making sure that we are not excluding people from becoming...

**Gwen:** Who they are. You're not ascribing an identity to someone. Allowing people to be who they are without ascribing an identity.

*(tea break)*

**Gwen:** Let's talk about Timiga Ikumajuq ("My body, the light within") then. A practical example of applying the model is the development of the Timiga Ikumajuq workshops. In Nunavut, we have a problem with sexually transmitted infections (STIs). The rates of infection are between 10 and 15 times higher than the rest of Canada. We have a strong arts community and amazing performance artists, visual artists. It's a beautiful way of telling stories and sharing experiences. Our young people carry the burden of the STIs, the 15- to 25-year-olds. We wanted to develop an intervention that incorporated our strengths, the arts, into a workshop that would help young people talk about what's going on for them in sexual health and relationships. We came from a place of knowing that sexual health is also a mental health issue. There was more to it than just whether or not someone has access to a condom and knows how to use it or birth control. It was about agency, self-esteem, and communication among young people.

   Timiga Ikumajuq grew out of that. Laakkuluk Williamson-Bathory, Sylvia Cloutier, and me, we developed a workshop for 14- and 15-year-olds using the arts as the starting point for discussions about sexual health. In the public health literature, nobody talks about love in sexual health. Risk dominates the discourse, and we wanted love to be part of the conversation. Old Inuit stories have elements of sexuality, and we wanted to reconnect youth with that part of their history as well. These conversations can be open, funny, creative, and silly. Laakkuluk specializes in Uajeerneq, Greenlandic mask dancing, which is very sexual—you have body parts right on your face in the mask. They're literally drawn on the mask (testicles and vagina) along with connections to the ancestors and spirit world. We thought that could be a fun starting place for teenagers to get involved in the workshop. We developed and piloted the workshop in three two-hour sessions with a group of grade 9 students about six years ago. It went well and was so exciting. Then we struggled with getting funding to keep it going. Two years ago, we were able to secure funding to expand to other communities. The workshop follows our model: operating from a place of kindness, respect, compassion, story. We follow a heart-centred approach toward the young people we work with. We talk to them, learn about them, engage with them in different activities over the course of the day, and collect information about their experiences through both paper evaluations and through a sharing circle. We do it together so no one's isolated, left alone, or doesn't have help. We talk to them about their resources, listen to their stories, and we share our own stories. It's based in storytelling. By the end of the day, they come to a place of realization and understanding. They turn into different characters when they put on the mask and they're telling stories about the sun and the moon or Nuliajuk (Sedna). Maybe they had heard the story before but didn't shout it out with pride the way they do at the end of the workshop. They grab on to the arts and it becomes an avenue to talk about relationships, be proud of themselves, develop skills. There are many positive outcomes that address key determinants of sexual health in Nunavut.

**Moriah:** It's key that Inuit art and culture are at the heart of the workshop. During the sharing circle at the end of the workshop the youth talked about how they don't learn about Inuit creation stories. That's something that maybe they are not getting from home or from school. It's something that they want more of. When they see themselves—their identities—reflected in the content that humans actually are sexual beings, they get to discuss that openly. They get to bring their full selves to that interaction. It's very impactful and it's so fun to see them come out of their shells.

**Gwen:** We see students who barely said a word all year long jumping out of themselves to perform or make art. The other part of the workshop is the theatre, where the Brazilian Theatre of the Oppressed method is used (Boal, 1979). They develop skits and perform them. They have to be based in reality. The characters have to make real decisions. In those stories, they talk about jealousy, bullying, and financial problems at home—about real moments that affect sexual decision-making. We're so proud of them at the end of the day. We see them bursting to tell stories, whereas a more "conventional" research process would be to sit down with a 14-year-old and interview them to learn about this topic. But they don't respond to that method. They're not comfortable. It's not a way to meaningfully talk about what's going on. We want to cultivate a space to talk in a way that takes the pressure off the individual. In the workshop, they focus on four main questions: What does sexual diversity mean to you? How does a relationship affect our emotions? What are the gendered roles for men and women that you see around you? What does a healthy relationship look like? Then they develop skits or storyboards from their discussion. I remember there was a young girl who was quiet, then when we got to doing skits she was telling everyone where to stand: "You've gotta do this and you've gotta put something in her drink and then you've gotta pass out and you've gotta…." She was the director. Her teacher was speechless. In our debrief, she told us, "This has to go into the school curriculum. This was so amazing." This is an example of how we implement a project based on our model. Our process derives more meaningful information, operates on our terms, the way we do it here. It's a really good example of that.

**Moriah:** Going back to the question around reconciliation, I'm very interested in projects that explore sexuality, sexual health, and healthy relationships. It's important to me to understand better how colonization and subsequent intergenerational trauma has adversely impacted my understanding and Inuit understandings of what healthy sexuality looked like, can look like, what we want it to look like, and trying to reconcile with that. Doing this work, it can help me reconcile, but it can also help young folks. Like the all-knowing coming into one and having these incredible "ah-ha" moments after doing the work and taking part in the workshop.

**Gwen:** I think you have really articulated the essence of why our work is so exciting and rewarding—because we get to have those "ah-ha" moments or that Iqqaumaqatigiinniq experience every day. What we work on, it furthers us as humans and our understanding of the world. I think all of us at Qaujigiartiit appreciate and value that. It's our privilege that we get to do this amazing work in service for our communities; it helps us grow as human beings in our understanding of the world. Even though we have no core funding and we wing it every year. At the end of the day, it's the human experience—that essence of being us on this earth that we actually get to live out in our work. That we're not just punching in letters on a keyboard, mindlessly or meaninglessly, we're cultivating meaning every day. You have helped me to see that just now in this conversation (*laughter*). Maybe that's why we are so excited about our centre and our work—because we grow as human beings in our communities with every project that we work on. Is that too romantic?

**Moriah:** Not at all. That's a benefit of being able to do this work—whatever we get out of some of these programs or workshops that we host or research projects that we do, we're helping other people along their journeys. Because we're here to work for the communities and answer the questions that they have.

**Gwen:** Maybe another way of looking at it is that what we do is therapeutic. The way people talk about research and how research communities perpetuate a narrative is that it must be unbiased, isolated, and insular, and it can't be seen to impact your population or your study group in any way. For us, it's the opposite. We're embedded and involved. We're humans who have experienced things, not robots without feelings. We embrace that. I know I do. As I grow and develop as a researcher, I find the work we do is therapeutic. Ultimately, we're working toward answering questions people will bring to us and helping to release the stories people want to share as part of their own therapeutic experience, too.

**Moriah:** It's part of the teachings from our communities of Makimautiksat Youth Wellness and Empowerment Camps (Healey, Mearns, & Noah, 2016): if our communities are unwell, then we're going to be unwell. If our communities are well, then we're going to be well as individuals (Egan, 1998). That impacts the community in a positive way. That unique understanding that we have to take care of ourselves and our community members, and that our community members have to do the same for us.

**Gwen:** It's reciprocal and circular. In regard to reconciliation—incorporating different methodologies in Timiga Ikujamuq—there's the Inuit performance arts, Inuit creation stories, visual art, body-mapping, Theatre of the Oppressed from Brazil, and sexual health discussions; we're doing it in a formal school-based education setting. There's a diversity of activities and spaces that come together in a really fun and exciting workshop where we get to hang out with teenagers all day, make art, and tell stories and everybody leaves the end of the day feeling better. I think that is a perfect depiction of where our centre fits in the reconciliation spectrum.

# REFERENCES

Boal, A. (1979). *Theatre of the oppressed.* C. A. McBride & M. O. L. McBride (Trans.). New York: Theatre Communications Group.

Egan, C. (1998). Points of view: Inuit women's perceptions of pollution. *International Journal of Circumpolar Health, 57,* 550–554.

Healey, G. K., Mearns, C., & Noah, J. L. (2016). The eight *Ujarait* model: Supporting Inuit adolescent mental health with an intervention model based on Inuit knowledge and ways of knowing. *International Journal of Indigenous Health, 11*(1), 92–101.

Healey, G. K., & Tagak Sr., A. (2014). *Piliriqatigiinniq* "working in a collaborative way for the common good": A perspective on the space where health research methodology and Inuit epistemology come together. *International Journal of Critical Indigenous Studies, 7*(1), 1–8.

McGrath, J. T. (2004). *Translating ethics across the cultural divide in Arctic research: Pittiarniq.* Unpublished manuscript.

Reconciliation. (2018). Merriam-Webster Dictionary.

## CHAPTER 17

# Kinship as Research Methodology: Travels to Truth and Reconciliation

*by Kim Anderson and Rene Meshake*

––––––––

I am Kim Anderson, a Métis writer and researcher, working as an associate professor in the Department of Family Relations and Applied Nutrition at the University of Guelph. Rene Meshake is an Anishinaabe multidisciplinary artist living in Guelph, Ontario. Rene and I work together frequently, most recently on his forthcoming memoir, *Injichaag: My Soul in Story* (University of Manitoba Press, 2019).

––––––––

February 2018

When the final report of the Truth and Reconciliation Commission of Canada (TRC) was released in 2016, it sparked a national discourse on how to address the legacy of Indian residential schools and the colonization of Indigenous Peoples in Canada on the whole. Much of the focus has been on the role of populations and institutions in promoting the truth about Indigenous Peoples' histories and on mending relationships between Indigenous and non-Indigenous peoples. But, in this chapter, we will reflect on a different process: uncovering truth and fostering reconciliation through the research-centred relationship of the authors: Kim and Rene, two Indigenous individuals (Métis and Anishinaabe, respectively) coming from the same greater colonial history but affected differently through personal circumstances. Through collaborative knowledge production, and in our capacities as an Indigenous studies scholar (Kim) and an oral historian, artist, and Elder (Rene), we have been practicing a research methodology that advances our personal truths and opens reconciliation pathways. As co-researchers we have used engagement with land, language, ceremony, and storytelling on multiple projects, and, as a result, have created new forms of kinship in the wake of our own disrupted kin experiences. We have done a lot of this work in the city where we live as neighbours—Guelph, Ontario—but we've also shared some pivotal moments through travel, and will focus on a few of those stories in this chapter.

For stylistic purposes, Kim will serve as the narrator.

## BACKGROUND TO THE "RESEARCH KIN"

I (Kim) was born in 1964 and raised in Ottawa by a Métis father and an Anglo-Canadian mother. During my upbringing I had very little engagement with Indigenous peoples other than the few aunts and uncles who lived in Ontario. Upon arriving at the University in Toronto in 1984, I began to build relationships with the thriving urban Native community there. Since my early 20s, I have spent much of my personal and professional life working in Indigenous identity construction, with a focus on gender and kinship. I completed a PhD in history in 2010, but have been doing oral history research with Maria Campbell and other Elders and Indigenous Knowledge Keepers for over 20 years. I identify as an Indigenous writer, scholar, and community-based researcher.

Rene was born in the railway town of Nakina in northwestern Ontario in 1948. He grew up in Anishinaabeg/Treaty Three territory, with family at Longlac 58 First Nation and Aroland First Nation. Rene spent his early years living off-reserve with his grandmother in a matriarchal land-based community he calls Pagwashing. He was raised through his grandmother's "bush university," periodically attending Indian day school, but at the age of 10 was scooped into the Indian residential school system. He attended MacIntosh Residential School for six years, where he suffered sexual abuse at the hands of a lay brother. This residential school experience was life changing, as it suffocated Rene's artistic expression and resulted in decades of struggle and recovery. Now, at 70 years old and with almost 30 years of sobriety, Rene is a successful multidisciplinary artist, musician, and writer who has written three children's books and two books of poetry. He has an active online and performing presence and lives in Guelph with his wife, Joan.

Rene and I met shortly after I arrived in Guelph in 1997, where Rene and Joan had been living for a few years already. We had both moved with our families out of Toronto to find a quieter community, and both families had toddler sons born in 1995. Our first encounter was at a "schmoozefest" networking event that the local arts council had sponsored. As the only Native people in the room, we noticed each other right away, and as Rene remembers it, "I said, 'I'm an artist' and you said, 'I'm a writer'—but I don't remember what else we talked about ... I guess we were schmoozing!"

Rene and I have now been friends within the small Native community in Guelph for over 20 years. On occasion, we did readings or arts events together, but we only started doing concentrated collaborative work in 2007 when I began my PhD research on life stages and Native women. Rene served as an oral historian on that project, sharing lots of stories about the matriarchs who raised him. From there, we continued to do more oral history on an Indigenous masculinities project, co-producing a booklet of art and stories on the subject. All of this oral history and relationship building has lent itself to collaborating on Rene's memoir, which we are now publishing with the University of Manitoba Press (2019) after over seven years of shared storytelling.

Somewhere in between all this work, we started to travel together. In an effort to show how our travelling has advanced our personal and often intertwining paths of truth and reconciliation, I will share some memories from two of these trips. The first was to Catalunya, which was Rene's first international trip, and the second was to Rene's home territory in Treaty Three.

# CATALUNYA: VISITING, EXILE, BORDERS, RECONCILIATION

It's 2014 and Rene; his wife, Joan; my son, Rajan; and I are in La Jonquera, on the border of France and Spain in Catalunya. We've come to the Museu Memorial de L'Exili (Exile Memorial Museum) so Rene and I can present at a conference called Memory and Testimony in the 21st Century. The job is to dig into "the border of memory and memory at the border," and the conference is populated by European scholars who speak mostly of atrocities committed in their territories. People are speaking Catalan, Spanish, French, and English interchangeably as we learn about dispossession from these and other lands.

My presentation is on "Storytelling and Canadian Aboriginal Memory," but when I get to it on the last day of the conference, I am unable to speak. After stumbling through some introductory remarks about my work as a historian/story gatherer, I am stopped by the unleashing of tears brought on by something Rene had spoken of earlier in the trip: *forgiveness*. Bonendamowin. Reconciling and Truth. As Rene had explained it, forgiveness in Anishinabemowin carries a word bundle: Bone (stop or end), endam (indignant mind), damaw (toward another).

I can't stop crying; I am stuck in this notion of forgiveness as I attempt to give my presentation, and so I stop and simply stand in front of the crowd in what becomes a long silence, supported by a fellow presenter, who rises to stand with me. As Trickster would have it, Rene isn't there to witness this outpouring or the silence that follows—he and Joan are off in search of bacon and eggs, a fitting Mishoomis response to culture shock after a week or so of continental breakfasts! But Rene had already presented his truths the night before, framed for this audience by my introductory remarks about colonization in Canada. He had played the traditional flute, told stories, and read poetry to an enraptured crowd as they learned about Indigenous recovery: his personal reconciliation after removal and loss of home territory, sexual abuse, residential school trauma, alcoholism, and six years of living homeless under the Bathurst Street Bridge in Toronto. Rene knows a lot about Bonendamowin.

I am intimately familiar this story; it is part of the collective story of Turtle Island's peoples, but this time it shakes me. I'm worn and weary from spending these days immersed in presentations about the exile of Spanish and Catalonian republicans, about the Holocaust, migrants and refugees in Italy, closed borders, human rights. We'd visited the internment camp across the French border at Rivesaltes, which housed Spanish and Catalan refugees, Jews, and, most recently, unwanted migrants. And as we walked around the dusty camp, Rene had revisited his own experiences of internment as an Indigenous child in Canada. The terra cotta shades that were so cheerful on the rooftops in Barcelona suddenly felt like bloodshed under our feet. And through all of this, I had been struggling to reconcile those words that Rene had said to me on the afternoon we'd arrived:

"Four-teen nine-t-y two! It all started here. And here I am, in 2014. *This trip is about forgiveness.*"

℞ ℠

It's 2014, Rene is in his late 60s, and it's the first time he has been out of Canada. Until recently, he has not been ready to cross the Atlantic, that border between Turtle Island and the shores of early colonial imaginings. But now we've arrived in Barcelona and I am perched beside Rene on an old couch in our rented apartment, a place of high ceilings, long corridors, and tiled floors. Even though it's 35 degrees outside we don't need a fan, as the wind blows gently and steadily through the wooden windows that flank the wall of the adjoining sunroom. Joan and Rajan recover from jet lag with a siesta while Rene and I record an interview, part of our ongoing work toward his memoir. Rene has a quiet manner of speaking, so I place my phone on the back of the leather couch to catch our voices.

"They are telling me stories," he says, referring to the architecture we had been craning our necks to see in our exploratory trip around the neighbourhood. "The language. I may not speak Catalan, but I understand the buildings. They are speaking to me, they are telling me a story."

I've been to Europe several times, but I've never toured with an artist, and certainly not an Anishinaabe artist who is seeing the so-called old world for the first time. Rene talks about the excitement of coming across his first palm tree and the haunting splendour of churches built by black robes, birthplace of those dark missions.

Borders and memories.

There are no empty lands. For Rene it's about multiple old worlds and stories and the places where they are lodged. He muses, "If I took somebody from Catalonia—an artist, a writer—to my country and go out there and fish for our supper, I wonder what kind of story they would tell me? You see what I mean by the language in the land? Every rock out there, every island, the mouths and bends in the rivers, every one has a story—they have a history. Some say most of our elders are dead—the language, our history is dead. There is nobody there to tell me a story. But it's still the land that tells me a story."

This discussion moves into an expression of gratitude for being in Europe for the first time, and then Rene arrives at that word, *forgiveness*. That's when I feel those spontaneous tears roll down my face, a surprise visit with what sits below my own indignant mind.

℘ ℭ

"You've gotta be tough," my father once told me. That was the night he punched the wall in our bathroom, leaving little indented knuckle marks on the drywall. Those surprises arrived in drunken moments of release, versions I recognize in other Indigenous men; in Rene, releasing 30 years of rage, repeatedly punching a pillow at Pedauhbun Lodge, the Indigenous treatment centre where he finally found healing. My dad went there too, but he never made it. He drank himself to death over that long terrible year that preceded his passing. I still grieve for him at that border, for he will always be in exile from the old man he could have been. But I give thanks that Rene and others are able to tell a story that has choked too many of our relations. This is the sadness in my bones that sometimes seeps out through the rolling tear, or the flood of unexpected emotion.

"Forgiveness is the job of the Creator," another residential school survivor and friend replies when I send her an email later, trying to sort through my struggle at the conference. I don't question her. But what about reconciliation?

In his presentation, Rene had talked about exile of the self and returning. He'd read a poem.

## MCINTOSH

by Rene Meshake

> March 19th, 1967.
> I checked the article again.
> March 19th, 1967,
> The year the school burnt down.
>
> For me, McIntosh never burnt down.
> Back then,
> Brother J, my Supervisor's

petting impaled my body
to the dormitory bed.
Disembowelled, I died.

*Old J had a little lamb*
*Branded it Twenty-Three*
*Old J sheared its wool and skin*
*Its fleece grew filthily*

*Twenty-Three won't graze no more*
*Graze no more along the stream*
*Twenty-Three was unworthy to dream*

From the article,
I clipped the picture
of the white, 3 story residence.
I ran outside, broke a cedar branch,
and set the bough and clipping ablaze.
As I stoked the fire,
my body emerged from the burning page
to reunite with me.

಼ ೮೪

Art and creativity offer one way through that long Indigenous path of uncovering truths, as I have discovered in the memory work I do with Rene. His story begins in that land of underground rivers, off-reserve and in a community run by grandmothers. This was the foundation of his artistic practice, where, as he says, "The old ladies used to sit around and tell stories. And then us kids would go out and play in the dirt—draw them. That was woodlands art—we all did it. The girls would make little communities out of mud. They would invite us in for play—but they were always in charge. They made tea. I drank so much tea!"

A violent, colonial shift happened when his community was moved onto a reserve in the early 1960s. The old ladies died off, their governing authority lost. The uncles began to drink. Violence set in. And Rene was sent to residential school. There were no grandmothers or woodland stories there, only nuns who insisted on a different kind of art.

"We were not allowed to draw anything with animals. It had to be all these boxy things: crosses and churches and Santa Claus … I liked doing Christmas trees because at least you could put an owl in there or something."

Rene did his best to resist, but the owls couldn't perch on Santa's shoulder or the roof of the church. That was pagan. Evil. And this sentiment, combined with the sexual and other abuses endured in residential school, led to years of self-doubt and feelings of inferiority, stifling artistic expression. It took decades to return, it took Indigenous healing, land, language, and moving into spaces where Rene found other artists who had pushed beyond boundaries.

For Rene, discovering Salvador Dali in art school also launched a transition back into his own work. And now, magically, we sit in Dali's home territory, Catalunya, where I listen to Rene talk about cycles and border busting and coming home. On this trip we will make visits to Guell Park, sit among mosaic and swirls, and feel gratitude for the whimsical. We will also visit the Dali museum and pay homage to the old man. And as Rene anticipates our visit to the resting place of Dali, he says, "I will read his originals, his handprints, his hand on his art. It seems like my soul travels ahead of me, just thinking of that!"

੪ ੩

One thing that Rene has often told me is, "I always believe that art has legs. One foot tells the story—the other one heals. It's got to heal, too." And now he tells me, "I think my healing here has been the forgiveness. 1492. Forgive. It was very hard for me to do, but now I'm beginning to relax in my forgiveness and sobriety and journey."

I can feel a personal realigning, a giant, slow shifting with this generous arrival.

"It's these people I must forgive," he says. "If you can see that connection with history. So, there's layers to this. Art. Language. Forgiveness."

There are lessons here about how I'm still young on the trail to reconciliation and forgiveness. But there is healing, too. During the break after my tearful, silent presentation, one of the community activists comes up to me and Joan, who is now by my side. He stands in front of us, an elderly Catalonian man who has lived through war, totalitarian regimes, and exile. He tells us in Catalan that he has a present. He tells me I am strong. And then he carefully hands over two folded Catalan flags. One for me, and one for Rene. As he does this, he offers one more word, in English: "*Forgiveness*."

I take this precious gift and thank him—and then I thank the old man spirit, the land, and the territories that have brought me to this place of Bonendamowin—or at least to the border of it.

## PAGWASHING: PURPOSE, DIPPING, AND RISING

It's 2015 and Rene, Joan, and I have come to Rene's home territory to do research on traditional naming. Joan has already started looking through church records to find the historic Anishinaabek names from Rene's home communities of Longlac 58 and Aroland First Nations, and Rene carries oral history about Elders sitting together to name the newborns. There are names like Betasamigijigweb (the sky walking toward us) and Wakeabanok (light coming from many directions), Rene's paternal great-grandparents, both born in 1878. "One name—like royalty," Rene has told me. "And these names carry purpose."

We, too, have purpose. As Rene explained:

> I have younger cousins back home that I see on Facebook, and they are having babies. I ask them, "Why are you giving your babies names that sound like crystals and chandeliers? Why not give them Anishinaabe names?"
>
> But then they say, "Well, give us names!"—and now I don't know what to do.
>
> I think I need fellow Elders to sit around and see this baby, and maybe one of us might have a vision—but I need land. So, I have to go back up north. And once I'm there perhaps that kind of vision will work. I know there's a ceremony of giving a name. But then, as well, there is becoming responsible for it.

Going back is not easy; Rene left his homeland in his early 30s after his father died, launching him into years of exile and wandering. This is only the second time he has been back in over 30 years. It's a long road home, and we don't know what will result.

We plan a 10-day trip, and Joan and Rene head out a few days before me. I feel comfort and relief when I see them waiting for me on the chilly night I step off the bus at the gas station motel. It's been a lonely four-hour ride out of Thunder Bay, but the car is warm and inviting as we hurtle eastward down the Trans-Canada. We have rented a cabin 30 minutes out of town and this will become our "lodge" for the next seven days—a ceremonial place as well as the home we eventually share with the chipmunk Joan names "Gaston"—a visitor who appears periodically through a hole in the flooring.

The first morning we visit the dilapidated church that is still standing, but barely, on the land where Rene and his grandmother used to camp on their visits to Longlac. We step gingerly into the ramshackle building, and Rene points out the stage in the basement where he did some of his early theatrical work as "funnyman," hamming it up for his mates after watching the Laurel and Hardy movies that the nuns would occasionally show. There's also the tomb of Father Couture, the priest who gave Rene his Christian name—the only one he now carries.

Outside and across the point there is a small and abandoned graveyard. I am humbled to visit the burial site of Rene's uncle Biidaan—the one so vivid to me from the stories we recorded for our Indigenous masculinities project. Biidaan is the one I met at Rene's house one day with the jarring experience of turning around to find him looking right through me out of one of Rene's paintings. That gaze now guards over me from where the painting hangs behind my desk at work.

The next day we take the road over to the settler town of Caramat, which Rene explains is "Tamarac" spelled backwards. We've come this way with Rene's cousin to find where they lived with their grannies in the bush, alongside the CNR railroad tracks and at a point where the creek of Pagwashing passes underneath. I feel like I know this place because Rene has often told me about Pagwashing with its dips and rises, snaking its way through the land and creating a series of lakes that eventually spill into Lake Superior. I think of Rene's last name, Meshake, which is short for Mehsakegishig, the motion of the damselfly as it dips and rises above the water and the horizon.

Having scoped out the area, we return the next day to make the offerings. The land is soft under my red rubber boots as we go in, full of the moss that the old ladies used to hang up to mark the trails or to make diapers for the babies. Rene explains several medicines as we pass, telling stories of the time his grandmother healed him from a burn or a cut or a sore stomach. We soon find the river that sustained Rene's childhood community—"and spirit," he says—until some authority burnt down all the houses in the 1950s and moved his grandmothers onto the reserve. We carefully unwrap the brightly coloured kerchiefs we brought from home, and as we tie them in the trees, like flags, I can see all the old ladies laughing and visiting and trading among themselves. As we leave, Rene tells us to keep looking forward.

With this ceremony done, we feel a key part of our purpose here is complete, and the next day we travel to Rene's paternal community to attend a fall feast. It is a wonderful celebration involving races to see who can be the fastest to filet a fish or pluck a duck, or who can do the best moose call. We feast on what community members have brought in: duck soup, moose stew over the fire, partridge, fried fish, "dirty porridge" (porridge made with the duck gravy), and more. We relax and visit with relatives until the organizers announce they are ready to give away the splashy door prizes. As we gather with the crowd to join in on the excitement, one of the organizers makes a pointed and very loud statement that the prizes "are for *Band members* only." This deeply hurts, because of course the only prize we had been looking for was a welcoming from the community in the wake of our multiple displacements.

We find acceptance with other kin, however, when they visit our lodge on the following night, loaded up with more wild meat and dirty porridge. It's a full blood moon, and in between us all laughing at the beloved toddler doing her best moose calls, we find ceremony. At one point, Rene's niece goes outside our little cabin to smoke a cigarette in the lightly falling rain, and Rene tells a story about the time his grandmother made a sweat lodge under the kitchen table. "She told my aunt Christine to go and smoke outside while they prayed," he says.

Our lodge serves up one final ceremony. On one of the sunny mornings while Rene and I are sitting having scrambled eggs, he announces that he is going to name me. He talks about how he has been watching me ever since our meeting at the schmoozefest, 17 years previous. Now that he is in his homeland, he says, and on the land, he has the authority to give me an Anishinaabe name— "but we'll wait until Joan gets out of the shower."

The ceremony, like our lodge, is simple. It begins as he tells the story of my name, which "jumped out at him" while he and Joan were doing our naming research. Wakeabanok, light coming from many directions.

"Over the years I've watched you travel," Rene says. "It's *wake*, circuitous. You're looking for stories and healing medicine, and you go everywhere for it. Wakeabanok. In times of need, this woman would have gathered medicines from around the globe, taking a longer journey because it wasn't a direct route. Patience. Perseverance. Light."

I hold back the tears as he continues to talk about purpose and names, and then he says, "So I'll give that name to you here, and you can take it with you wherever you go." And then he gently adds, "Giving you that name brings me a sense of who I am."

On our last night, I can't sleep and so I go outside to talk to the moon, engaging in a makeshift full moon ceremony. Rene tells me that he couldn't sleep either; that he lay awake until I came in, worrying that a spirit might take me away in the night. But he eventually fell asleep, and close to dawn, he tells me, he dreamt of his dad. And it wasn't long before he woke up, fell out of bed, and we were ready to go.

## CONCLUSION

It's 2017 and Rene and I are sharing stories in his living room. We've finished our soup and he pushes his slippered feet skyward as he pulls back the lever on his recliner. Listening to us laugh uproariously as she passes through on her way to the kitchen, Joan says, "I think you two are good for each other." And I think she is right.

Maybe research as reconciliation means that co-researchers are good for each other: that we can eat together, find shared humour, listen carefully to each other's stories, travel, co-create knowledge, build new expression, and, most of all, develop kinship. Reconciliation can involve creating new kin relations out of a legacy of loss, a process that can sometimes take decades of building trust and relationship. I suppose any community-based researcher knows this. But as Indigenous individuals living in this time, what particular truths can we uncover through our research processes, and how do they foster reconciliation?

"It's like peeling back an onion," Rene has told me on multiple occasions. "There's always another layer." But on these trips at least, we have moved one layer deeper. There's new knowledge about the grief of losing fathers, or the consequences of being displaced from land, or the pain of feeling alienated from community. We have also learned about people with colonial pathways similar to our own, even in those places we presumed to be on the other side of choppy waters. We've deepened our appreciation for art as healer and confirmed the universal lessons to be learned from old men and old ladies here and there. We've approached new borders of forgiveness and found there were friends waiting for us on the other side. We have left our ceremonial flags and been given new ones. We've strengthened our purpose. We've named, and have learned about the responsibilities that come with kinship. And above all we have been reminded that language and stories are never lost, but rather grounded in land and place, in all its bloodshed as well as its whimsical beauty.

So, Rene and I have become rich again through our research work, as has Joan, who is part of everything we do. And we will continue to research and produce knowledge and art as we travel to lands new and old in our search for truths; as we follow our intertwining pathways to reconciliation.

## ACKNOWLEDGEMENTS

Sections of this chapter have previously appeared in "Bonendamowin Is Forgiveness: A Reconciliation Bundle from Kim Anderson and Rene Meshake," *Muskrat Magazine*, April 7, 2017, http:/muskratmagazine.com/author/kimanderson.

## After Major Trans Mountain Setback, Furious Trudeau Threatens First Nations with "Fiery Reconciliation"

After a federal court quashed the expansion of the Trans Mountain pipeline, a furious Prime Minister Justin Trudeau threatened to increase reconciliation with First Nations.

"If you thought we were reconciling hard with our Indigenous Peoples before this, you are sorely mistaken," Trudeau told reporters.

"Mark my words, we will rain fiery reconciliation upon Indigenous communities until this pipeline is built."

In an emergency cabinet meeting earlier on Thursday, Trudeau had to be restrained by senior party members after he threatened to "go down to BC to build that pipeline my damn self."

In a statement, the federal government also blamed "crafty, smooth-talking" First Nations for derailing the multi-billion-dollar project.